Mediterranean Diet Cookbook

1500+ Days of Easy & Tasty Recipes that Anyone Can Cook at Home. With 60-Day Meal Plan and Shopping List.

Jessica Marciante

TABLE OF CONTENTS

MEDITERRANEAN GREEK SALAD WRAPS...................................34
PIZZA POCKETS...34
GRILLED CAESAR SALAD SANDWICHES....................................34
CHICKPEA LETTUCE WRAPS...34
VEGETABLE AND CHEESE LAVASH PIZZA...................................35
GREEK VEGETABLE SALAD PITA..35
ARTICHOKE AND CUCUMBER HOAGIES.....................................35
MINI PORK AND CUCUMBER LETTUCE WRAPS..........................35
OPEN-FACED MARGHERITA SANDWICHES.................................36
ZUCCHINI HUMMUS WRAPS...36
ROASTED VEGETABLE PANINI...36

CHAPTER 5 BEANS RECIPES, GRAINS RECIPES, & PASTAS RECIPES 37

BAKED ROLLED OAT WITH PEARS AND PECANS.......................37
BROWN RICE PILAF WITH PISTACHIOS AND RAISINS...............37
PEARL BARLEY RISOTTO WITH PARMESAN CHEESE.................38
CRANBERRY AND ALMOND QUINOA...38
ISRAELI COUSCOUS WITH ASPARAGUS.....................................38
GOUDA BEEF AND SPINACH FETTUCCINE.................................38
ITALIAN SAUTÉD CANNELLINI BEANS......................................39
LENTIL AND VEGETABLE CURRY STEW......................................39
RITZY VEGGIE CHILI...39
WALNUT AND RICOTTA SPAGHETTI..39
CHICKPEA, VEGETABLE, AND FRUIT STEW...............................40
PESTO PASTA...40
QUINOA AND CHICKPEA VEGETABLE BOWLS...........................40
BLACK-EYED PEAS SALAD WITH WALNUTS...............................40
SPICY ITALIAN BEAN BALLS WITH MARINARA.........................41
WILD RICE, CELERY, AND CAULIFLOWER PILAF........................41
BULGUR PILAF WITH GARBANZO...41
MASHED BEANS WITH CUMIN...42
QUINOA WITH BABY POTATOES AND BROCCOLI.......................42
TURKISH CANNED PINTO BEAN SALAD....................................42
BROCCOLI AND CARROT PASTA SALAD....................................42
TRIPLE-GREEN PASTA WITH CHEESE.......................................43
LENTIL RISOTTO...43
CAPRESE PASTA WITH ROASTED ASPARAGUS..........................43
FREEKEH PILAF WITH DATES AND PISTACHIOS........................44
BLACK-EYED PEA AND VEGETABLE STEW..................................44
CHICKPEA SALAD WITH TOMATOES AND BASIL.......................44
MEDITERRANEAN LENTILS...44
ROASTED RATATOUILLE PASTA..45
TOMATO BASIL PASTA...45
PORK AND SPINACH SPAGHETTI...45
PAPAYA, JICAMA, AND PEAS RICE BOWL..................................46
BLACK BEAN CHILI WITH MANGOES.......................................46
ISRAELI STYLE EGGPLANT AND CHICKPEA SALAD...................46
PESTO ARBORIO RICE AND VEGGIE BOWLS.............................47
RICE AND BEAN STUFFED ZUCCHINI.......................................47
CHARD AND MUSHROOM RISOTTO..47
CHEESY TOMATO LINGUINE..47
BEEF AND BEAN STUFFED PASTA SHELLS................................48
PESTO CHICKEN PASTA (ITALIAN)...48
CHICKEN AND SPAGHETTI RAGÙ BOLOGNESE.........................48

ITALIAN CHICKEN PASTA (ITALIAN)...48
SHRIMP AND LEEK SPAGHETTI (ITALIAN)................................49
GARLIC SHRIMP FETTUCCINE (ITALIAN)..................................49
ASPARAGUS PASTA (ITALIAN)..49

CHAPTER 6 VEGETABLE RECIPES....................50

STUFFED PORTOBELLO MUSHROOMS WITH SPINACH..............50
CHICKPEA LETTUCE WRAPS WITH CELERY...............................50
ZOODLES WITH WALNUT PESTO...50
MUSHROOM AND SPINACH STUFFED PEPPERS........................51
BLACK BEAN AND CORN TORTILLA BOWLS..............................51
POTATO, CORN, AND SPINACH MEDLEY....................................51
MUSHROOM AND POTATO OAT BURGERS.................................51
VEGGIE-STUFFED PORTABELLO MUSHROOMS.........................52
CAULIFLOWER AND BROCCOLI BOWLS....................................52
STIR-FRIED EGGPLANT...52
RADISH AND CABBAGE CONGEE...52
RICE, CORN, AND BEAN STUFFED PEPPERS............................53
CARROT AND TURNIP PURÉE...53
BRUSSELS SPROUTS LINGUINE...53
BABY KALE AND CABBAGE SALAD...53
PEANUT AND COCONUT STUFFED EGGPLANTS.......................54
CAULIFLOWER WITH SWEET POTATO......................................54
SWEET POTATO AND TOMATO CURRY.....................................54
ZOODLES WITH BEET PESTO...55
CAULIFLOWER HASH WITH CARROTS......................................55
FRIED EGGPLANT ROLLS...55
ZOODLES...55
ROASTED VEGGIES AND BROWN RICE BOWL..........................56
GARLICKY ZUCCHINI CUBES WITH MINT.................................56
ZUCCHINI AND ARTICHOKES BOWL WITH FARRO...................56
WILTED DANDELION GREENS WITH SWEET ONION..................56
CHEESY SWEET POTATO BURGERS...57
QUICK STEAMED BROCCOLI...57
EGGPLANT AND ZUCCHINI GRATIN...57
ASPARAGUS WITH FETA (GREEK)..58
ROSEMARY SWEET POTATO MEDALLIONS (SPANISH)..............58
GARLIC EGGPLANT SLICES (SPANISH).....................................58
DELICIOUS TOMATO BROTH (SPANISH)...................................58

CHAPTER 7 POULTRY RECIPES & MEATS RECIPES.59

HERBED-MUSTARD-COATED PORK TENDERLOIN.....................59
GRILLED PORK CHOPS...59
MACADAMIA PORK...59
BEEF, TOMATO, AND LENTILS STEW.......................................59
GYRO BURGERS WITH TAHINI SAUCE.....................................60
QUICK CHICKEN SALAD WRAPS...60
SAUTÉED GROUND TURKEY WITH BROWN RICE......................60
ROASTED CHICKEN THIGHS WITH BASMATI RICE....................61
ROASTED PORK MEAT (SPANISH)...61
YOGURT CHICKEN BREASTS..61
LEMON BEEF (SPANISH)...61
GREEK CHICKEN SALAD (GREEK)..62
SEASONED PORK CHOPS (SPANISH).......................................62
BEEF STROGANOFF (SPANISH)...62

MEDITERRANEAN DIET SHOPPING LIST

STAPLES

Oils
- [ ] Olive Oil
- [ ] Extra-virgin olive oil

Vinegar
- [ ] Balsamic
- [ ] Red wine
- [ ] White wine

A variety of dried herbs & spices
- [ ] Basil
- [ ] Parsley
- [ ] Oregano
- [ ] Cayenne pepper
- [ ] Cinnamon
- [ ] Cloves
- [ ] Cumin
- [ ] Coriander
- [ ] Dill
- [ ] Fennel seed
- [ ] Ginger
- [ ] Rosemary
- [ ] Red and white wine
- [ ] Garlic

MEAT & SEAFOOD

- [ ] Clams
- [ ] Cod
- [ ] Crab meat
- [ ] Halibut
- [ ] Mussels
- [ ] Salmon
- [ ] Scallops
- [ ] Shrimp
- [ ] Tilapia
- [ ] Tuna
- [ ] Chicken breast*
- [ ] Chicken thighs*
- [ ] Lean red meat**

CANNED & PACKAGED

- [ ] Olives
- [ ] Canned Tomatoes

Dried & canned beans
- [ ] Cannellini beans
- [ ] Navy beans
- [ ] Chickpeas
- [ ] Black beans
- [ ] Kidney beans
- [ ] Lentils
- [ ] Canned tuna

Whole Grains
- [ ] Whole grain pasta
- [ ] Bulgur
- [ ] Whole wheat couscous
- [ ] Quinoa
- [ ] Brown rice
- [ ] Barley
- [ ] Faro
- [ ] Polenta
- [ ] Oats
- [ ] Whole wheat bread or pita
- [ ] Whole grain crackers

Nuts & seeds
- [ ] Almonds
- [ ] Hazelnuts
- [ ] Pine nuts
- [ ] Walnuts
- [ ] Cashews
- [ ] Sunflower seeds
- [ ] Sesame seeds

REFRIGERATED

Cheese
- [ ] Cream cheese
- [ ] Feta
- [ ] Goat cheese
- [ ] Mozzarella
- [ ] Parmesan
- [ ] Ricotta
- [ ] Low-fat milk
- [ ] Plain or Greek yogurt
- [ ] Eggs

PRODUCE

- [ ] Apples
- [ ] Artichokes
- [ ] Asparagus
- [ ] Avocado
- [ ] Bananas
- [ ] Beets
- [ ] Bell peppers
- [ ] Berries (all types)
- [ ] Broccoli
- [ ] Brussels sprouts
- [ ] Cabbage
- [ ] Carrots
- [ ] Celery
- [ ] Cherries
- [ ] Cucumbers
- [ ] Dates
- [ ] Eggplant
- [ ] Fennel
- [ ] Figs
- [ ] Grapes
- [ ] Green beans
- [ ] Kiwi
- [ ] Leafy greens
- [ ] Lemons
- [ ] Lettuce
- [ ] Limes
- [ ] Melons
- [ ] Mushrooms
- [ ] Nectarines
- [ ] Onions
- [ ] Oranges
- [ ] Peas
- [ ] Peaches
- [ ] Pears
- [ ] Plums
- [ ] Pomegranate
- [ ] Potatoes
- [ ] Shallots
- [ ] Spinach
- [ ] Squash
- [ ] Tomatoes
- [ ] Zucchini

* In moderation, once to twice per week
** On rare occasions, once to twice monthly

INTRODUCTION

"Mediterranean diet" is a generic term based on the traditional eating habits in the countries bordering the Mediterranean Sea. There's not one standard Mediterranean diet. At least 16 countries border the Mediterranean. Eating styles vary among these countries and even among regions within each country because of differences in culture, ethnic background, religion, economy, geography and agricultural production. However, there are some common factors.

Interest in the Mediterranean diet began in the 1960s with the observation that coronary heart disease caused fewer deaths in Mediterranean countries, such as Greece and Italy, than in the U.S. and northern Europe. Subsequent studies found that the Mediterranean diet is associated with reduced risk factors for cardiovascular disease. The Mediterranean diet is a way of eating based on the traditional cuisine of countries bordering the Mediterranean Sea. The foundation of the Mediterranean diet is vegetables, fruits, herbs, nuts, beans and whole grains. Meals are built around these plant-based foods. Moderate amounts of dairy, poultry and eggs are also central to the Mediterranean Diet, as is seafood. In contrast, red meat is eaten only occasionally. Healthy fats are a mainstay of the Mediterranean diet. They're eaten instead of less healthy fats, such as saturated and trans fats, which contribute to heart disease.

Olive oil is the primary source of added fat in the Mediterranean diet. Olive oil provides monounsaturated fat, which has been found to lower total cholesterol and low-density lipoprotein (LDL or "bad") cholesterol levels. The Mediterranean diet typically allows red wine in moderation. Although alcohol has been associated with a reduced risk of heart disease in some studies, it's by no means risk free. Below you can find the shopping list of the most common in the Mediterranean diet. They are divided by category; they are the most used but you will also find recipes with not present in this list.

By combining all the recipes in this book, we calculated that you can make different meals for over 1500 days! I hope you will enjoy the recipes and find the nutrition plan useful. As for the nutrition plan, we decided to set it on an average of kcal ranging from 1400 to 1500.

Chapter 1
The 60-Day Meal Plan

	Breakfast	Lunch	Dinner	Total Calories
DAY 1	Baked Eggs in Avocado Calories: 301	Black Bean Chili with Mangoes Calories: 430	Roasted Veggies and Brown Rice Bowl Calories: 453 Cheesy Sweet Potato Burgers Calories: 290	1474
DAY 2	Mediterranean Eggs Calories: 223	Italian Sautéd Cannellini Beans Calories: 435	Asian-Inspired Tuna Lettuce Wraps Calories: 270 Vegetable and Cheese Lavash Pizza Calories: 431	1359
DAY 3	Breakfast Yogurt Sundae Calories: 236	Turkish Canned Pinto Bean Salad Calories: 402	Roasted Chicken Thighs With Basmati Rice Calories: 400 Glazed Mushroom and Vegetable Fajitas Calories: 403	1441
DAY 4	Savory Breakfast Oatmeal Calories: 197	Bulgur Pilaf with Garbanzo Calories: 462 Walnut and Ricotta Spaghetti Calories: 264	Quick Chicken Salad Wraps Calories: 428 Cauliflower Hash with Carrots Calories: 108	1459
DAY 5	Tomato and Egg Scramble Calories: 260 Kale and Apple Smoothie Calories: 177	Garlic Shrimp Fettuccine Calories: 615	Mango and Coconut Frozen Pie Calories: 426	1478
DAY 6	Baked Eggs in Avocado Calories: 301	Tomato Basil Pasta Calories: 415 Cheesy Tomato Linguine Calories: 311	Macadamia Pork Calories: 436	1463
DAY 7	Crustless Tiropita Calories: 181 Avocado and Egg Toast Calories: 297	Ritzy Veggie Chili Calories: 633	Pecan and Carrot Cake Calories: 255	1366

DAY 8	Avocado Toast with Goat Cheese Calories: 136 Ricotta Toast with Strawberries Calories:274	Caprese Fusilli Calories: 589	Brussels Sprouts Linguine Calories: 502	**1501**
DAY 9	Berry and Nut Parfait Calories: 507	Ritzy Veggie Chili Calories: 633	Garlicky Zucchini Cubes with Mint Calories: 146 Cauliflower Hash with Carrots Calories: 158	**1444**
DAY 10	Kale and Apple Smoothie Calories: 177 Baked Eggs in Avocado Calories: 301	Chard and Mushroom Risotto Calories: 420 Walnut and Ricotta Spaghetti Calories: 264	Parsley-Dijon Chicken and Potatoes Calories: 324	**1486**
DAY 11	Apple-Tahini Toast Calories: 358	Pesto Pasta Calories: 1067	Cauliflower Hash with Carrots Calories: 158	**1583**
DAY 12	Mediterranean Eggs Calories: 223	Grana Padano Risotto Calories: 307 Tomato Basil Pasta Calories: 415	Lemony Shrimp with Orzo Salad Calories: 565	**1510**
DAY 13	Avocado Toast with Goat Cheese Calories: 136	Garlic Shrimp Fettuccine Calories: 615	Sweet Potato and Tomato Curry Calories: 224 Vegetable and Cheese Lavash Pizza Calories: 431	**1406**
DAY 14	Banana-Blueberry Breakfast Cookies Calories: 264	Lentil Risotto Calories: 261 Lentil and Vegetable Curry Stew Calories: 530	Macadamia Pork Calories: 436	**1491**
DAY 15	Crustless Tiropita Calories: 181	Pesto Pasta Calories: 1067	Glazed Mushroom and Vegetable Fajitas Calories: 403	**1651**
DAY 16	Spinach Cheese Pie Calories: 417 Savory Breakfast Oatmeal Calories: 197	Chicken and Spaghetti Ragù Bolognese Calories: 477	Spicy Tofu Tacos with Cherry Tomato Salsa Calories: 240	**1331**

DAY 17	Baked Eggs in Avocado Calories: 301 Ricotta Toast with Strawberries Calories:274	Black Bean Chili with Mangoes Calories: 430	Cheesy Sweet Potato Burgers Calories: 290	1295
DAY 18	Mediterranean Eggs Calories: 223	Italian Sautéd Cannellini Beans Calories: 435	Asian-Inspired Tuna Lettuce Wraps Calories: 270 Vegetable and Cheese Lavash Pizza Calories: 431	1359
DAY 19	Breakfast Yogurt Sundae Calories: 236	Turkish Canned Pinto Bean Salad Calories: 402	Roasted Chicken Thighs With Basmati Rice Calories: 400 Glazed Mushroom and Vegetable Fajitas Calories: 403	1441
DAY 20	Savory Breakfast Oatmeal Calories: 197	Bulgur Pilaf with Garbanzo Calories: 462 Walnut and Ricotta Spaghetti Calories: 264	Quick Chicken Salad Wraps Calories: 428 Cauliflower Hash with Carrots Calories: 108	1459
DAY 21	Baked Eggs in Avocado Calories: 301	Tomato Basil Pasta Calories: 415 Cheesy Tomato Linguine Calories: 311	Potato Lamb and Olive Stew Calories: 309	1336
DAY 22	Crustless Tiropita Calories: 181 Avocado and Egg Toast Calories: 297	Ritzy Veggie Chili Calories: 633	Pecan and Carrot Cake Calories: 255	1366
DAY 23	Avocado Toast with Goat Cheese Calories: 136 Ricotta Toast with Strawberries Calories:274	Caprese Fusilli Calories: 589	Brussels Sprouts Linguine Calories: 502	1501
DAY 24	Banana-Blueberry Breakfast Cookies Calories: 264	Lentil Risotto Calories: 261 Lentil and Vegetable Curry Stew Calories: 530	Macadamia Pork Calories: 436	1491

DAY 25	Mediterranean Eggs Calories: 223 Berry and Nut Parfait Calories: 507	Italian Sautéd Cannellini Beans Calories: 435	Asian-Inspired Tuna Lettuce Wraps Calories: 270	**1435**
DAY 26	Breakfast Yogurt Sundae Calories: 236 Spinach Cheese Pie Calories: 417	Turkish Canned Pinto Bean Salad Calories: 402	Roasted Chicken Thighs With Basmati Rice Calories: 400	**1455**
DAY 27	Tomato and Egg Scramble Calories: 260 Kale and Apple Smoothie Calories: 177	Garlic Shrimp Fettuccine Calories: 615	Mango and Coconut Frozen Pie Calories: 426	**1478**
DAY 28	Avocado Toast with Goat Cheese Calories: 136 Spinach Cheese Pie Calories: 417	Garlic Shrimp Fettuccine Calories: 615	Sweet Potato and Tomato Curry Calories: 224	**1392**
DAY 29	Berry and Nut Parfait Calories: 507	Ritzy Veggie Chili Calories: 633	Garlicky Zucchini Cubes with Mint Calories: 146 Cauliflower Hash with Carrots Calories: 158	**1444**
DAY 30	Baked Eggs in Avocado Calories: 301	Black Bean Chili with Mangoes Calories: 430	Roasted Veggies and Brown Rice Bowl Calories: 453 Cheesy Sweet Potato Burgers Calories: 290	**1474**

Please note: refer to the index to find the number of the page corresponding to the recipe.

Repeat for another 30 days from the beginning. We trust that this 60-day nutritional plan is to your liking!

Chapter 2
Breakfast Recipes

Spinach and Egg Breakfast Wraps

Prep Time: 10 minutes | **Cooking Time:** 7 minutes | **Servings:** 2

Ingredients

1 tablespoon olive oil
¼ cup minced onion
3 to 4 tablespoons minced sun-dried tomatoes in olive oil and herbs
3 large eggs, whisked
1½ cups packed baby spinach
1 ounce (28 g) crumbled feta cheese
Salt, to taste
2 (8-inch) whole-wheat tortillas

Directions

1. Heat the olive oil in a large skillet over medium-high heat.
2. Sauté the onion and tomatoes for about 3 minutes, stirring occasionally, until softened.
3. Reduce the heat to medium. Add the whisked eggs and stir-fry for 1 to 2 minutes.
4. Stir in the baby spinach and scatter with the crumbled feta cheese. Season as needed with salt.
5. Remove the egg mixture from the heat to a plate. Set aside.
6. Working in batches, place 2 tortillas on a microwave-safe dish and microwave for about 20 seconds to make them warm.
7. Spoon half of the egg mixture into each tortilla. Fold them in half and roll up, then serve.

Per Serving

calories: 434 | fat: 28.1g | protein: 17.2g | carbs: 30.8g | fiber: 6.0g | sodium: 551mg

Ricotta Toast with Strawberries

Prep Time: 10 minutes | **Cooking Time:** 0 minutes | **Servings:** 2

Ingredients

½ cup crumbled ricotta cheese
1 tablespoon honey, plus additional as needed
Pinch of sea salt, plus additional as needed
4 slices of whole-grain bread, toasted
1 cup sliced fresh strawberries
4 large fresh basil leaves, sliced into thin shreds

Directions

1. Mix together the cheese, honey, and salt in a small bowl until well incorporated.
2. Taste and add additional salt and honey as needed.
3. Spoon 2 tablespoons of the cheese mixture onto each slice of bread and spread it all over.
4. Sprinkle the sliced strawberry and basil leaves on top before serving.

Per Serving calories: 274 | fat: 7.9g | protein: 15.1g | carbs: 39.8g | fiber: 5.0g | sodium: 322mg

Mediterranean Eggs (Shakshuka)

Prep Time: 5 minutes | **Cooking Time:** 20 minutes | **Servings:** 4

Ingredients

2 tablespoons extra-virgin olive oil
1 cup chopped shallots
1 teaspoon garlic powder
1 cup finely diced potato
1 cup chopped red bell peppers
1 (14.5-ounce/ 411-g) can diced tomatoes, drained
¼ teaspoon ground cardamom
¼ teaspoon paprika
¼ teaspoon turmeric
4 large eggs
¼ cup chopped fresh cilantro

Directions

1. Preheat the oven to 350ºF (180ºC).
2. Heat the olive oil in an ovenproof skillet over medium-high heat until it shimmers.
3. Add the shallots and sauté for about 3 minutes, stirring occasionally, until fragrant.
4. Fold in the garlic powder, potato, and bell peppers and stir to combine.
5. Cover and cook for 10 minutes, stirring frequently.
6. Add the tomatoes, cardamon, paprika, and turmeric and mix well.
7. When the mixture begins to bubble, remove from the heat and crack the eggs into the skillet.
8. Transfer the skillet to the preheated oven and bake for 5 to 10 minutes, or until the egg whites are set and the yolks are cooked to your liking.
9. Remove from the oven and garnish with the cilantro before serving.

Per Serving

calories: 223 | fat: 11.8g | protein: 9.1g | carbs: 19.5g | fiber: 3.0g | sodium: 277mg

Crustless Tiropita (Greek Cheese Pie)

Prep Time: 10 minutes | **Cooking Time:** 35 to 40 mins | **Servings:** 6

Ingredients

4 tablespoons extra-virgin olive oil, divided
½ cup whole-milk ricotta cheese
1¼ cups crumbled feta cheese
2 tablespoons chopped fresh mint
½ teaspoon lemon zest
¼ teaspoon freshly ground black pepper
2 large eggs
½ teaspoon baking powder
1 tablespoon chopped fresh dill

Directions

1. Preheat the oven to 350°F (180°C). Coat the bottom and sides of a baking dish with 2 tablespoons of olive oil. Set aside.
2. Mix together the ricotta and feta cheese in a medium bowl and stir with a fork until well combined. Add the dill, mint, lemon zest, and black pepper and mix well. In a separate bowl, whisk together the eggs and baking powder. Pour the whisked eggs into the bowl of cheese mixture. Blend well.
3. Slowly pour the mixture into the coated baking dish and drizzle with the remaining 2 tablespoons of olive oil.
4. Bake in the preheated oven for about 35 to 40 minutes, or until the pie is browned around the edges and cooked through.
5. Cool for 5 minutes before slicing into wedges.

Per Serving

calories: 181 | fat: 16.6g | protein: 7.0g | carbs: 1.8g | fiber: 0g | sodium: 321mg

Fluffy Almond Flour Pancakes with Strawberries

Prep Time: 5 minutes | **Cooking Time:** 15 minutes | **Servings:** 4

Ingredients

1 cup plus 2 tablespoons unsweetened almond milk
1 cup almond flour
2 large eggs, whisked ⅓ cup honey
1 teaspoon baking soda
¼ teaspoon salt
2 tablespoons extra-virgin olive oil
1 cup sliced strawberries

Directions

1. Combine the almond milk, almond flour, whisked eggs, honey, baking soda, and salt in a large bowl and whisk to incorporate.
2. Heat the olive oil in a large skillet over medium-high heat.
3. Make the pancakes: Pour ⅓ cup of batter into the hot skillet and swirl the pan so the batter covers the bottom evenly. Cook for 2 to 3 minutes until the pancake turns golden brown around the edges. Gently flip the pancake with a spatula and cook for 2 to 3 minutes until cooked through. Repeat with the remaining batter.
4. Serve the pancakes with the sliced strawberries on top.

Per Serving

calories: 298 | fat: 11.7g | protein: 11.8g | carbs: 34.8g | fiber: 3.9g | sodium: 195mg

Breakfast Yogurt Sundae

Prep Time: 5 minutes | **Cooking Time:** 0 minutes | **Servings:** 1

Ingredients

¾ cup plain Greek yogurt
¼ cup fresh mixed berries (blueberries, strawberries, blackberries)
2 tablespoons walnut pieces
1 tablespoon ground flaxseed
2 fresh mint leaves, shredded

Directions

1. Pour the yogurt into a tall parfait glass and sprinkle with the mixed berries, walnut pieces, and flaxseed.
2. Garnish with the shredded mint leaves and serve immediately.

Per Serving

calories: 236 | fat: 10.8g | protein: 21.1g | carbs: 15.9g | fiber: 4.1g | sodium: 63mg

Avocado Toast with Goat Cheese

Prep Time: 5 minutes | **Cooking Time:** 2 to 3 minutes | **Servings:** 2

Ingredients

2 slices whole-wheat thin-sliced bread
½ avocado
2 tablespoons crumbled goat cheese
Salt, to taste

Directions

1. Toast the bread slices in a toaster for 2 to 3 minutes on each side until browned.
2. Scoop out the flesh from the avocado into a medium bowl and mash it with a fork to desired consistency. Spread the mash onto each piece of toast.
3. Scatter the crumbled goat cheese on top and season as needed with salt.
4. Serve immediately.

Per Serving

calories: 136 | fat: 5.9g | protein: 5.0g | carbs: 17.5g | fiber: 5.1g | sodium: 194mg

Healthy Chia Pudding

Prep Time: 5 minutes | **Cooking Time:** 0 minutes | **Servings:** 4

Ingredients

4 cups unsweetened almond milk
¾ cup chia seeds
1 teaspoon ground cinnamon
Pinch sea salt

Directions

1. In a medium bowl, whisk together the almond milk, chia seeds, cinnamon, and sea salt until well incorporated.
2. Cover and transfer to the refrigerator to thicken for about 1 hour, or until a pudding-like texture is achieved.
3. Serve chilled.

Per Serving calories: 236 | fat: 9.8g | protein: 13.1g | carbs: 24.8g | fiber: 11.0g | sodium: 133mg

Banana-Blueberry Breakfast Cookies

Prep Time: 10 minutes | **Cooking Time:** 13 minutes | **Servings:** 4

Ingredients

2 medium bananas, sliced
4 tablespoons almond butter
4 large eggs, lightly beaten
½ cup unsweetened applesauce
1 teaspoon vanilla extract
⅔ cup coconut flour
¼ teaspoon salt
1 cup fresh or frozen blueberries

Directions

1. Preheat the oven to 375°F (190°C). Line a baking sheet with parchment paper.
2. Stir together the bananas and almond butter in a medium bowl until well incorporated.
3. Fold in the beaten eggs, applesauce, and vanilla and blend well.
4. Add the coconut flour and salt and mix well. Add the blueberries and stir to just incorporate.
5. Drop about 2 tablespoons of dough onto the parchment paper-lined baking sheet for each cookie. Using your clean hand, flatten each into a rounded biscuit shape, until it is 1 inch thick.
6. Bake in the preheated oven for about 13 minutes, or until the top is golden brown and a toothpick inserted in the center comes out clean.
7. Let the cookies cool for 5 to 10 minutes before serving.

Per Serving (3 cookies)
calories: 264 | fat: 13.9g | protein: 7.3g | carbs: 27.6g | fiber: 5.2g | sodium: 219mg

Blackberry-Yogurt Green Smoothie

Prep Time: 5 minutes | **Cooking Time:** 0 minutes | **Servings:** 2

Ingredients

1 cup plain Greek yogurt
1 cup baby spinach
½ cup frozen blackberries
½ cup unsweetened almond milk
½ teaspoon peeled and grated fresh ginger
¼ cup chopped pecans

Directions

1. Process the yogurt, baby spinach, blackberries, almond milk, and ginger in a food processor until smoothly blended.
2. Divide the mixture into two bowls and serve topped with the chopped pecans.

Per Serving
calories: 201 | fat: 14.5g | protein: 7.1g | carbs: 14.9g | fiber: 4.3g | sodium: 103mg

Buckwheat Porridge

Prep Time: 5 minutes | **Cooking Time:** 40 minutes | **Servings:** 4

Ingredients

3 cups water
2 cups raw buckwheat groats
Pinch sea salt
1 cup unsweetened almond milk

Directions

1. In a medium saucepan, add the water, buckwheat groats, and sea salt and bring to a boil over medium-high heat.
2. Once it starts to boil, reduce the heat to low. Cook for about 20 minutes, stirring occasionally, or until most of the water is absorbed.
3. Fold in the almond milk and whisk well. Continue cooking for about 15 minutes, or until the buckwheat groats are very softened. Ladle the porridge into bowls and serve warm.

Per Serving calories: 121 | fat: 1.0g | protein: 6.3g | carbs: 21.5g | fiber: 3.0g | sodium: 47mg

Creamy Vanilla Oatmeal

Prep Time: 5 minutes | **Cooking Time:** 40 minutes | **Servings:** 4

Ingredients

4 cups water
Pinch sea salt
1 cup steel-cut oats
¾ cup unsweetened almond milk
2 teaspoons pure vanilla extract

Directions

1. Add the water and salt to a large saucepan over high heat and bring to a boil.
2. Once boiling, reduce the heat to low and add the oats. Mix well and cook for 30 minutes, stirring occasionally.
3. Fold in the almond milk and vanilla and whisk to combine. Continue cooking for about 10 minutes, or until the oats are thick and creamy.
4. Ladle the oatmeal into bowls and serve warm.

Per Serving calories: 117 | fat: 2.2g | protein: 4.3g | carbs: 20.0g | fiber: 3.8g | sodium: 38mg

Spinach Cheese Pie

Prep Time: 5 minutes | **Cooking Time:** 25 minutes | **Servings:** 8

Ingredients

2 tablespoons extra-virgin olive oil
1 onion, chopped
1 pound (454 g) frozen spinach, thawed
¼ teaspoon ground nutmeg
¼ teaspoon garlic salt
¼ teaspoon freshly ground black pepper
4 large eggs, divided
1 cup grated Parmesan cheese, divided
2 puff pastry doughs, at room temperature
4 hard-boiled eggs, halved
Nonstick cooking spray

Directions

1. Preheat the oven to 350ºF (180ºC). Spritz a baking sheet with nonstick cooking spray and set aside.
2. Heat a large skillet over medium-high heat. Add the olive oil and onion and sauté for about 5 minutes, stirring occasionally, or until translucent. Squeeze the excess water from the spinach, then add to the skillet and cook, uncovered, so that any excess water from the spinach can evaporate.
3. Season with the nutmeg, garlic salt, and black pepper. Remove from heat and set aside to cool.
4. Beat 3 eggs in a small bowl. Add the beaten eggs and ½ cup of Parmesan cheese to the spinach mixture, stirring well. Roll out the pastry dough on the prepared baking sheet. Layer the spinach mixture on top of the dough, leaving 2 inches around each edge.
5. Once the spinach is spread onto the pastry dough, evenly place the hard-boiled egg halves throughout the pie, then cover with the second pastry dough. Pinch the edges closed. Beat the remaining 1 egg in the bowl. Brush the egg wash over the pastry dough. Bake in the preheated oven for 15 to 20 minutes until golden brown. Sprinkle with the remaining ½ cup of Parmesan cheese. Cool for 5 minutes before cutting and serving.

Per Serving
calories: 417 | fat: 28.0g | protein: 17.0g | carbs: 25.0g | fiber: 3.0g | sodium: 490mg

Baked Ricotta with Honey Pears

Prep Time: 5 minutes | **Cooking Time:** 22 to 25 minutes | **Servings:** 4

Ingredients

1 (1-pound / 454-g) container whole-milk ricotta cheese
2 large eggs
¼ cup whole-wheat pastry flour
1 tablespoon sugar
1 teaspoon vanilla extract
¼ teaspoon ground nutmeg
1 pear, cored and diced
2 tablespoons water
1 tablespoon honey
Nonstick cooking spray

Directions

1. Preheat the oven to 400ºF (205ºC). Spray four ramekins with nonstick cooking spray.
2. Beat together the ricotta, eggs, flour, sugar, vanilla, and nutmeg in a large bowl until combined. Spoon the mixture into the ramekins.Bake in the preheated oven for 22 to 25 minutes, or until the ricotta is just set.
3. Meanwhile, in a small saucepan over medium heat, simmer the pear in the water for 10 minutes, or until slightly softened. Remove from the heat, and stir in the honey.
4. Remove the ramekins from the oven and cool slightly on a wire rack. Top the ricotta ramekins with the pear and serve.

Per Serving calories: 329 | fat: 19.0g | protein: 17.0g | carbs: 23.0g | fiber: 3.0g | sodium: 109mg

Quinoa Breakfast Bowls

Prep Time: 5 minutes | **Cooking Time:** 17 minutes | **Servings:** 1

Ingredients

¼ cup quinoa, rinsed
¾ cup water, plus additional as needed
1 carrot, grated
½ small broccoli head, finely chopped
¼ teaspoon salt
1 tablespoon chopped fresh dill

Directions

1. Add the quinoa and water to a small pot over high heat and bring to a boil. Once boiling, reduce the heat to low. Cover and cook for 5 minutes, stirring occasionally.
2. Stir in the carrot, broccoli, and salt and continue cooking for 1o to 12 minutes, or until the quinoa is cooked though and the vegetables are fork- tender. If the mixture gets too thick, you can add additional water as needed.
3. Add the dill and serve warm.

Per Serving calories: 219 | fat: 2.9g | protein: 10.0g | carbs: 40.8g | fiber: 7.1g | sodium: 666mg

Breakfast Pancakes with Berry Sauce

Prep Time: 5 minutes | **Cooking Time:** 10 minutes | **Servings:** 4

Ingredients

Pancakes:
1 cup almond flour
1 teaspoon baking powder
¼ teaspoon salt
6 tablespoon extra-virgin olive oil, divided
2 large eggs, beaten

Zest and juice of 1 lemon
½ teaspoon vanilla extract
Berry Sauce:
1 cup frozen mixed berries
1 tablespoon water, plus more as needed
½ teaspoon vanilla extract

Directions

Make the Pancakes
1. In a large bowl, combine the almond flour, baking powder, and salt and stir to break up any clumps.
2. Add 4 tablespoons olive oil, beaten eggs, lemon zest and juice, and vanilla extract and stir until well mixed.
3. Heat 1 tablespoon of olive oil in a large skillet. Spoon about 2 tablespoons of batter for each pancake. Cook until bubbles begin to form, 4 to 5 minutes. Flip and cook for another 2 to 3 minutes. Repeat with the remaining 1 tablespoon of olive oil and batter.

Make the Berry Sauce
4. Combine the frozen berries, water, and vanilla extract in a small saucepan and heat over medium-high heat for 3 to 4 minutes until bubbly, adding more water as needed. Using the back of a spoon or fork, mash the berries and whisk until smooth. Serve the pancakes with the berry sauce.

Per Serving calories: 275 | fat: 26.0g | protein: 4.0g | carbs: 8.0g | fiber: 2.0g | sodium: 271mg

Marinara Poached Eggs

Prep Time: 5 minutes | **Cooking Time:** 15 minutes | **Servings:** 6

Ingredients

1 tablespoon extra-virgin olive oil
1 cup chopped onion
2 garlic cloves, minced
2 (14.5-ounce / 411-g) cans no-salt-added

Italian diced tomatoes, undrained
6 large eggs
½ cup chopped fresh flat-leaf parsley

Directions

1. Heat the olive oil in a large skillet over medium-high heat.
2. Add the onion and sauté for 5 minutes, stirring occasionally. Add the garlic and cook for 1 minute more.
3. Pour the tomatoes with their juices over the onion mixture and cook for 2 to 3 minutes until bubbling.
4. Reduce the heat to medium and use a large spoon to make six indentations in the tomato mixture. Crack the eggs, one at a time, into each indentation. Cover and simmer for 6 to 7 minutes, or until the eggs are cooked to your preference.
5. Serve with the parsley sprinkled on top.

Per Serving
calories: 89 | fat: 6.0g | protein: 4.0g | carbs: 4.0g | fiber: 1.0g | sodium: 77mg

Feta and Spinach Frittata

Prep Time: 10 minutes | **Cooking Time:** 15 minutes | **Servings:** 2

Ingredients

4 large eggs, beaten
2 tablespoons fresh chopped herbs, such as rosemary, thyme, oregano, basil or 1 teaspoon dried herbs
¼ teaspoon salt
Freshly ground black pepper, to taste
4 tablespoons extra-virgin olive oil, divided

1 cup fresh spinach, arugula, kale, or other leafy greens
4 ounces (113 g) quartered artichoke hearts, rinsed, drained, and thoroughly dried
8 cherry tomatoes, halved
½ cup crumbled soft goat cheese

Directions

1. Preheat the broiler to Low. In a small bowl, combine the beaten eggs, herbs, salt, and pepper and whisk well with a fork
2. In an ovenproof skillet, heat 2 tablespoons of olive oil over medium heat. Add the spinach, artichoke hearts, and cherry tomatoes and sauté until just wilted, 1 to 2 minutes.
3. Pour in the egg mixture and let it cook undisturbed over medium heat for 3 to 4 minutes, until the eggs begin to set on the bottom.
4. Sprinkle the goat cheese across the top of the egg mixture and transfer the skillet to the oven.
5. Broil for 4 to 5 minutes, or until the frittata is firm in the center and golden brown on top.
6. Remove from the oven and run a rubber spatula around the edge to loosen the sides. Slice the frittata in half and serve drizzled with the remaining 2 tablespoons of olive oil.

Per Serving
calories: 529 | fat: 46.5g | protein: 21.4g | carbs: 7.1g | fiber: 3.1g | sodium: 762mg

Savory Breakfast Oatmeal

Prep Time: 5 minutes | **Cooking Time:** 15 minutes | **Servings:** 2

Ingredients

½ cup steel-cut oats
1 cup water
1 medium cucumber, chopped
1 large tomato, chopped
1 tablespoon olive oil

Pinch freshly grated Parmesan cheese
Sea salt and freshly ground pepper, to taste
Flat-leaf parsley or mint, chopped, for garnish

Directions

1. Combine the oats and water in a medium saucepan and bring to a boil over high heat, stirring continuously, or until the water is absorbed, about 15 minutes.
2. Divide the oatmeal between 2 bowls and scatter the tomato and cucumber on top. Drizzle with the olive oil and sprinkle with the Parmesan cheese.
3. Season with salt and pepper to taste. Serve garnished with the parsley.

Per Serving
calories: 197| fat: 8.9g | protein: 6.3g | carbs: 23.1g | fiber: 6.4g | sodium: 27mg

Avocado and Egg Toast

Prep Time: 5 minutes | **Cooking Time:** 8 minutes | **Servings:** 2

Ingredients

2 tablespoons ground flaxseed
½ teaspoon baking powder
2 large eggs, beaten
1 teaspoon salt, plus additional for serving
½ teaspoon freshly ground black pepper, plus additional for serving

½ teaspoon garlic powder, sesame seed, caraway seed, or other dried herbs (optional)
3 tablespoons extra-virgin olive oil, divided
1 medium ripe avocado, peeled, pitted, and sliced
2 tablespoons chopped ripe tomato

Directions

1. In a small bowl, combine the flaxseed and baking powder, breaking up any lumps in the baking powder.
2. Add the beaten eggs, salt, pepper, and garlic powder (if desired) and whisk well. Let sit for 2 minutes.
3. In a small nonstick skillet, heat 1 tablespoon of olive oil over medium heat. Pour the egg mixture into the skillet and let cook undisturbed until the egg begins to set on bottom, 2 to 3 minutes.
4. Using a rubber spatula, scrape down the sides to allow uncooked egg to reach the bottom. Cook for an additional 2 to 3 minutes.
5. Once almost set, flip like a pancake and allow the top to fully cook, another 1 to 2 minutes.
6. Remove from the skillet and allow to cool slightly, then slice into 2 pieces.
7. Top each piece with avocado slices, additional salt and pepper, chopped tomato, and drizzle with the remaining 2 tablespoons of olive oil. Serve immediately.

Per Serving

calories: 297 | fat: 26.1g | protein: 8.9g | carbs: 12.0g | fiber: 7.1g | sodium: 1132mg

Tomato and Egg Breakfast Pizza

Prep Time: 5 minutes | **Cooking Time:** 15 minutes | **Servings:** 2

Ingredients

2 (6- to 8-inch-long) slices of whole-wheat naan bread
2 tablespoons prepared pesto

1 medium tomato, sliced
2 large eggs

Directions

1. Heat a large nonstick skillet over medium-high heat. Place the naan bread in the skillet and let warm for about 2 minutes on each side, or until softened.
2. Spread 1 tablespoon of the pesto on one side of each slice and top with tomato slices.
3. Remove from the skillet and place each one on its own plate.
4. Crack the eggs into the skillet, keeping them separated, and cook until the whites are no longer translucent and the yolk is cooked to desired doneness.
5. Using a spatula, spoon one egg onto each bread slice. Serve warm.

Per Serving

calories: 429 | fat: 16.8g | protein: 18.1g | carbs: 12.0g | fiber: 4.8g | sodium: 682mg

Parmesan Oatmeal with Greens

Prep Time: 10 minutes | **Cooking Time:** 18 minutes | **Servings:** 2

Ingredients

1 tablespoon olive oil
¼ cup minced onion
2 cups greens (arugula, baby spinach, chopped kale, or Swiss chard)
¾ cup gluten-free old-fashioned oats

1½ cups water, or low-sodium chicken stock
2 tablespoons Parmesan cheese
Salt, to taste
Pinch freshly ground black pepper

Directions

1. Heat the olive oil in a saucepan over medium-high heat. Add the minced onion and sauté for 2 minutes, or until softened.
2. Add the greens and stir until they begin to wilt. Transfer this mixture to a bowl and set aside.
3. Add the oats to the pan and let them toast for about 2 minutes. Add the water and bring the oats to a boil.
4. Reduce the heat to low, cover, and let the oats cook for 10 minutes, or until the liquid is absorbed and the oats are tender.
5. Stir the Parmesan cheese into the oats, and add the onion and greens back to the pan. Add additional water if needed, so the oats are creamy and not dry.
6. Stir well and season with salt and black pepper to taste. Serve warm.

Per Serving

calories: 257 | fat: 14.0g | protein: 12.2g | carbs: 30.2g | fiber: 6.1g | sodium: 262mg

Pita Chicken Salad (Greek)

Prep Time: 18 minutes | **Cooking Time:** 4 minutes |
Servings: 4

Ingredients

1 tbsp. olive oil	1 piece of chicken breast
Dried basil to taste	3 tbsps. natural yogurt
2 pieces pita	1 tbsp. lemon juice
1 garlic clove	1 bunch (7 oz.) green salad
1 tomato	2 chives
1 cucumber Salt to taste	Ground black pepper to taste

Directions

1. Rub the chicken slices with salt, pepper, and dried basil, fry in a pan until cooked.
2. Put the chicken, slices of tomato, cucumber, and onion in half the pits.
3. Mix the yogurt with lemon juice and garlic, add to the salad in Pita. Garnish with chives then serve.

Nutrition:

Calories: 94 Fat: 1.8 g. Protein: 6 g.

Chorizo & Cheese Omelet (Italian)

Prep Time: 10 minutes **Cooking Time:** 10 minutes
Servings: 2

Ingredients

4 eggs, beaten	4 oz. mozzarella, grated
8 chorizo slices, thin	Salt and black pepper to taste
1 tomato, sliced	
1 tbsp. butter	

Directions

1. Whisk the eggs with salt and pepper.
2. In a cast-iron skillet, add the butter and cook the eggs for 30 seconds. Create a layer with the chorizo slices.
3. Arrange the sliced tomato and mozzarella over the chorizo and cook for about 3 minutes. Cover the skillet and continue cooking for 3 more minutes, or until the omelet is completely set.
4. With a spatula, run around the edges of the omelet and flip it onto a plate folded-side down. Serve.

Nutrition:

Calories: 451 g. Fats: 36.5 g. Protein: 30g.

Cheesy Yogurt (Greek)

Prep Time: 4 hours and 5 minutes **Cooking Time:** 0 minutes
Servings: 4

Ingredients

1 cup Greek yogurt	1 tablespoon honey
½ cup feta cheese, crumbled	

Directions

1. In a blender, combine the yogurt with the honey and the cheese and pulse well.
2. Divide into bowls and freeze for 4 hours before serving for breakfast.

Nutrition:

Calories 161, fat 10, fiber 0, carbs 11.8, protein 6.6

Kale and Apple Smoothie

Prep Time: 5 minutes | **Cooking Time:** 0 minutes |
Servings: 2

Ingredients

2 cups shredded kale	½ Granny Smith apple, unpeeled, cored and chopped
1 cup unsweetened almond milk	½ avocado, diced 3 ice cubes
¼ cup 2 percent plain Greek yogurt	

Directions

1. Put all in a blender and blend until smooth and thick.
2. Pour into two glasses and serve immediately.

Per Serving

calories: 177 | fat: 6.8g | protein: 8.2g | carbs: 22.0g | fiber: 4.1g | sodium: 112mg

Healthy Chia and Oats Smoothie (Greek)

Prep Time: 10 minutes | **Cooking Time:** 0 minutes |
Servings: 2

Ingredients

6 tbsps. oats.	2 tbsps. chia seeds.
2 tbsps. hemp powder.	4 Medjool dates, pitted (optional).
2 bananas, chopped.	2big handful's spinach, torn.
1cup almond milk.	
1 cup frozen berries.	

Directions

1. Add all the to a blender and blend until smooth.
2. Pour in glasses and serve.

Nutrition:

Calories: 140. Fat: 7 g. Fiber: 4 g. Carbs: 12 g. Protein: 12 g.

Breakfast Tostadas (Spanish)

Prep Time: 15 minutes | **Cooking Time:** 16 minutes | **Servings:** 6

Ingredients

½ white onion, diced

1 tbsp. fresh cilantro, chopped

1 tomato, chopped

6 corn tortillas

2oz. Cheddar cheese, shredded

½ tsp. butter

6 eggs

1 cucumber, chopped

½ jalapeño pepper, chopped

1 tbsp. lime juice

1tbsp. canola oil

½ cup white beans, canned, drained

½ tsp. Sea salt

Directions

1. Make the Pico de Gallo:
2. In the salad bowl combine the diced white onion, tomato, cucumber, fresh cilantro, and jalapeño pepper.
3. Then add the lime juice and a ½ tbsp. canola oil. Mix up the mixture well. Pico de Gallo is ready.
4. After this, preheat the oven to 390°F.
5. Line the tray with baking paper.
6. Arrange the corn tortillas on the baking paper and brush with the remaining canola oil from both sides.
7. Bake for 10 minutes.
8. Chill the cooked crunchy tortillas well.
9. Meanwhile, toss the butter in the skillet.
10. Crack the eggs in the melted butter and sprinkle them with sea salt.
11. Fry the eggs for 3–5 minutes over medium heat.
12. After this, mash the beans until you get a puree texture.
13. Spread the bean puree on the corn tortillas.
14. Add the fried eggs.
15. Then top the eggs with the Pico de Gallo and shredded Cheddar cheese.

Nutrition:

Calories: 246 Fat: 11 g. Protein: 14 g.

Berry and Nut Parfait

Prep Time: 10 minutes | **Cooking Time:** 0 minutes | **Servings:** 2

Ingredients

2 cups plain Greek yogurt

2 tablespoons honey

1 cup fresh raspberries

1 cup fresh blueberries

½ cup walnut pieces

Directions

1. In a medium bowl, whisk the yogurt and honey. Spoon into 2 serving bowls.
2. Top each with ½ cup blueberries, ½ cup raspberries, and ¼ cup walnut pieces. Serve immediately.

Per Serving calories: 507 | fat: 23.0g | protein: 24.1g | carbs: 57.0g | fiber: 8.2g | sodium: 172mg

Butternut Squash Hummus (Greek)

Prep Time: 16 minutes | **Cooking Time:** 15 minutes | **Servings:** 4

Ingredients

2 lbs. (900 g.) seeded butternut squash, peeled

2 tbsps. lemon juice

¼ cup tahini

1 tbsp. olive oil

2 garlic cloves, minced Salt and pepper

Directions

1. Heat the oven to 300°F/148°C.
2. Coat the butternut squash with olive oil.
3. Set in a baking dish to bake for 15 minutes in the oven.
4. Once the squash is cooked, place it in a food processor together with the rest of the .
5. Pulse until smooth.
6. Serve with carrots and celery sticks.
7. For further use of place in individual containers, put a label and store it in the fridge.
8. Allow warming at room temperature before heating in the microwave oven.

Nutrition:

Calories: 115 Fat: 5.8 g. Protein: 2.5 g.

Basil and Tomato Soup (Spanish)

Prep Time: 7 minutes | **Cooking Time:** 25 minutes | **Servings:** 2

Ingredients

2 tbsps. vegetable broth

1 celery stalk, chopped

1 carrot, chopped

2 bay leaves

1 garlic clove, minced

½ cup white onion

3 cup tomatoes, chopped

Salt and pepper

1 ½ cup unsweetened almond milk

1/3 cup basil leaves

Directions

1. Cook the vegetable broth in a large saucepan over medium heat.
2. Add in the garlic and onions and cook for 4 minutes.
3. Add in the carrots and celery. Cook for 1 more minute.
4. Mix in the tomatoes and bring to a boil. Simmer for 15 minutes.
5. Add the almond milk, basil, and bay leaves.
6. Season and serve.

Nutrition:

Calories: 213 Fat: 3.9 g. Protein: 6.9 g.

Cauliflower Breakfast Porridge

Prep Time: 5 minutes | **Cooking Time:** 5 minutes | **Servings:** 2

Ingredients

2 cups riced cauliflower
¾ cup unsweetened almond milk
4 tablespoons extra-virgin olive oil, divided
2 teaspoons grated fresh orange peel (from ½ orange)
½ teaspoon almond extract or vanilla extract
½ teaspoon ground cinnamon
⅛ teaspoon salt
4 tablespoons chopped walnuts, divided
1 to 2 teaspoons maple syrup (optional)

Directions

1. Place the riced cauliflower, almond milk, 2 tablespoons of olive oil, orange peel, almond extract, cinnamon, and salt in a medium saucepan. Stir to incorporate and bring the mixture to a boil over medium-high heat, stirring.
2. Remove from the heat and add 2 tablespoons of chopped walnuts and maple syrup (if desired).Stir again and divide the porridge into bowls. Sprinkle each bowl evenly with remaining 2 tablespoons of walnuts and olive oil.

Per Serving calories: 381 | fat: 37.8g | protein: 5.2g | carbs: 10.9g | fiber: 4.0g | sodium: 228mg

Morning Overnight Oats with Raspberries

Prep Time: 5 minutes | **Cooking Time:** 0 minutes | **Servings:** 2

Ingredients

⅔ cup unsweetened almond milk
¼ cup raspberries
⅓ cup rolled oats
1 teaspoon honey
¼ teaspoon turmeric
⅛ teaspoon ground cinnamon
Pinch ground cloves

Directions

1. Place the almond milk, raspberries, rolled oats, honey, turmeric, cinnamon, and cloves in a mason jar. Cover and shake to combine. Transfer to the refrigerator for at least 8 hours, preferably 24 hours. Serve chilled.

Per Serving calories: 81 | fat: 1.9g | protein: 2.1g | carbs: 13.8g | fiber: 3.0g | sodium: 97mg

Tomato and Egg Scramble

Prep Time: 10 minutes | **Cooking Time:** 20 minutes | **Servings:** 4

Ingredients

2 tablespoons extra-virgin olive oil
¼ cup finely minced red onion
1½ cups chopped fresh tomatoes
2 garlic cloves, minced
½ teaspoon dried thyme
½ teaspoon dried oregano
8 large eggs
½ teaspoon salt
¼ teaspoon freshly ground black pepper
¾ cup crumbled feta cheese
¼ cup chopped fresh mint leaves

Directions

1. Heat the olive oil in a large skillet over medium heat.
2. Sauté the red onion and tomatoes in the hot skillet for 10 to 12 minutes, or until the tomatoes are softened. Stir in the garlic, thyme, and oregano and sauté for 2 to 4 minutes, or until the garlic is fragrant. Meanwhile, beat the eggs with the salt and pepper in a medium bowl until frothy. Pour the beaten eggs into the skillet and reduce the heat to low. Scramble for 3 to 4 minutes, stirring constantly, or until the eggs are set. Remove from the heat and scatter with the feta cheese and mint. Serve warm.

Per Serving calories: 260 | fat: 21.9g | protein: 10.2g | carbs: 5.8g | fiber: 1.0g | sodium: 571mg

Baked Eggs in Avocado

Prep Time: 5 minutes | **Cooking Time:** 10 to 15 minutes | **Servings:** 2

Ingredients

1 ripe large avocado
2 large eggs
Salt and freshly ground black pepper, to taste
4 tablespoons jarred pesto, for serving
2 tablespoons chopped tomato, for serving
2 tablespoons crumbled feta cheese, for serving (optional)

Directions

1. Preheat the oven to 425ºF (220ºC).
2. Slice the avocado in half, remove the pit and scoop out a generous tablespoon of flesh from each half to create a hole big enough to fit an egg.
3. Transfer the avocado halves (cut-side up) to a baking sheet.
4. Crack 1 egg into each avocado half and sprinkle with salt and pepper.
5. Bake in the preheated oven for 10 to 15 minutes, or until the eggs are cooked to your preferred doneness.
6. Remove the avocado halves from the oven. Scatter each avocado half evenly with the jarred pesto, chopped tomato, and crumbled feta cheese (if desired). Serve immediately.

Per Serving
calories: 301 | fat: 25.9g | protein: 8.1g | carbs: 9.8g | fiber: 5.0g | sodium: 435mg

Cheesy Broccoli and Mushroom Egg Casserole
Prep Time: 10 minutes | **Cooking Time:** 40 minutes | **Servings:** 4

Ingredients
2 tablespoons extra-virgin olive oil
½ sweet onion, chopped
1 teaspoon minced garlic
1 cup sliced button mushrooms
1 cup chopped broccoli
8 large eggs
¼ cup unsweetened almond milk
1 tablespoon chopped fresh basil
1 cup shredded Cheddar cheese
Sea salt and freshly ground black pepper, to taste

Directions
1. Preheat the oven to 375ºF (190ºC).
2. Heat the olive oil in a large ovenproof skillet over medium-high heat.
3. Add the onion, garlic, and mushrooms to the skillet and sauté for about 5 minutes, stirring occasionally. Stir in the broccoli and sauté for 5 minutes until the vegetables start to soften.
4. Meanwhile, beat the eggs with the almond milk and basil in a small bowl until well mixed.
5. Remove the skillet from the heat and pour the egg mixture over the top. Scatter the Cheddar cheese all over.
6. Bake uncovered in the preheated oven for about 30 minutes, or until the top of the casserole is golden brown and a fork inserted in the center comes out clean.
7. Remove from the oven and sprinkle with the sea salt and pepper. Serve hot.

Per Serving
calories: 326 | fat: 27.2g | protein: 14.1g | carbs: 6.7g | fiber: 0.7g | sodium: 246mg

Warm Bulgur Breakfast Bowls with Fruits
Prep Time: 5 minutes | **Cooking Time:** 15 minutes | **Servings:** 6

Ingredients
2 cups unsweetened almond milk
1½ cups uncooked bulgur
1 cup water
½ teaspoon ground cinnamon
2 cups frozen (or fresh, pitted) dark sweet cherries
8 dried (or fresh) figs, chopped
½ cup chopped almonds
¼ cup loosely packed fresh mint, chopped

Directions
1. Combine the milk, bulgur, water, and cinnamon in a medium saucepan, stirring, and bring just to a boil.
2. Cover, reduce the heat to medium-low, and allow to simmer for 10 minutes, or until the liquid is absorbed.
3. Turn off the heat, but keep the pan on the stove, and stir in the frozen cherries (no need to thaw), figs, and almonds. Cover and let the hot bulgur thaw the cherries and partially hydrate the figs, about 1 minute.
4. Fold in the mint and stir to combine, then serve.

Per Serving
calories: 207 | fat: 6.0g | protein: 8.0g | carbs: 32.0g | fiber: 4.0g | sodium: 82mg

Avocado Smoothie
Prep Time: 2 minutes | **Cooking Time:** 0 minutes | **Servings:** 2

Ingredients
1 large avocado
1½ cups unsweetened coconut milk
2 tablespoons honey

Directions
1. Place all in a blender and blend until smooth and creamy.
2. Serve immediately.

Per Serving
calories: 686 | fat: 57.6g | protein: 6.2g | carbs: 35.8g | fiber: 10.7g | sodium: 35mg

Cinnamon Pistachio Smoothie
Prep Time: 5 minutes | **Cooking Time:** 0 minutes | **Servings:** 1

Ingredients
½ cup unsweetened almond milk, plus more as needed
½ cup plain Greek yogurt
Zest and juice of ½ orange
1 tablespoon extra-virgin olive oil
1 tablespoon shelled pistachios, coarsely chopped
¼ to ½ teaspoon ground allspice
¼ teaspoon vanilla extract
¼ teaspoon ground cinnamon

Directions
1. In a blender, combine ½ cup almond milk, yogurt, orange zest and juice, olive oil, pistachios, allspice, vanilla, and cinnamon. Blend until smooth and creamy, adding more almond milk to achieve your desired consistency.
2. Serve chilled.

Per Serving calories: 264 | fat: 22.0g | protein: 6.0g | carbs: 12.0g | fiber: 2.0g | sodium: 127mg

Apple-Tahini Toast
Prep Time: 5 minutes | **Cooking Time:** 0 minutes | **Servings:** 1

Ingredients
2 slices whole-wheat bread, toasted
2 tablespoons tahini
1 small apple of your choice, cored and thinly sliced
1 teaspoon honey

Directions
1. Spread the tahini on the toasted bread.
2. Place the apple slices on the bread and drizzle with the honey. Serve immediately.

Per Serving
calories: 458 | fat: 17.8g | protein: 11.0g | carbs: 63.5g | fiber: 10.5g | sodium: 285mg

Chapter 3
Sides Recipes, Salads Recipes, & Soups Recipes

Sumptuous Greek Vegetable Salad

Prep Time: 20 minutes | **Cooking Time:** 0 minutes | **Servings:** 6

Ingredients

Salad:
1 (15-ounce / 425-g) can chickpeas, drained and rinsed
1 (14-ounce / 397-g) can artichoke hearts, drained and halved
1 head Bibb lettuce, chopped (about 2½ cups)
1 cucumber, peeled deseeded, and chopped (about 1½ cups)
1½ cups grape tomatoes, halved
¼ cup chopped basil leaves
½ cup sliced black olives

½ cup cubed feta cheese
Dressing:
1 tablespoon freshly squeezed lemon juice (from about ½ small lemon)
¼ teaspoon freshly ground black pepper
1 tablespoon chopped fresh oregano
2 tablespoons extra-virgin olive oil
1 tablespoon red wine vinegar
1 teaspoon honey

Directions
1. Combine the for the salad in a large salad bowl, then toss to combine well.
2. Combine the for the dressing in a small bowl, then stir to mix well.
3. Dress the salad and serve immediately.

Per Serving
calories: 165 | fat: 8.1g | protein: 7.2g | carbs: 17.9g | fiber: 7.0g | sodium: 337mg

Brussels Sprout and Apple Slaw

Prep Time: 15 minutes | **Cooking Time:** 0 minutes | **Servings:** 4

Ingredients

Salad:
1 pound (454 g) Brussels sprouts, stem ends removed and sliced thinly
1 apple, cored and sliced thinly
½ red onion, sliced thinly
Dressing:
1 teaspoon Dijon mustard

2 teaspoons apple cider vinegar
1 tablespoon raw honey
1 cup plain coconut yogurt
1 teaspoon sea salt
For Garnish:
½ cup pomegranate seeds
½ cup chopped toasted hazelnuts

Directions
1. Combine the for the salad in a large salad bowl, then toss to combine well.
2. Combine the for the dressing in a small bowl, then stir to mix well.
3. Dress the salad let sit for 10 minutes. Serve with pomegranate seeds and toasted hazelnuts on top.

Per Serving
calories: 248 | fat: 11.2g | protein: 12.7g | carbs: 29.9g | fiber: 8.0g | sodium: 645mg

Butternut Squash and Cauliflower Soup

Prep Time: 15 minutes | **Cooking Time:** 4 hours | **Servings:** 4 to 6

Ingredients

1 pound (454 g) butternut squash, peeled and cut into 1-inch cubes
1 small head cauliflower, cut into 1-inch pieces
1 onion, sliced
2 cups unsweetened coconut milk
1 tablespoon curry powder

4 cups low-sodium vegetable soup
2 tablespoons coconut oil
1 teaspoon sea salt
¼ teaspoon freshly ground white pepper
¼ cup chopped fresh cilantro, divided
½ cup no-added-sugar apple juice

Directions
1. Combine all the , except for the cilantro, in the slow cooker. Stir to mix well. Cook on high heat for 4 hours or until the vegetables are tender.
2. Pour the soup in a food processor, then pulse until creamy and smooth. Pour the puréed soup in a large serving bowl and garnish with cilantro before serving.

Per Serving
calories: 415 | fat: 30.8g | protein: 10.1g | carbs: 29.9g | fiber: 7.0g | sodium: 1386mg

Paella Soup

Prep Time: 6 minutes | **Cooking Time:** 24 minutes | **Servings:** 6

Ingredients

2 tablespoons extra-virgin olive oil
1 cup chopped onion
1½ cups coarsely chopped green bell pepper
1½ cups coarsely chopped red bell pepper
2 garlic cloves, chopped
1 teaspoon ground turmeric
1 teaspoon dried thyme
2 teaspoons smoked paprika
2½ cups uncooked instant brown rice
2 cups low-sodium or no-salt-added chicken broth
2½ cups water
1 cup frozen green peas, thawed
1 (28-ounce / 794-g) can low-sodium or no-salt-added crushed tomatoes
1 pound (454 g) fresh raw medium shrimp, shells and tails removed

Directions

1. In a large stockpot over medium-high heat, heat the oil. Add the onion, bell peppers, and garlic. Cook for 8 minutes, stirring occasionally. Add the turmeric, thyme, and smoked paprika, and cook for 2 minutes more, stirring often. Stir in the rice, broth, and water. Bring to a boil over high heat. Cover, reduce the heat to medium-low, and cook for 10 minutes.
2. Stir the peas, tomatoes, and shrimp into the soup. Cook for 4 minutes, until the shrimp is cooked, turning from gray to pink and white. The soup will be very thick, almost like stew, when ready to serve.
3. Ladle the soup into bowls and serve hot.

Per Serving

calories: 431 | fat: 5.7g | protein: 26.0g | carbs: 69.1g | fiber: 7.4g | sodium: 203mg

Sautéed Kale with Olives

Prep Time: 10 minutes | **Cooking Time:** 10 minutes | **Servings:** 2

Ingredients

1 bunch kale, leaves chopped and stems minced
½ cup celery leaves, roughly chopped, or additional parsley
½ bunch flat-leaf parsley, stems, leaves roughly
4 garlic cloves, chopped
2 teaspoons olive oil
¼ cup pitted Kalamata olives, chopped
Grated zest and juice of 1 lemon
Salt and pepper, to taste

Directions

1. Place the kale, celery leaves, parsley, and garlic in a steamer basket set over a medium saucepan. Steam over medium-high heat, covered, for 15 minutes. Remove from the heat and squeeze out any excess moisture. Place a large skillet over medium heat. Add the oil, then add the kale mixture to the skillet. Cook, stirring often, for 5 minutes. Remove from the heat and add the olives and lemon zest and juice. Season with salt and pepper and serve.

Per Serving calories: 86 | fat: 6.4g | protein: 1.8g | carbs: 7.5g | fiber: 2.1g | sodium: 276mg

Balsamic Brussels Sprouts and Delicata Squash

Prep Time: 10 minutes | **Cooking Time:** 30 minutes | **Servings:** 2

Ingredients

½ pound (227 g) Brussels sprouts, ends trimmed and outer leaves removed
1 medium delicata squash, halved lengthwise, seeded, and cut into 1-inch pieces
1 cup fresh cranberries
2 teaspoons olive oil
Salt and freshly ground black pepper, to taste
½ cup balsamic vinegar
2 tablespoons roasted pumpkin seeds
2 tablespoons fresh pomegranate arils (seeds)

Directions

1. Preheat oven to 400°F (205°C). Line a sheet pan with parchment paper. Combine the Brussels sprouts, squash, and cranberries in a large bowl. Drizzle with olive oil, and season lightly with salt and pepper. Toss well to coat and arrange in a single layer on the sheet pan.
2. Roast in the preheated oven for 30 minutes, turning vegetables halfway through, or until Brussels sprouts turn brown and crisp in spots. Meanwhile, make the balsamic glaze by simmering the vinegar for 10 to 12 minutes, or until mixture has reduced to about ¼ cup and turns a syrupy consistency. Remove the vegetables from the oven, drizzle with balsamic syrup, and sprinkle with pumpkin seeds and pomegranate arils before serving.

Per Serving calories: 203 | fat: 6.8g | protein: 6.2g | carbs: 22.0g | fiber: 8.2g | sodium: 32mg

Cucumber Gazpacho

Prep Time: 10 minutes | **Cooking Time:** 0 minutes | **Servings:** 4

Ingredients

2 cucumbers, peeled, deseeded, and cut into chunks
½ cup mint, finely chopped
2 cups plain Greek yogurt
2 garlic cloves, minced
2 cups low-sodium vegetable soup
1 tablespoon no-salt-added tomato paste
3 teaspoons fresh dill
Sea salt and freshly ground pepper, to taste

Directions

1. Put the cucumber, mint, yogurt, and garlic in a food processor, then pulse until creamy and smooth.
2. Transfer the puréed mixture in a large serving bowl, then add the vegetable soup, tomato paste, dill, salt, and ground black pepper. Stir to mix well.
3. Keep the soup in the refrigerator for at least 2 hours, then serve chilled.

Per Serving

calories: 133 | fat: 1.5g | protein: 14.2g | carbs: 16.5g | fiber: 2.9g | sodium: 331mg

Avgolemono (Lemon Chicken Soup)

Prep Time: 15 minutes | **Cooking Time:** 60 minutes |
Servings: 2

Ingredients

½ large onion	3 tablespoons freshly
2 medium carrots	squeezed lemon juice
1 celery stalk	1 egg yolk
1 garlic clove	2 tablespoons chopped
5 cups low-sodium chicken	fresh dill
stock	2 tablespoons chopped
¼ cup brown rice	fresh parsley
1½ cups (about 5 ounces /	Salt, to taste
142 g) shredded rotisserie	
chicken	

Directions

1. Put the onion, carrots, celery, and garlic in a food processor and pulse until the vegetables are minced.
2. Add the vegetables and chicken stock to a stockpot and bring it to a boil over high heat.
3. Reduce the heat to medium-low and add the rice, shredded chicken and lemon juice. Cover and let the soup simmer for 40 minutes, or until the rice is cooked.
4. In a small bowl, whisk the egg yolk lightly. Slowly, while whisking with one hand, pour about ½ of a ladle of the broth into the egg yolk to warm, or temper, the yolk. Slowly add another ladle of broth and continue to whisk.
5. Remove the soup from the heat and pour the whisked egg yolk–broth mixture into the pot. Stir well to combine.
6. Add the fresh dill and parsley. Season with salt to taste and serve.

Per Serving

calories: 172 | fat: 4.2g | protein: 18.2g | carbs: 16.1g | fiber: 2.1g | sodium: 232mg

Garlicky Roasted Grape Tomatoes (Spanish)

Prep Time: 10 minutes **Cooking Time:** 45 minutes
Servings: 2

Ingredients

1-pint grape tomatoes	10 whole garlic cloves, skins
1 fresh thyme sprig	removed
¼ cup olive oil	½ teaspoon salt
1 fresh rosemary sprig	

Directions

1. Preheat oven to 350ºF (180ºC).
2. Toss tomatoes, garlic cloves, oil, salt, and herb sprigs in a baking dish.
3. Roast tomatoes until they are soft and begin to caramelize, about 45 minutes.
4. Remove herbs before serving.

Nutrition: calories: 271 fats: 26g protein: 3g carbs: 12g fiber: 3g sodium: 593mg

Herb-Roasted Vegetables (Italian)

Prep Time: 15 minutes **Cooking Time:** 45 minutes
Servings: 6

Ingredients

Nonstick cooking spray	1eggplants, peeled and
1 zucchini, sliced ¼ inch	sliced 1/8 inch thick
thick	black pepper to taste
1yellow summer squash,	¼ cup, plus 2 tablespoons
sliced ¼ inch thick 2 Roma	extra-virgin olive oil,
tomatoes, sliced 1/8 inch	divided 1 tablespoon garlic
thick	powder
¼ teaspoon dried oregano	¼ teaspoon dried basil
¼ teaspoon salt	

Directions

1. Preheat the oven to 400ºF (205ºC).
2. Spray a 9-by-13-inch baking dish with cooking spray. In the dish, toss the eggplant, zucchini, squash, and tomatoes with 2 tablespoons oil, garlic powder, oregano, basil, salt, and pepper. Standing the vegetables up (like little soldiers), alternate layers of eggplant, zucchini, squash, and Roma tomato.
3. Drizzle the top with the remaining ¼ cup of olive oil.
4. Bake, uncovered, for 40 to 45 minutes, or until vegetables are golden brown.

Nutrition: calories: 186 fats: 14g protein: 3g carbs: 15g fiber: 5g sodium: 110mg

Mediterranean Bruschetta Hummus Platter(Greek)

Prep Time: 15 minutes **Cooking Time:** 0 minutes
Servings: 6

Ingredients

1/3 cup finely diced	½ cup finely diced fresh
seedless English cucumber	tomato
4 warmed pitas, cut into	1 tablespoon fresh chopped
wedges, for serving	parsley or basil
1 (10-ounce / 283-g)	1 teaspoon extra-virgin olive
container plain hummus	oil
Carrot sticks, for serving	¼ cup Herbed Olive Oil
2 tablespoons crumbled feta	2 tablespoons balsamic
cheese	glaze
Celery sticks, for serving	Sliced bell peppers for serving
Purple cauliflower, for serving	Broccoli, for serving

Directions

1. In a small bowl, mix the tomato and cucumber and toss with the olive oil. Pile the cucumber mixture over a fresh container of hummus. Drizzle the hummus and vegetables with the balsamic glaze. Top with crumbled feta and fresh parsley.
2. Put the hummus on a large cutting board. Pour the Herbed Olive Oil in a small bowl and put it on the cutting board. Surround the bowls with the pita wedges and cut carrot sticks, celery sticks, sliced bell peppers, broccoli, and cauliflower.

Nutrition: calories: 345 fats: 19g protein: 9g carbs: 32g fiber: 3g sodium: 473mg

Pumpkin Soup with Crispy Sage Leaves
Prep Time: 15 minutes | **Cooking Time:** 10 minutes | **Servings:** 4

Ingredients
1 tablespoon olive oil
2 garlic cloves, cut into ⅛-inch-thick slices
1 onion, chopped
2 cups freshly puréed pumpkin
4 cups low-sodium vegetable soup
2 teaspoons chipotle powder
1 teaspoon sea salt
½ teaspoon freshly ground black pepper
½ cup vegetable oil
12 sage leaves, stemmed

Directions
1. Heat the olive oil in a stockpot over high heat until shimmering.
2. Add the garlic and onion, then sauté for 5 minutes or until the onion is translucent.
3. Pour in the puréed pumpkin and vegetable soup in the pot, then sprinkle with chipotle powder, salt, and ground black pepper. Stir to mix well.
4. Bring to a boil. Reduce the heat to low and simmer for 5 minutes.
5. Meanwhile, heat the vegetable oil in a nonstick skillet over high heat.
6. Add the sage leaf to the skillet and sauté for a minute or until crispy. Transfer the sage on paper towels to soak the excess oil.
7. Gently pour the soup in three serving bowls, then divide the crispy sage leaves in bowls for garnish. Serve immediately.

Per Serving
calories: 380 | fat: 20.1g | protein: 8.9g | carbs: 45.2g | fiber: 18.0g | sodium: 1364mg

Green Beans with Tahini-Lemon Sauce
Prep Time: 5 minutes | **Cooking Time:** 10 minutes | **Servings:** 2

Ingredients
1 pound (454 g) green beans, washed and trimmed
2 tablespoons tahini
1 garlic clove, minced
Grated zest and juice of 1 lemon
Salt and black pepper, to taste
1 teaspoon toasted black or white sesame seeds (optional)

Directions
1. Steam the beans in a medium saucepan fitted with a steamer basket (or by adding ¼ cup water to a covered saucepan) over medium-high heat. Drain, reserving the cooking water. Mix the tahini, garlic, lemon zest and juice, and salt and pepper to taste. Use the reserved cooking water to thin the sauce as desired.
2. Toss the green beans with the sauce and garnish with the sesame seeds, if desired. Serve immediately.

Per Serving calories: 188 | fat: 8.4g | protein: 7.2g | carbs: 22.2g | fiber: 7.9g | sodium: 200mg

Mushroom Barley Soup
Prep Time: 5 minutes | **Cooking Time:** 20 to 23 minutes | **Servings:** 6

Ingredients
2 tablespoons extra-virgin olive oil
1 cup chopped carrots
1 cup chopped onion
5½ cups chopped mushrooms
6 cups no-salt-added vegetable broth
1 cup uncooked pearled barley
¼ cup red wine
2 tablespoons tomato paste
4 sprigs fresh thyme or ½ teaspoon dried thyme
1 dried bay leaf
6 tablespoons grated Parmesan cheese

Directions
1. In a large stockpot over medium heat, heat the oil. Add the onion and carrots and cook for 5 minutes, stirring frequently. Turn up the heat to medium-high and add the mushrooms. Cook for 3 minutes, stirring frequently.
2. Add the broth, barley, wine, tomato paste, thyme, and bay leaf. Stir, cover, and bring the soup to a boil. Once it's boiling, stir a few times, reduce the heat to medium-low, cover, and cook for another 12 to 15 minutes, until the barley is cooked through.
3. Remove the bay leaf and serve the soup in bowls with 1 tablespoon of cheese sprinkled on top of each.
Per Serving
calories: 195 | fat: 4.0g | protein: 7.0g | carbs: 34.0g | fiber: 6.0g | sodium: 173mg

Sautéed White Beans with Rosemary
Prep Time: 10 minutes | **Cooking Time:** 12 minutes | **Servings:** 2

Ingredients
1 tablespoon olive oil
2 garlic cloves, minced
1 (15-ounce / 425-g) can white cannellini beans, drained and rinsed
1 teaspoon minced fresh rosemary plus 1 whole fresh rosemary sprig
¼ teaspoon dried sage
½ cup low-sodium chicken stock
Salt, to taste

Directions
1. Heat the olive oil in a saucepan over medium-high heat.
2. Add the garlic and sauté for 30 seconds until fragrant.
3. Add the beans, minced and whole rosemary, sage, and chicken stock and bring the mixture to a boil.
4. Reduce the heat to medium and allow to simmer for 10 minutes, or until most of the liquid is evaporated. If desired, mash some of the beans with a fork to thicken them. Season with salt to taste. Remove the rosemary sprig before serving.
Per Serving calories: 155 | fat: 7.0g | protein: 6.0g | carbs: 17.0g | fiber: 8.0g | sodium: 153mg

Quinoa and Garbanzo Salad (Spanish)

Prep Time: 10 minutes **Cooking Time:** 30 minutes
Servings: 8

Ingredients

4 cups water
1 cup thinly sliced onions (red or white)
2 teaspoons salt, divided
1 teaspoon freshly ground black pepper
¼ cup lemon juice
2 cups red or yellow quinoa
1 (16-ounce / 454-g) can garbanzo beans, rinsed and drained
1/3 cup extra-virgin olive oil

Directions

1. In a 3-quart pot over medium heat, bring the water to a boil.
2. Add the quinoa and 1 teaspoon of salt to the pot. Stir, cover, and let cook over low heat for 15 to 20 minutes.
3. Turn off the heat, fluff the quinoa with a fork, cover again, and let stand for 5 to 10 more minutes.
4. Put the cooked quinoa, onions, and garbanzo beans in a large bowl.
5. In a separate small bowl, whisk together the olive oil, lemon juice, remaining 1 teaspoon of salt, and black pepper.
6. Add the dressing to the quinoa mixture and gently toss everything together. Serve warm or cold.

Nutrition: calories: 318 fat: 6g protein: 9g carbs: 43g fiber: 13g sodium: 585mg

Mediterranean Salad with Peppers and Tomatoes(Greek)

Prep Time: 35 minutes **Cooking Time:** 30 minutes
Servings: 2

Ingredients

1 eggplant
1 bell pepper
1 onion
3 tbsp olive oil
4 stalks of sage
1 zucchini
4 tomatoes
4 sprigs of rosemary
6 sprigs of thyme
3 tbsp balsamic vinegar salt and pepper

Directions

1. Quarter tomatoes. Cut the remaining vegetables into bite-sized pieces, halve the onion and chop it into small pieces. Line a baking sheet with parchment paper, place the vegetables on top, drizzle with olive oil and mix well.
2. Season with salt and pepper. Scatter the herbs over the vegetables. Put the vegetables in the oven and bake at 200 degrees for about 30 minutes.
3. Remove and transfer to a large bowl and mix with olive oil with balsamic vinegar. Season with salt and pepper.
4. Let it draw covered. When the salad is still lukewarm, add the tomato quarters and mix well.
5. Serve the salad lukewarm.

Nutrition: Calories: 355 Carbohydrates: 39.43g Protein: 6.51g Fat: 21.43g

Israeli Salad (Greek)

Prep Time: 15 minutes **Cooking Time:** 6 mins
Servings: 4

Ingredients

¼ cup pine nuts
¼ cup coarsely chopped walnuts
¼ cup shelled sunflower seeds
1 pint cherry tomatoes, finely chopped
½ small red onion, finely chopped
¼ cup extra-virgin olive oil
4 cups baby arugula
¼ teaspoon freshly ground black pepper
¼ cup shelled pistachios
¼ cup shelled pumpkin seeds
2 large English cucumbers, unpeeled and finely chopped
1 teaspoon salt
½ cup finely chopped fresh flat-leaf Italian parsley
2 to 3 tablespoons freshly squeezed lemon juice

Directions

1. In a large dry skillet, toast the pine nuts, pistachios, walnuts, pumpkin seeds, and sunflower seeds over medium-low heat until golden and fragrant, 5 to 6 minutes, being careful not to burn them. Remove from the heat and set aside.
2. In a large bowl, combine the cucumber, tomatoes, red onion, and parsley.
3. In a small bowl, whisk together olive oil, lemon juice, salt, and pepper. Pour over the chopped vegetables and toss to coat.
4. Add the toasted nuts and seeds and arugula and toss with the salad to blend well. Serve at room temperature or chilled.

Nutrition: calories: 414 fat: 34g protein: 10g carbs: 17g fiber: 6g sodium: 642mg

Healthy Detox Salad (Italian)

Prep Time: 5 minutes **Cooking Time:** 0 minutes
Servings: 4

Ingredients

4 cups mixed greens
2 tbsp lemon juice
2 tbsp almonds, chopped
1 large apple, diced
2 tbsp pumpkin seed oil
1 tbsp chia seeds
1 large carrot, coarsely grated
1 large beet, coarsely grated

Directions

1. In a medium salad bowl, except for mixed greens, combine all thoroughly.
2. Into 4 salad plates, divide the mixed greens.
3. Evenly top mixed greens with the salad bowl mixture.
4. Serve and enjoy.

Nutrition: Calories: 141; Protein: 2.1g; Carbs: 14.7g; Fat: 8.2g

Bulgur, Kale and Cheese Mix (Italian)

Prep Time: 10 minutes
Cooking Time: 10 minutes
Servings: 6

Ingredients

4 ounces bulgur	4 ounces kale, chopped
1 tablespoon mint, chopped	1 cucumber, chopped
A pinch of allspice, ground	4 ounces feta cheese, crumbled
2 tablespoons olive oil	
Zest and juice of ½ lemon	3 spring onions, chopped

Directions

1. Put bulgur in a bowl, cover with hot water, aside for 10 minutes, and fluff with a fork. Heat a pan with the oil over medium heat, add the onions and the allspice and cook for 3 minutes.
2. Add the bulgur and the rest of the , cook everything for 5-6 minutes more, divide between plates, and serve.

Nutrition: 200 Calories 6.7g Fat 3.4g Fiber 15.4g Carbs 4.5g protein

Spicy Green Beans Mix (Greek)

Prep Time: 5 minutes **Cooking Time:** 15 minutes
Servings: 4

Ingredients

4 teaspoons olive oil	½ teaspoon hot paprika
¾ cup veggie stock	1 yellow onion, sliced
1-pound green beans, trimmed and halved	½ cup goat cheese, shredded
1 garlic clove, minced	2 teaspoon balsamic vinegar

Directions

1. Heat a pan with the oil over medium heat, add the garlic, stir, and cook for 1 minute.
2. Add the green beans and the rest of the , toss, cook everything for 15 minutes more, divide between plates, and serve as a side dish.

Nutrition: 188 Calories 4g Fat 3g Fiber 12.4g Carbs 4.4g protein

Beans and Rice (Spanish)

Prep Time: 10 minutes **Cooking Time:** 55 minutes
Servings: 6

Ingredients

1 tablespoon olive oil	1 yellow onion, chopped
2 celery stalks, chopped	2 cups brown rice
2 garlic cloves, minced	4 cups water
1 and ½ cup canned black beans, rinsed and drained	Salt and black pepper to the taste

Directions

1. Heat a pan with the oil over medium heat, add the celery, garlic, and onion, stir, and cook for 10 minutes.
2. Add the rest of the , stir, bring to a simmer, and cook over medium heat for 45 minutes. Divide between plates and serve.

Nutrition: 224 Calories 8.4g Fat 3.4g Fiber 15.3g Carbs 6.2g protein

Lime Cucumber Mix (Greek)

Prep Time: 10 minutes
Cooking Time: 0 minute
Servings: 8

Ingredients

4 cucumbers, chopped	½ cup green bell pepper, chopped
1 yellow onion, chopped	
1 chili pepper, chopped	1 teaspoon parsley, chopped
1 garlic clove, minced	2 tablespoons lime juice
1 tablespoon dill, chopped	Salt and black pepper to the taste
1 tablespoon olive oil	

Directions

1. In a large bowl, mix the cucumber with the bell peppers and the rest of the , toss, and serve as a side dish.

Nutrition: 123 Calories 4.3g Fat 2.3g Fiber 5.6g Carbs 2g protein

Walnuts Cucumber Mix (Greek)

Prep Time: 5 minutes **Cooking Time:** 0 minute
Servings: 2

Ingredients

1cucumbers, chopped	Salt and black pepper to the taste
1 tablespoon olive oil	
1 tablespoon lemon juice	1 tablespoon balsamic vinegar
3 tablespoons walnuts, chopped	
1 red chili pepper, dried	1 teaspoon chives, chopped

Directions

1. In a bowl, mix the cucumbers with the oil and the rest of the , toss, and serve as a side dish.

Nutrition: 121 Calories 2.3g Fat 2g Fiber 6.7g Carbs 2.4g protein

Balsamic Asparagus (Greek)

Prep Time: 10 minutes **Cooking Time:** 15 minutes
Servings: 4

Ingredients

3 tablespoons olive oil	Salt and black pepper to the taste
3 garlic cloves minced	
2 tablespoons shallot chopped	2 teaspoons balsamic vinegar
1 and ½ pound asparagus trimmed	

Directions

1. Heat a pan with the oil over medium-high heat, add the garlic and the shallot and sauté for 3 minutes.
2. Add the rest of the , cook for 12 minutes more, divide between plates, and serve as a side dish.

Nutrition: 100 Calories 10.5g Fat 1.2g Fiber 2.3g Carbs 2.1g protein

Lemony Carrots (Italian)

Prep Time: 10 minutes **Cooking Time:** 40 minutes
Servings: 4

Ingredients

1tablespoons olive oil
1 tablespoon dill, chopped
½ teaspoon lemon zest, grated
1 tablespoon lemon juice
1 teaspoon cumin, ground

2 pounds baby carrots, trimmed
1/3 cup Greek yogurt
1 garlic clove, minced
Salt and black pepper to the taste

Directions

1. In a roasting pan, combine the carrots with the oil, salt, pepper and the rest of the except the dill, toss and bake at 400 degrees F for 20 minutes.
2. Reduce the temperature to 375 degrees F and cook for 20 minutes more.
3. Divide the mix between plates, sprinkle the dill on top and serve.

Nutrition: calories 192, fat 5.4, fiber 3.4, carbs 7.3, protein 5.6

Oregano Potatoes (Spanish)

Prep Time: 10 minutes **Cooking Time:** 40 minutes
Servings: 4

Ingredients

6 red potatoes, peeled and cut into wedges
Salt and black pepper to the taste
1 teaspoon lemon zest, grated

2 tablespoons olive oil ½ cup chicken stock
1 teaspoon oregano, dried
1tablespoon chives, chopped

Directions

1. In a roasting pan, combine the potatoes with salt, pepper, the oil and the rest of the except the chives, toss, introduce in the oven and cook at 425 degrees F for 40 minutes.
2. Divide the mix between plates, sprinkle the chives on top and serve as a side dish.

Nutrition: calories 245, fat 4.5, fiber 2.8, carbs 7.1, protein 6.4

Chives Rice Mix (Spanish)

Prep Time: 5 minutes **Cooking Time:** 5 mins
Servings: 4

Ingredients

2tablespoons avocado oil
2 tablespoons chives, chopped

1 cup Arborio rice cooked
Salt and black pepper to the taste
2 teaspoons lemon juice

Directions

1. Heat up a pan with the avocado oil over medium high heat, add the rice and the rest of the , toss, cook for 5 minutes, divide the mix between plates and serve as a side dish.

Nutrition: calories 236, fat 9, fiber 12.4, carbs 17.5, protein 4.5

Baby Squash and Lentils Mix (Greek)

Prep Time: 10 minutes **Cooking Time:** 10 minutes
Servings: 4

Ingredients

1tablespoons olive oil
10 ounces baby squash, sliced
1 tablespoon balsamic vinegar
1 tablespoon dill, chopped

½ teaspoon sweet paprika
15 ounces canned lentils, drained and rinsed Salt and black pepper to the taste

Directions

1. Heat up a pan with the oil over medium heat, add the squash, lentils and the rest of the , toss and cook over medium heat for 10 minutes.
2. Divide the mix between plates and serve as a side dish.

Nutrition: calories 438, fat 8.4, fiber 32.4, carbs 65.5, protein 22.4

Parmesan Quinoa and Mushrooms (Spanish)

Prep Time: 10 minutes **Cooking Time:** 20 minutes
Servings: 4

Ingredients

1cup quinoa, cooked
2tablespoons olive oil
1 teaspoon garlic, minced
Salt and black pepper to the taste
2 tablespoons cilantro, chopped

½ cup chicken stock
6 ounces white mushrooms, sliced
½ cup parmesan, grated

Directions

1. Heat up a pan with the oil over medium heat, add the garlic and mushrooms, stir and sauté for 10 minutes. Add the quinoa and the rest of the , toss, cook over medium heat for 10 minutes more, divide between plates and serve as a side dish.

Nutrition: calories 233, fat 9.5, fiber 6.4, carbs 27.4, protein 12.5

Green Beans and Peppers Mix (Greek)

Prep Time: 10 minutes **Cooking Time:** 10 minutes
Servings: 4

Ingredients

2 tablespoons olive oil
1 tablespoon dill, chopped
1 tablespoon lime juice
2 red bell peppers, cut into strips

1and ½ pounds green beans, trimmed and halved
Salt and black pepper to the taste
2 tablespoons rosemary, chopped

Directions

1. Heat up a pan with the oil over medium heat, add the bell peppers and the green beans, toss and cook for 5 minutes.
2. Add the rest of the , toss, cook for 5 minutes more, divide between plates and serve as a side dish.

Nutrition: calories 222, fat 8.6, fiber 3.4, carbs 8.6, protein 3.4

Garlic Snap Peas Mix (Greek)

Prep Time: 10 minutes **Cooking Time:** 10 minutes
Servings: 4

Ingredients

½ cup walnuts, chopped
1 and ½ teaspoons garlic, minced
1 pound sugar snap peas
¼ cup olive oil
½ cup veggie stock
2 teaspoons lime juice
Salt and black pepper to the taste
1 tablespoon chives, chopped

Directions

1. Heat up a pan with the stock over medium heat, add the snap peas and cook for 5 minutes.
2. Add the rest of the except the chives, cook for 5 minutes more and divide between plates.
3. Sprinkle the chives on top and serve as a side dish.
Nutrition: calories 200, fat 7.6, fiber 3.5, carbs 8.5, protein 4.3

Corn and Olives (Spanish)

Prep Time: 5 minutes **Cooking Time:** 0 min
Servings: 4

Ingredients

2 cups corn
2 tablespoons extra virgin olive oil
½ teaspoon balsamic vinegar
Salt and black pepper to the taste
4 ounces green olives, pitted and halved
1 teaspoon thyme, chopped
1 tablespoon oregano, chopped

Directions

1. In a bowl, combine the corn with the olives and the rest of the , toss and serve as a side dish.
Nutrition: calories 154, fat 10, fiber 3.4, carbs 17, protein 9.3

Rosemary Red Quinoa (Greek)

Prep Time: 10 minutes **Cooking Time:** 25 minutes
Servings: 6

Ingredients

4 cups chicken stock
2 tablespoons olive oil
1 teaspoon lemon zest, grated
2 tablespoons lemon juice
1 red onion, chopped
2 cups red quinoa, rinsed
1 tablespoon garlic, minced
Salt and black pepper to the taste
2 tablespoons rosemary, chopped

Directions

1. Heat up a pan with the oil over medium heat, add the onion and the garlic and sauté for 5 minutes.
2. Add the quinoa, the stock and the rest of the , bring to a simmer and cook for 20 minutes stirring from time to time.
3. Divide the mix between plates and serve.
Nutrition: calories 193, fat 7.9, fiber 1.4, carbs 5.4, protein 1.3

Thyme Corn and Cheese Mix (Greek)

Prep Time: 5 minutes **Cooking Time:** 0 min
Servings: 4

Ingredients

1 tablespoon olive oil
2cups corn
1 cup scallions, sliced
2 tablespoons blue cheese, crumbled
1teaspoon thyme, chopped
Salt and black pepper to the taste
1 tablespoon chives, chopped

1. In a salad bowl, combine the corn with scallions, thyme and the rest of the , toss, divide between plates and serve.
Nutrition: calories 183, fat 5.5, fiber 7.5, carbs 14.5

Olives and Carrots Sauté (Greek)

Prep Time: 10 minutes **Cooking Time:** 20 minutes
Servings: 4

Ingredients

1tablespoon green olives, pitted and sliced
½ teaspoon lemon zest, grated
¼ teaspoon rosemary, dried
Salt and black pepper to the taste
2 pounds carrots, sliced
1 tablespoon parsley, chopped
2teaspoons capers, drained and chopped
1and ½ teaspoons balsamic vinegar
¼ cup veggie stock
2spring onions, chopped
3 tablespoons olive oil

Directions

1. Heat up a pan with the oil over medium heat, add the carrots and brown for 5 minutes.
2. Add green olives, capers and the rest of the except the parsley and the chives, stir and cook over medium heat for 15 minutes.
3. Add the chives and parsley, toss, divide the mix between plates and serve as a side dish.
Nutrition: calories 244, fat 11, fiber 3.5, carbs 5.6, protein 6.3

Lemon Endives (Greek)

Prep Time: 10 minutes **Cooking Time:** 35 minutes
Servings: 4

Ingredients

Juice of 1 and ½ lemons
3 tablespoons olive oil
¼ cup veggie stock
Salt and black pepper to the taste
4 endives, halved lengthwise
1 tablespoon dill, chopped

Directions

1. In a roasting pan, combine the endives with the rest of the, introduce in the oven and cook at 375 degrees F for 35 minutes.
2. Divide the endives between plates and serve as a side dish.
Nutrition: calories 221, fat 5.4, fiber 6.4, carbs 15.4, protein 14.3

Yogurt Peppers Mix (Greek)

Prep Time: 10 minutes **Cooking Time:** 15 minutes
Servings: 4

Ingredients

1red bell peppers, cut into thick strips
3 garlic cloves, minced
1 tablespoon cilantro, chopped
½ cup Greek yogurt
2shallots, chopped
2 tablespoons olive oil
Salt and black pepper to the taste

Directions

1. Heat up a pan with the oil over medium heat, add the shallots and garlic, stir and cook for 5 minutes.
2. Add the rest of the , toss, cook for 10 minutes more, divide the mix between plates and serve as a side dish.

Nutrition: calories 274, fat 11, fiber 3.5, protein 13.3, carbs 6.5

Basil Artichokes (Italian)

Prep Time: 10 minutes **Cooking Time:** 12 minutes
Servings: 4

Ingredients

1red onion, chopped
Salt and black pepper to the taste
10 ounces canned artichoke hearts, drained
2tablespoons basil, chopped
2garlic cloves, minced
½ cup veggie stock
1teaspoon lemon juice
1 tablespoon olive oil

Directions

1. Heat up a pan with the oil over medium high heat, add the
2. onion and the garlic, stir and sauté for 2 minutes.
3. Add the artichokes and the rest of the , toss, cook for 10 minutes more, divide between plates and serve as a side dish.

Nutrition: calories 105, fat 7.6, fiber 3, carbs 6.7, protein 2.5

Broccoli and Roasted Peppers (Greek)

Prep Time: 10 minutes **Cooking Time:** 10 minutes
Servings: 4

Ingredients

1 pound broccoli florets.
1 tablespoon olive oil
2 tablespoons balsamic vinegar.
1 tablespoon cilantro, chopped
2 garlic cloves, minced.
¼ cup roasted peppers, chopped.
Salt and black pepper to the taste.

Directions

1. Heat up a pan with the oil over medium high heat, add the garlic and the peppers and cook for 2 minutes.
2. Add the broccoli and the rest of the , toss, cook over medium heat for 8 minutes more, divide between plates and serve as a side dish.

Nutrition: calories 193, fat 5.6, fiber 3.45, carbs 8.6, protein 4.5

Cauliflower Quinoa (Greek)

Prep Time: 5 minutes **Cooking Time:** 10 minutes
Servings: 4

Ingredients

1 and ½ cups quinoa
3 cups cauliflower florets
2 spring onions
1 tablespoon red wine vinegar
1 tablespoon parsley
3 tablespoons olive oil
chopped Salt and pepper to the taste
chopped
1 tablespoon chives
chopped

Directions

1. Heat up a pan with the oil over medium-high heat, add the spring onions and cook for 2 minutes.
2. Add the cauliflower, quinoa and the rest of the , toss, cook over medium heat for 8-9 minutes, divide between plates and serve as a side dish.

Nutrition: calories 220, fat 16.7, fiber 5.6, carbs 6.8, protein 5.4

Mixed Veggies and Chard (Greek)

Prep Time: 10 minutes **Cooking Time:** 20 minutes
Servings: 4

Ingredients

½ cup celery, chopped
½ cup red onion, chopped
1 cup veggie stock
1 tablespoon olive oil
Salt and black pepper to the taste
½ cup carrot, chopped
½ cup red bell pepper, chopped
½ cup black olives, pitted and chopped
10 ounces ruby chard, torn
1 teaspoon balsamic vinegar

Directions

1. Heat up a pan with the oil over medium-high heat, add the celery, carrot, onion, bell pepper, salt and pepper, stir and sauté for 5 minutes.
2. Add the rest of the , toss, cook over medium heat for 15 minutes more, divide between plates and serve as a side dish.

Nutrition: calories 150, fat 6.7, fiber 2.6, carbs 6.8, protein 5.4

Spicy Broccoli and Almonds (Greek)

Prep Time: 10 minutes **Cooking Time:** 30 minutes
Servings: 4

Ingredients

1 broccoli head, florets separated
1tablespoon chili powder
2tablespoons almonds, toasted and chopped
1 tablespoon olive oil
2 garlic cloves, minced
Salt and black pepper to the taste
1 tablespoon mint, chopped

Directions

1. In a roasting pan, combine the broccoli with the garlic, oil and the rest of the , toss, introduce in the oven and cook at 390 degrees F for 30 minutes.
2. Divide the mix between plates and serve as a side dish.

Nutrition: calories 156, fat 5.4, fiber 1.2, carbs 4.3, protein 2

Broccoli Salad with Caramelized Onions (Italian)

Prep Time: 10 minutes **Cooking Time:** 25 minutes
Servings: 4

Ingredients

3 tablespoons extra-virgin olive oil	1 teaspoon dried thyme
2 tablespoons balsamic vinegar	2 red onions, sliced
Salt and pepper to taste	1-pound broccoli, cut into florets

Directions

1. Heat the oil and add in sliced onions. Cook until the onions are caramelized. Stir in vinegar and thyme, and then remove from the stove.
2. Mix together the broccoli and onion mixture in a bowl, adding salt and pepper if desired. Serve and eat salad as soon as possible.

Nutrition: Calories: 113 Fat: 9 g Fiber: 8 g Carbs: 13 g Protein: 18 g

Olives and Lentils Salad (Greek)

Prep Time: 10 minutes **Cooking Time:** 0 minutes
Servings: 2

Ingredients

1/3 cup canned green lentils	1 cups baby spinach
1 tablespoon olive oil	1 cup black olives
2 tablespoons sunflower seeds	2 tablespoons balsamic vinegar
1 tablespoon Dijon mustard	2 tablespoons olive oil

Directions

1. Mix the lentils with the spinach, olives, and the rest of the in a salad bowl, toss and serve cold.

Nutrition: Calories: 279 Fat: 6.5 g Protein: 12 g

Tomato Salad (Spanish)

Prep Time: 22 minutes **Cooking Time:** 0 minute
Servings: 4

Ingredients

1 cucumber, sliced	¼ cup sun-dried tomatoes, chopped
1 lb. tomatoes, cubed	
½ cup black olives	1 tablespoon balsamic vinegar
1 red onion, sliced	
¼ cup parsley, fresh & chopped	2 tablespoons olive oil

Directions

1. Get out a bowl and combine all your vegetables. To make your dressing mix all your seasoning, olive oil, and vinegar.
2. Toss with your salad and serve fresh.

Nutrition: 126 Calories 2.1g Protein 9.2g Fat

Chicken and Cabbage Salad (Italian)

Prep Time: 10 minutes **Cooking Time:** 6 minutes
Servings: 4

Ingredients

1 medium chicken breasts	5 tablespoon extra-virgin olive oil
4 ounces green cabbage	
2 tablespoons sherry vinegar tablespoon chives	¼ cup feta cheese, crumbled
¼ cup barbeque sauce	Bacon slices, cooked and crumbled
Salt and black pepper to taste	

Directions

1. In a bowl, mix 4 tablespoon oils with vinegar, salt and pepper to taste and stir well.
2. Add the shredded cabbage, toss to coat, and leave aside for now.
3. Season chicken with salt and pepper, heat a pan with remaining oil over medium-high heat, add chicken, cook for 6 minutes, take off heat, transfer to a bowl and mix well with barbeque sauce.
4. Arrange salad on serving plates, add chicken strips, sprinkle cheese, chives, and crumbled bacon, and serve right away.

Nutrition: 200 Calories 15g Fat 33g Protein

Roasted Broccoli Salad (Italian)

Prep Time: 9 minutes **Cooking Time:** 17 minutes
Servings: 4

Ingredients

1 lb. broccoli	3 tablespoons olive oil, divided 1-pint cherry tomatoes
1 tablespoon balsamic vinegar	
1 ½ teaspoons honey	3 cups cubed bread
½ teaspoon black pepper	¼ teaspoon sea salt, fine grated parmesan

Directions

1. Set the oven to 450, and then place a rimmed baking sheet.
2. Drizzle your broccoli with a tablespoon of oil, and toss to coat.
3. Take out from the oven, and spoon the broccoli. Leave oil at the bottom of the bowl and add in your tomatoes, toss to coat, then mix tomatoes with a tablespoon of honey. place on the same baking sheet.
4. Roast for fifteen minutes, and stir halfway through your cooking time.
5. Add in your bread, and then roast for three more minutes.
6. Whisk two tablespoons of oil, vinegar, and remaining honey. Season. Pour this over your broccoli mix to serve.

Nutrition: 226 Calories 7g Protein 12g Fat

Chapter 4
Sandwiches Recipes, Pizzas Recipes, & Wraps Recipes

Falafel Balls with Tahini Sauce

Prep Time: 2 hours 20 minutes | **Cooking Time:** 20 minutes | **Servings:** 4

Ingredients

Tahini Sauce:
½ cup tahini
2 tablespoons lemon juice
¼ cup finely chopped flat-leaf parsley
2 cloves garlic, minced
½ cup cold water, as needed

Falafel:
1 cup dried chickpeas, soaked overnight, drained
¼ cup chopped flat-leaf parsley

¼ cup chopped cilantro
1 large onion, chopped
1 teaspoon cumin
½ teaspoon chili flakes
4 cloves garlic
1 teaspoon sea salt
5 tablespoons almond flour
1½ teaspoons baking soda, dissolved in 1 teaspoon water
2 cups peanut oil
1 medium bell pepper, chopped
1 medium tomato, chopped
4 whole-wheat pita breads

Directions

Make the Tahini Sauce
1. Combine the for the tahini sauce in a small bowl. Stir to mix well until smooth.
2. Wrap the bowl in plastic and refrigerate until ready to serve.

Make the Falafel
3. Put the chickpeas, parsley, cilantro, onion, cumin, chili flakes, garlic, and salt in a food processor. Pulse to mix well but not puréed.
4. Add the flour and baking soda to the food processor, then pulse to form a smooth and tight dough.
5. Put the dough in a large bowl and wrap in plastic. Refrigerate for at least 2 hours to let it rise.
6. Divide and shape the dough into walnut-sized small balls.
7. Pour the peanut oil in a large pot and heat over high heat until the temperature of the oil reaches 375°F (190°C).
8. Drop 6 balls into the oil each time, and fry for 5 minutes or until golden brown and crispy. Turn the balls with a strainer to make them fried evenly.
9. Transfer the balls on paper towels with the strainer, then drain the oil from the balls.
10. Roast the pita breads in the oven for 5 minutes or until golden brown, if needed, then stuff the pitas with falafel balls and top with bell peppers and tomatoes. Drizzle with tahini sauce and serve immediately.

Per Serving
calories: 574 | fat: 27.1g | protein: 19.8g | carbs: 69.7g | fiber: 13.4g | sodium: 1246mg

Glazed Mushroom and Vegetable Fajitas

Prep Time: 20 minutes | **Cooking Time:** 20 minutes
Makes 6

Ingredients

Spicy Glazed Mushrooms:
1 teaspoon olive oil
1 (10- to 12-ounce / 284- to 340-g) package cremini mushrooms, rinsed and drained, cut into thin slices
to 1 teaspoon chili powder
Sea salt and freshly ground black pepper, to taste
1 teaspoon maple syrup

Fajitas:
2 teaspoons olive oil
1 onion, chopped
Sea salt, to taste
1 bell pepper, any color, deseeded and sliced into long strips
1 zucchini, cut into large matchsticks
6 whole-grain tortilla
2 carrots, grated
3 to 4 scallions, sliced
½ cup fresh cilantro, finely chopped

Directions

Make the Spicy Glazed Mushrooms
1. Heat the olive oil in a nonstick skillet over medium heat until shimmering.
2. Add the mushrooms and sauté for 10 minutes or until tender.
3. Sprinkle the mushrooms with chili powder, salt, and ground black pepper. Drizzle with maple syrup. Stir to mix well and cook for 5 to 7 minutes or until the mushrooms are glazed. Set aside until ready to use.

Make the Fajitas
4. Heat the olive oil in the same skillet over medium heat until shimmering.
5. Add the onion and sauté for 5 minutes or until translucent. Sprinkle with salt.
6. Add the bell pepper and zucchini and sauté for 7 minutes or until tender.
7. Meanwhile, toast the tortilla in the oven for 5 minutes or until golden brown.
8. Allow the tortilla to cool for a few minutes until they can be handled, then assemble the tortilla with glazed mushrooms, sautéed vegetables and remaining vegetables to make the fajitas. Serve immediately.

Per Serving
calories: 403 | fat: 14.8g | protein: 11.2g | carbs: 7.9g | fiber: 7.0g | sodium: 230mg

Green Veggie Sandwiches

Prep Time: 20 minutes | **Cooking Time:** 0 minutes | **Servings:** 2

Ingredients

Spread:
1 (15-ounce / 425-g) can cannellini beans, drained and rinsed
⅓ cup packed fresh basil leaves
⅓ cup packed fresh parsley
⅓ cup chopped fresh chives
2 garlic cloves, chopped
Zest and juice of ½ lemon
1 tablespoon apple cider vinegar

Sandwiches:
4 whole-grain bread slices, toasted
8 English cucumber slices
1 large beefsteak tomato, cut into slices
1 large avocado, halved, pitted, and cut into slices
1 small yellow bell pepper, cut into slices
2 handfuls broccoli sprouts
2 handfuls fresh spinach

Directions
Make the Spread
1. In a food processor, combine the cannellini beans, basil, parsley, chives, garlic, lemon zest and juice, and vinegar. Pulse a few times, scrape down the sides, and purée until smooth. You may need to scrape down the sides again to incorporate all the basil and parsley. Refrigerate for at least 1 hour to allow the flavors to blend. Assemble the Sandwiches
2. Build your sandwiches by spreading several tablespoons of spread on each slice of bread. Layer two slices of bread with the cucumber, tomato, avocado, bell pepper, broccoli sprouts, and spinach. Top with the remaining bread slices and press down lightly. Serve immediately.

Per Serving
calories: 617 | fat: 21.1g | protein: 28.1g | carbs: 86.1g | fiber: 25.6g | sodium: 593mg

Mushroom-Pesto Baked Pizza

Prep Time: 5 minutes | **Cooking Time:** 15 minutes | **Servings:** 2

Ingredients
1 teaspoon extra-virgin olive oil
½ cup sliced mushrooms
½ red onion, sliced
Salt and freshly ground black pepper
¼ cup store-bought pesto sauce
2 whole-wheat flatbreads
¼ cup shredded Mozzarella cheese

Directions
1. Preheat the oven to 350°F (180°C). In a small skillet, heat the oil over medium heat. Add the mushrooms and onion, and season with salt and pepper. Sauté for 3 to 5 minutes until the onion and mushrooms begin to soften. Spread 2 tablespoons of pesto on each flatbread. Divide the mushroom-onion mixture between the two flatbreads. Top each with 2 tablespoons of cheese. Place the flatbreads on a baking sheet and bake for 10 to 12 minutes until the cheese is melted and bubbly. Serve warm.

Per Serving calories: 348 | fat: 23.5g | protein: 14.2g | carbs: 28.1g | fiber: 7.1g | sodium: 792mg

Tuna and Hummus Wraps

Prep Time: 10 minutes | **Cooking Time:** 0 minutes | **Servings:** 2

Ingredients
Hummus:
1 cup from 1 (15-ounce / 425-g) can low-sodium chickpeas, drained and rinsed
2 tablespoons tahini
1 tablespoon extra-virgin olive oil
1 garlic clove
Juice of ½ lemon
2 tablespoons water

Wraps:
4 large lettuce leaves
1 (5-ounce / 142-g) can chunk light tuna packed in water, drained
1 red bell pepper, seeded and cut into strips
1 cucumber, sliced
¼ teaspoon salt

Directions
Make the Hummus
1. In a blender jar, combine the chickpeas, tahini, olive oil, garlic, lemon juice, salt, and water. Process until smooth. Taste and adjust with additional lemon juice or salt, as needed.

Make the Wraps
2. On each lettuce leaf, spread 1 tablespoon of hummus, and divide the tuna among the leaves. Top each with several strips of red pepper and cucumber slices.
3. Roll up the lettuce leaves, folding in the two shorter sides and rolling away from you, like a burrito. Serve immediately.

Per Serving calories: 192 | fat: 5.1g | protein: 26.1g | carbs: 15.1g | fiber: 4.1g | sodium: 352mg

Tuna and Olive Salad Sandwiches

Prep Time: 10 minutes | **Cooking Time:** 0 minutes | **Servings:** 4

Ingredients
3 tablespoons freshly squeezed lemon juice
2 tablespoons extra-virgin olive oil
1 garlic clove, minced
½ teaspoon freshly ground black pepper
2 (5-ounce / 142-g) cans tuna, drained
1 (2.25-ounce / 64-g) can sliced olives, any green or black variety
½ cup chopped fresh fennel, including fronds
8 slices whole-grain crusty bread

Directions
1. In a medium bowl, whisk together the lemon juice, oil, garlic, and pepper. Add the tuna, olives and fennel to the bowl. Using a fork, separate the tuna into chunks and stir to incorporate all the .
2. Divide the tuna salad equally among 4 slices of bread. Top each with the remaining bread slices.
3. Let the sandwiches sit for at least 5 minutes so the zesty filling can soak into the bread before serving.

Per Serving
calories: 952 | fat: 17.0g | protein: 165.0g | carbs: 37.0g | fiber: 7.0g | sodium: 2572mg

Mediterranean Greek Salad Wraps

Prep Time: 15 minutes | **Cooking Time:** 0 minutes | **Servings:** 4

Ingredients

1½ cups seedless cucumber, peeled and chopped
1 cup chopped tomato
½ cup finely chopped fresh mint
¼ cup diced red onion
1 (2.25-ounce / 64-g) can sliced black olives, drained
2 tablespoons extra-virgin olive oil
1 tablespoon red wine vinegar
¼ teaspoon kosher salt
¼ teaspoon freshly ground black pepper
½ cup crumbled goat cheese
4 whole-wheat flatbread wraps or soft whole-wheat tortillas

Directions

1. In a large bowl, stir together the cucumber, tomato, mint, onion and olives.
2. In a small bowl, whisk together the oil, vinegar, salt, and pepper. Spread the dressing over the salad. Toss gently to combine.
3. On a clean work surface, lay the wraps. Divide the goat cheese evenly among the wraps. Scoop a quarter of the salad filling down the center of each wrap.
4. Fold up each wrap: Start by folding up the bottom, then fold one side over and fold the other side over the top. Repeat with the remaining wraps.
5. Serve immediately.

Per Serving

calories: 225 | fat: 12.0g | protein: 12.0g | carbs: 18.0g | fiber: 4.0g | sodium: 349mg

Pizza Pockets

Prep Time: 10 minutes | **Cooking Time:** 0 minutes | **Servings:** 2

Ingredients

½ cup tomato sauce
½ teaspoon oregano
½ teaspoon garlic powder
½ cup chopped black olives
2 canned artichoke hearts, drained and chopped
2 ounces (57 g) pepperoni, chopped
½ cup shredded Mozzarella cheese
1 whole-wheat pita, halved

Directions

1. In a medium bowl, stir together the tomato sauce, oregano, and garlic powder.
2. Add the olives, artichoke hearts, pepperoni, and cheese. Stir to mix.
3. Spoon the mixture into the pita halves and serve.

Per Serving

calories: 375 | fat: 23.5g | protein: 17.1g | carbs: 27.1g | fiber: 6.1g | sodium: 1080mg

Grilled Caesar Salad Sandwiches

Prep Time: 5 minutes | **Cooking Time:** 5 minutes | **Servings:** 2

Ingredients

¾ cup olive oil, divided
2 romaine lettuce hearts, left intact
3 to 4 anchovy fillets
Juice of 1 lemon
2 to 3 cloves garlic, peeled
1 teaspoon Dijon mustard
¼ teaspoon Worcestershire sauce
Sea salt and freshly ground pepper, to taste
2 slices whole-wheat bread, toasted
Freshly grated Parmesan cheese, for serving

Directions

1. Preheat the grill to medium-high heat and oil the grates.
2. On a cutting board, drizzle the lettuce with 1 to 2 tablespoons of olive oil and place on the grates.
3. Grill for 5 minutes, turning until lettuce is slightly charred on all sides. Let lettuce cool enough to handle.
4. In a food processor, combine the remaining olive oil with the anchovies, lemon juice, garlic, mustard, and Worcestershire sauce.
5. Pulse the until you have a smooth emulsion. Season with sea salt and freshly ground pepper to taste. Chop the lettuce in half and place on the bread.
6. Drizzle with the dressing and serve with a sprinkle of Parmesan cheese.

Per Serving

calories: 949 | fat: 85.6g | protein: 12.9g | carbs: 34.1g | fiber: 13.9g | sodium: 786mg

Chickpea Lettuce Wraps

Prep Time: 15 minutes | **Cooking Time:** 0 minutes | **Servings:** 2

Ingredients

1 (15-ounce / 425-g) can chickpeas, drained and rinsed well
1 celery stalk, diced
½ shallot, minced
1 green apple, cored and diced
3 tablespoons tahini (sesame paste)
2 teaspoons freshly squeezed lemon juice
1 teaspoon raw honey
1 teaspoon Dijon mustard
Dash salt
Filtered water, to thin
4 romaine lettuce leaves

Directions

1. In a medium bowl, stir together the chickpeas, celery, shallot, apple, tahini, lemon juice, honey, mustard, and salt. If needed, add some water to thin the mixture.
2. Place the romaine lettuce leaves on a plate. Fill each with the chickpea filling, using it all. Wrap the leaves around the filling. Serve immediately.

Per Serving calories: 397 | fat: 15.1g | protein: 15.1g | carbs: 53.1g | fiber: 15.3g | sodium: 409mg

Vegetable and Cheese Lavash Pizza

Prep Time: 15 minutes | **Cooking Time:** 11 minutes | **Servings:** 4

Ingredients

2 (12 by 9-inch) lavash breads
2 tablespoons extra-virgin olive oil
10 ounces (284 g) frozen spinach, thawed and squeezed dry
1 cup shredded fontina cheese
1 tomato, cored and cut into ½-inch pieces
½ cup pitted large green olives, chopped
¼ teaspoon red pepper flakes
3 garlic cloves, minced
¼ teaspoon sea salt
¼ teaspoon ground black pepper
½ cup grated Parmesan cheese

Directions

1. Preheat oven to 475ºF (246ºC).
2. Brush the lavash breads with olive oil, then place them on two baking sheet. Heat in the preheated oven for 4 minutes or until lightly browned. Flip the breads halfway through the cooking time.
3. Meanwhile, combine the spinach, fontina cheese, tomato pieces, olives, red pepper flakes, garlic, salt, and black pepper in a large bowl. Stir to mix well.
4. Remove the lavash bread from the oven and sit them on two large plates, spread them with the spinach mixture, then scatter with the Parmesan cheese on top.
5. Bake in the oven for 7 minutes or until the cheese melts and well browned. Slice and serve warm.

Per Serving calories: 431 | fat: 21.5g | protein: 20.0g | carbs: 38.4g | fiber: 2.5g | sodium: 854mg

Greek Vegetable Salad Pita

Prep Time: 10 minutes | **Cooking Time:** 0 minutes | **Servings:** 4

Ingredients

½ cup baby spinach leaves
½ small red onion, thinly sliced
½ small cucumber, deseeded and chopped
1 tomato, chopped
1 cup chopped romaine lettuce
1 tablespoon extra-virgin olive oil
½ tablespoon red wine vinegar
1 teaspoon Dijon mustard
1 tablespoon crumbled feta cheese
Sea salt and freshly ground pepper, to taste
1 whole-wheat pita

Directions

1. Combine all the , except for the pita, in a large bowl. Toss to mix well. Stuff the pita with the salad, then serve immediately. **Per Serving** calories: 137 | fat: 8.1g | protein: 3.1g | carbs: 14.3g | fiber: 2.4g | sodium: 166mg

Artichoke and Cucumber Hoagies

Prep Time: 10 minutes | **Cooking Time:** 15 minutes
Makes 1

Ingredients

1 (12-ounce / 340-g) whole grain baguette, sliced in half horizontally
1 cup frozen and thawed artichoke hearts, roughly chopped
1 cucumber, sliced
2 tomatoes, sliced
1 red bell pepper, sliced
⅓ cup Kalamata olives, pitted and chopped
¼ small red onion, thinly sliced
Sea salt and ground black pepper, to taste
2 tablespoons pesto
Balsamic vinegar, to taste

Directions

1. arrange the baguette halves on a clean work surface, then cut off the top third from each half. Scoop some insides of the bottom half out and reserve as breadcrumbs.
2. Toast the baguette in a baking pan in the oven for 1 minute to brown lightly. Put the artichokes, cucumber, tomatoes, bell pepper, olives, and onion in a large bowl. Sprinkle with salt and ground black pepper. Toss to combine well.
3. Spread the bottom half of the baguette with the vegetable mixture and drizzle with balsamic vinegar, then smear the cut side of the baguette top with pesto. Assemble the two baguette halves. Wrap the hoagies in parchment paper and let sit for at least an hour before serving.

Per Serving (1 hoagies) calories: 1263 | fat: 37.7g | protein: 56.3g | carbs: 180.1g | fiber: 37.8g | sodium: 2137mg

Mini Pork and Cucumber Lettuce Wraps

Prep Time: 20 minutes | **Cooking Time:** 0 minutes
Makes 12 wraps

Ingredients

8 ounces (227 g) cooked ground pork
1 cucumber, diced
1 tomato, diced
1 red onion, sliced
1 ounce (28 g) low-fat feta cheese, crumbled
Juice of 1 lemon
1 tablespoon extra-virgin olive oil
Sea salt and freshly ground pepper, to taste
12 small, intact iceberg lettuce leaves

Directions

1. Combine the ground pork, cucumber, tomato, and onion in a large bowl, then scatter with feta cheese.
2. Drizzle with lemon juice and olive oil, and sprinkle with salt and pepper. Toss to mix well.
3. Unfold the small lettuce leaves on a large plate or several small plates, then divide and top with the pork mixture.
4. Wrap and serve immediately.

Per Serving (1 warp)
calories: 78 | fat: 5.6g | protein: 5.5g | carbs: 1.4g | fiber: 0.3g | sodium: 50mg

Open-Faced Margherita Sandwiches

Prep Time: 10 minutes | **Cooking Time:** 5 minutes | **Servings:** 4

Ingredients

2 (6- to 7-inch) whole-wheat submarine or hoagie rolls, sliced open horizontally
1 tablespoon extra-virgin olive oil
1 garlic clove, halved
1 large ripe tomato, cut into 8 slices
¼ teaspoon dried oregano
1 cup fresh Mozzarella, sliced
¼ cup lightly packed fresh basil leaves, torn into small pieces
¼ teaspoon freshly ground black pepper

Directions

1. Preheat the broiler to High with the rack 4 inches under the heating element. Put the sliced bread on a large, rimmed baking sheet and broil for 1 minute, or until the bread is just lightly toasted. Remove from the oven.
2. Brush each piece of the toasted bread with the oil, and rub a garlic half over each piece. Put the toasted bread back on the baking sheet. Evenly divide the tomato slices on each piece. Sprinkle with the oregano and top with the cheese.
3. Place the baking sheet under the broiler. Set the timer for 1½ minutes, but check after 1 minute. When the cheese is melted and the edges are just starting to get dark brown, remove the sandwiches from the oven. Top each sandwich with the fresh basil and pepper before serving.

Per Serving calories: 93 | fat: 2.0g | protein: 10.0g | carbs: 8.0g | fiber: 2.0g | sodium: 313mg

Zucchini Hummus Wraps

Prep Time: 15 minutes | **Cooking Time:** 6 minutes | **Servings:** 2

Ingredients

1 zucchini, ends removed, thinly sliced lengthwise
¼ teaspoon freshly ground black pepper
¼ cup hummus
2 Roma tomatoes, cut lengthwise into slices
2 tablespoons chopped red onion
½ teaspoon dried oregano
¼ teaspoon garlic powder
2 whole wheat tortillas
1 cup chopped kale
½ teaspoon ground cumin

Directions

1. In a skillet over medium heat, add the zucchini slices and cook for 3 minutes per side. Sprinkle with the oregano, pepper, and garlic powder and remove from the heat.
2. Spread 2 tablespoons of hummus on each tortilla. Lay half the zucchini in the center of each tortilla. Top with tomato slices, kale, red onion, and ¼ teaspoon of cumin. Wrap tightly and serve.

Per Serving
calories: 248 | fat: 8.1g | protein: 9.1g | carbs: 37.1g | fiber: 8.1g | sodium: mg

Roasted Vegetable Panini

Prep Time: 10 minutes | **Cooking Time:** 15 minutes | **Servings:** 4

2 tablespoons extra-virgin olive oil, divided
1½ cups diced broccoli
1 cup diced zucchini
¼ cup diced onion
¼ teaspoon dried oregano
⅛ teaspoon kosher or sea salt
⅛ teaspoon freshly ground black pepper
1 (12-ounce / 340-g) jar roasted red peppers, drained and finely chopped
2 tablespoons grated Parmesan or Asiago cheese
1 cup fresh Mozzarella (about 4 ounces / 113 g), sliced
1 (2-foot-long) whole-grain Italian loaf, cut into 4 equal lengths Cooking spray

Directions

1. Place a large, rimmed baking sheet in the oven. Preheat the oven to 450°F (235°C) with the baking sheet inside.
2. In a large bowl, stir together 1 tablespoon of the oil, broccoli, zucchini, onion, oregano, salt and pepper.
3. Remove the baking sheet from the oven and spritz the baking sheet with cooking spray. Spread the vegetable mixture on the baking sheet and roast for 5 minutes, stirring once halfway through cooking. Remove the baking sheet from the oven. Stir in the red peppers and Parmesan cheese. In a large skillet over medium-high heat, heat the remaining 1 tablespoon of the oil.
4. Cut open each section of bread horizontally, but don't cut all the way through. Fill each with the vegetable mix (about ½ cup), and layer 1 ounce (28 g) of sliced Mozzarella cheese on top. Close the sandwiches, and place two of them on the skillet. Place a heavy object on top and grill for 2½ minutes. Flip the sandwiches and grill for another 2½ minutes. Repeat the grilling process with the remaining two sandwiches. Serve hot.

Per Serving calories: 116 | fat: 4.0g | protein: 12.0g | carbs: 9.0g | fiber: 3.0g | sodium: 569mg

Chapter 5
Beans Recipes, Grains Recipes, & Pastas Recipes

Baked Rolled Oat with Pears and Pecans

Prep Time: 15 minutes | **Cooking Time:** 30 minutes | **Servings:** 6

Ingredients

2 tablespoons coconut oil, melted, plus more for greasing the pan

3 ripe pears, cored and diced

2 cups unsweetened almond milk

1 tablespoon pure vanilla extract

¼ cup pure maple syrup

2 cups gluten-free rolled oats

½ cup raisins

¾ cup chopped pecans

¼ teaspoon ground nutmeg

1 teaspoon ground cinnamon

½ teaspoon ground ginger

¼ teaspoon sea salt

Directions

1. Preheat the oven to 350ºF (180ºC). Grease a baking dish with melted coconut oil, then spread the pears in a single layer on the baking dish evenly.
2. Combine the almond milk, vanilla extract, maple syrup, and coconut oil in a bowl. Stir to mix well.
3. Combine the remaining in a separate large bowl. Stir to mix well. Fold the almond milk mixture in the bowl, then pour the mixture over the pears.
4. Place the baking dish in the preheated oven and bake for 30 minutes or until lightly browned and set.
5. Serve immediately.

Per Serving

calories: 479 | fat: 34.9g | protein: 8.8g | carbs: 50.1g | fiber: 10.8g | sodium: 113mg

Brown Rice Pilaf with Pistachios and Raisins

Prep Time: 5 minutes | **Cooking Time:** 15 minutes | **Servings:** 6

Ingredients

1 tablespoon extra-virgin olive oil

1 cup chopped onion

½ cup shredded carrot

½ teaspoon ground cinnamon

1 teaspoon ground cumin

2 cups brown rice

1¾ cups pure orange juice

¼ cup water

½ cup shelled pistachios

1 cup golden raisins

½ cup chopped fresh chives

Directions

1. Heat the olive oil in a saucepan over medium-high heat until shimmering.
2. Add the onion and sauté for 5 minutes or until translucent.
3. Add the carrots, cinnamon, and cumin, then sauté for 1 minutes or until aromatic.
4. Pour int the brown rice, orange juice, and water. Bring to a boil. Reduce the heat to medium-low and simmer for 7 minutes or until the liquid is almost absorbed.
5. Transfer the rice mixture in a large serving bowl, then spread with pistachios, raisins, and chives. Serve immediately.

Per Serving

calories: 264 | fat: 7.1g | protein: 5.2g | carbs: 48.9g | fiber: 4.0g | sodium: 86mg

Pearl Barley Risotto with Parmesan Cheese

Prep Time: 5 minutes | **Cooking Time:** 20 minutes | **Servings:** 6

Ingredients

4 cups low-sodium or no-salt-added vegetable broth
1 tablespoon extra-virgin olive oil
1 cup chopped yellow onion
2 cups uncooked pearl barley
½ cup dry white wine
1 cup freshly grated Parmesan cheese, divided
¼ teaspoon kosher or sea salt
¼ teaspoon freshly ground black pepper
Fresh chopped chives and lemon wedges, for serving (optional)

Directions

1. Pour the broth into a medium saucepan and bring to a simmer.
2. Heat the olive oil in a large stockpot over medium-high heat. Add the onion and cook for about 4 minutes, stirring occasionally.
3. Add the barley and cook for 2 minutes, stirring, or until the barley is toasted. Pour in the wine and cook for about 1 minute, or until most of the liquid evaporates. Add 1 cup of the warm broth into the pot and cook, stirring, for about 2 minutes, or until most of the liquid is absorbed.
4. Add the remaining broth, 1 cup at a time, cooking until each cup is absorbed (about 2 minutes each time) before adding the next. The last addition of broth will take a bit longer to absorb, about 4 minutes.
5. Remove the pot from the heat, and stir in ½ cup of the cheese, and the salt and pepper.
6. Serve with the remaining ½ cup of the cheese on the side, along with the chives and lemon wedges (if desired).

Per Serving calories: 421 | fat: 11.0g | protein: 15.0g | carbs: 67.0g | fiber: 11.0g | sodium: 641mg

Cranberry and Almond Quinoa

Prep Time: 5 minutes | **Cooking Time:** 10 minutes | **Servings:** 2

Ingredients

2 cups water
1 cup quinoa, rinsed
¼ cup salted sunflower seeds
½ cup slivered almonds
1 cup dried cranberries

Directions

1. Combine water and quinoa in the Instant Pot.
2. Secure the lid. Select the Manual mode and set the cooking time for 10 minutes at High Pressure.
3. Once cooking is complete, do a quick pressure release. Carefully open the lid.
4. Add sunflower seeds, almonds, and dried cranberries and gently mix until well combined.
5. Serve hot.

Per Serving
calories: 445 | fat: 14.8g | protein: 15.1g | carbs: 64.1g | fiber: 10.2g | sodium: 113mg

Israeli Couscous with Asparagus

Prep Time: 5 minutes | **Cooking Time:** 25 minutes | **Servings:** 6

Ingredients

1½ pounds (680 g) asparagus spears, ends trimmed and stalks chopped into 1-inch pieces
1 garlic clove, minced
1 tablespoon extra-virgin olive oil
¼ teaspoon freshly ground black pepper
1¾ cups water
1 (8-ounce / 227-g) box uncooked whole-wheat or regular Israeli couscous (about 1⅓ cups)
¼ teaspoon kosher salt
1 cup garlic-and-herb goat cheese, at room temperature

Directions

1. Preheat the oven to 425ºF (220ºC).
2. In a large bowl, stir together the asparagus, garlic, oil, and pepper. Spread the asparagus on a large, rimmed baking sheet and roast for 10 minutes, stirring a few times. Remove the pan from the oven, and spoon the asparagus into a large serving bowl. Set aside.
3. While the asparagus is roasting, bring the water to a boil in a medium saucepan. Add the couscous and season with salt, stirring well.
4. Reduce the heat to medium-low. Cover and cook for 12 minutes, or until the water is absorbed.
5. Pour the hot couscous into the bowl with the asparagus. Add the goat cheese and mix thoroughly until completely melted. Serve immediately.

Per Serving calories: 103 | fat: 2.0g | protein: 6.0g | carbs: 18.0g | fiber: 5.0g | sodium: 343mg

Gouda Beef and Spinach Fettuccine

Prep Time: 10 minutes | **Cooking Time:** 15 minutes | **Servings:** 6

Ingredients

10 ounces (283 g) ground beef
1 pound (454 g) fettuccine pasta
1 cup gouda cheese, shredded
1 cup fresh spinach, torn
1 medium onion, chopped
2 cups tomatoes, diced
1 tablespoon olive oil
1 teaspoon salt
½ teaspoon ground black pepper

Directions

1. Heat the olive oil on Sauté mode in the Instant Pot. Stir-fry the beef and onion for 5 minutes. Add the pasta. Pour water enough to cover and season with salt and pepper. Cook on High Pressure for 5 minutes. Do a quick release. Press Sauté and stir in the tomato and spinach; cook for 5 minutes. Top with Gouda to serve.

Per Serving calories: 493 | fat: 17.7g | protein: 20.6g | carbs: 64.3g | fiber: 9.5g | sodium: 561mg

Italian Sautéd Cannellini Beans

Prep Time: 10 minutes | **Cooking Time:** 15 minutes | **Servings:** 6

Ingredients

2 teaspoons extra-virgin olive oil

½ cup minced onion

¼ cup red wine vinegar

1 (12-ounce / 340-g) can no-salt-added tomato paste

2 tablespoons raw honey

½ cup water

¼ teaspoon ground cinnamon

Directions

1. 2(15-ounce / 425-g) cans cannellini beans
1. Heat the olive oil in a saucepan over medium heat until shimmering.
2. Add the onion and sauté for 5 minutes or until translucent.
3. Pour in the red wine vinegar, tomato paste, honey, and water. Sprinkle with cinnamon. Stir to mix well. Reduce the heat to low, then pour all the beans into the saucepan. Cook for 10 more minutes. Stir constantly. Serve immediately.

Per Serving

calories: 435 | fat: 2.1g | protein: 26.2g | carbs: 80.3g | fiber: 24.0g | sodium: 72mg

Lentil and Vegetable Curry Stew

Prep Time: 20 minutes | **Cooking Time:** 4 hours 7 mins | **Servings:** 8

Ingredients

1 tablespoon coconut oil

1 yellow onion, diced

¼ cup yellow Thai curry paste

2 cups unsweetened coconut milk

2 cups dry red lentils, rinsed well and drained

3 cups bite-sized cauliflower florets

2 golden potatoes, cut into chunks

2 carrots, peeled and diced

8 cups low-sodium vegetable soup, divided

1 bunch kale, stems removed and roughly chopped

Sea salt, to taste

½ cup fresh cilantro, chopped

Pinch crushed red pepper flakes

Directions

1. Heat the coconut oil in a nonstick skillet over medium-high heat until melted. Add the onion and sauté for 5 minutes or until translucent. Pour in the curry paste and sauté for another 2 minutes, then fold in the coconut milk and stir to combine well. Bring to a simmer and turn off the heat.
2. Put the lentils, cauliflower, potatoes, and carrot in the slow cooker. Pour in 6 cups of vegetable soup and the curry mixture. Stir to combine well. Cover and cook on high for 4 hours or until the lentils and vegetables are soft. Stir periodically.
3. During the last 30 minutes, fold the kale in the slow cooker and pour in the remaining vegetable soup. Sprinkle with salt. Pour the stew in a large serving bowl and spread the cilantro and red pepper flakes on top before serving hot.

Per Serving calories: 530 | fat: 19.2g | protein: 20.3g | carbs: 75.2g | fiber: 15.5g | sodium: 562mg

Ritzy Veggie Chili

Prep Time: 15 minutes | **Cooking Time:** 5 hours | **Servings:** 4

Ingredients

1 (28-ounce / 794-g) can chopped tomatoes, with the juice

1 (15-ounce / 425-g) can black beans, drained and rinsed

1 (15-ounce / 425-g) can redly beans, drained and rinsed

1 medium green bell pepper, chopped

1 yellow onion, chopped

1 tablespoon onion powder

1 teaspoon paprika

1 teaspoon cayenne pepper

1 teaspoon garlic powder

½ teaspoon sea salt

½ teaspoon ground black pepper

1 tablespoon olive oil

1 large hass avocado, pitted, peeled, and chopped, for garnish

Directions

1. Combine all the , except for the avocado, in the slow cooker. Stir to mix well.
2. Put the slow cooker lid on and cook on high for 5 hours or until the vegetables are tender and the mixture has a thick consistency.
3. Pour the chili in a large serving bowl. Allow to cool for 30 minutes, then spread with chopped avocado and serve.

Per Serving calories: 633 | fat: 16.3g | protein: 31.7g | carbs: 97.0g | fiber: 28.9g | sodium: 792mg

Walnut and Ricotta Spaghetti

Prep Time: 15 minutes | **Cooking Time:** 10 minutes | **Servings:** 6

Ingredients

1 pound (454 g) cooked whole-wheat spaghetti

2 tablespoons extra-virgin olive oil

4 cloves garlic, minced

¾ cup walnuts, toasted and finely chopped

2 tablespoons ricotta cheese

¼ cup flat-leaf parsley, chopped

½ cup grated Parmesan cheese

Sea salt and freshly ground pepper, to taste

Directions

1. Reserve a cup of spaghetti water while cooking the spaghetti.
2. Heat the olive oil in a nonstick skillet over medium-low heat or until shimmering.
3. Add the garlic and sauté for a minute or until fragrant.
4. Pour the spaghetti water into the skillet and cook for 8 more minutes.
5. Turn off the heat and mix in the walnuts and ricotta cheese.
6. Put the cooked spaghetti on a large serving plate, then pour the walnut sauce over. Spread with parsley and Parmesan, then sprinkle with salt and ground pepper. Toss to serve.

Per Serving

calories: 264 | fat: 16.8g | protein: 8.6g | carbs: 22.8g | fiber: 4.0g | sodium: 336mg

Chickpea, Vegetable, and Fruit Stew

Prep Time: 20 minutes | **Cooking Time:** 6 hours 4 minutes | **Servings:** 6

Ingredients

1 large bell pepper, any color, chopped
6 ounces (170 g) green beans, trimmed and cut into bite-size pieces
3 cups canned chickpeas, rinsed and drained
1 (15-ounce / 425-g) can diced tomatoes, with the juice
1 large carrot, cut into ¼-inch rounds
2 large potatoes, peeled and cubed
1 large yellow onion, chopped

1 teaspoon grated fresh ginger
2 garlic cloves, minced
1¾ cups low-sodium vegetable soup
1 teaspoon ground cumin
1 tablespoon ground coriander
¼ tps ground red pepper flakes
Sea salt and ground black pepper, to taste
8 ounces (227 g) fresh baby spinach
¼ cup diced dried figs
¼ cup diced dried apricots
1 cup plain Greek yogurt

Directions

1. Place the bell peppers, green beans, chicken peas, tomatoes and juice, carrot, potatoes, onion, ginger, and garlic in the slow cooker. Pour in the vegetable soup and sprinkle with cumin, coriander, red pepper flakes, salt, and ground black pepper. Stir to mix well. Put the slow cooker lid on and cook on high for 6 hours or until the vegetables are soft. Stir periodically.
2. Open the lid and fold in the spinach, figs, apricots, and yogurt. Stir to mix well. Cook for 4 minutes or until the spinach is wilted. Pour them in a large serving bowl. Allow to cool for at least 20 minutes.

Per Serving

calories: 611 | fat: 9.0g | protein: 30.7g | carbs: 107.4g | fiber: 20.8g | sodium: 344mg

Pesto Pasta

Prep Time: 10 minutes | **Cooking Time:** 8 minutes | **Servings:** 4 to 6

Ingredients

1 pound (454 g) spaghetti
4 cups fresh basil leaves, stems removed
3 cloves garlic
1 teaspoon salt
1 cup extra-virgin olive oil

½ teaspoon freshly ground black pepper
½ cup toasted pine nuts
¼ cup lemon juice
½ cup grated Parmesan cheese

Directions

1. Bring a large pot of salted water to a boil. Add the spaghetti to the pot and cook for 8 minutes. In a food processor, place the remaining , except for the olive oil, and pulse.
2. While the processor is running, slowly drizzle the olive oil through the top opening. Process until all the olive oil has been added. Reserve ½ cup of the cooking liquid. Drain the pasta and put it into a large bowl. Add the pesto and cooking liquid to the bowl of pasta and toss everything together. Serve immediately.

Per Serving

calories: 1067 | fat: 72.0g | protein: 23.0g | carbs: 91..0g | fiber: 6.0g | sodium: 817mg

Quinoa and Chickpea Vegetable Bowls

Prep Time: 20 minutes | **Cooking Time:** 15 minutes | **Servings:** 4

Ingredients

1 cup red dry quinoa, rinsed and drained
2 cups low-sodium vegetable soup
2 cups fresh spinach
2 cups finely shredded red cabbage
1 (15-ounce / 425-g) can chickpeas, drained and rinsed
1 ripe avocado, thinly sliced
1 cup shredded carrots
1 red bell pepper, thinly sliced
4 tablespoons Mango Sauce
½ cup fresh cilantro, chopped

Mango Sauce:
1 mango, diced
¼ cup fresh lime juice
½ teaspoon ground turmeric
1 teaspoon finely minced fresh ginger
¼ teaspoon sea salt
Pinch of ground red pepper
1 teaspoon pure maple syrup
2 tablespoons extra-virgin olive oil

Directions

1. Pour the quinoa and vegetable soup in a saucepan. Bring to a boil. Reduce the heat to low. Cover and cook for 15 minutes or until tender. Fluffy with a fork.
2. Meanwhile, combine the for the mango sauce in a food processor. Pulse until smooth.
3. Divide the quinoa, spinach, and cabbage into 4 serving bowls, then top with chickpeas, avocado, carrots, and bell pepper. Dress them with the mango sauce and spread with cilantro. Serve immediately.

Per Serving calories: 366 | fat: 11.1g | protein: 15.5g | carbs: 55.6g | fiber: 17.7g | sodium: 746mg

Black-Eyed Peas Salad with Walnuts

Prep Time: 10 minutes | **Cooking Time:** 0 minutes | **Servings:** 4 to 6

Ingredients

3 tablespoons extra-virgin olive oil
3 tablespoons dukkah, divided
2 tablespoons lemon juice
2 tablespoons pomegranate molasses
¼ tbs salt, or more to taste
⅛ teaspoon pepper, or more to taste

2 (15-ounce / 425-g) cans black-eyed peas, rinsed
½ cup pomegranate seeds
½ cup minced fresh parsley
½ cup walnuts, toasted and chopped
4 scallions, sliced thinly

Directions

1. In a large bowl, whisk together the olive oil, 2 tablespoons of the dukkah, lemon juice, pomegranate molasses, salt and pepper. Stir in the remaining . Season with salt and pepper. Sprinkle with the remaining 1 tablespoon of the dukkah before serving.

Per Serving calories: 155 | fat: 11.5g | protein: 2.0g | carbs: 12.5g | fiber: 2.1g | sodium: 105mg

Spicy Italian Bean Balls with Marinara

Prep Time: 20 minutes | **Cooking Time:** 30 minutes | **Servings:** 2 to 4

Ingredients

Bean Balls:
1 tablespoon extra-virgin olive oil
½ yellow onion, minced
1 teaspoon fennel seeds
2 teaspoons dried oregano
½ teaspoon crushed red pepper flakes
1 teaspoon garlic powder
1 (15-ounce / 425-g) can white beans (cannellini or navy), drained and rinsed

½ cup whole-grain bread crumbs
Sea salt and ground black pepper, to taste
Marinara:
1 tablespoon extra-virgin olive oil
3 garlic cloves, minced
Handful basil leaves
1 (28-ounce / 794-g) can chopped tomatoes with juice reserved
Sea salt, to taste

Directions
Make the Bean Balls
1. Preheat the oven to 350°F (180°C). Line a baking sheet with parchment paper.
2. Heat the olive oil in a nonstick skillet over medium heat until shimmering.
3. Add the onion and sauté for 5 minutes or until translucent.
4. Sprinkle with fennel seeds, oregano, red pepper flakes, and garlic powder, then cook for 1 minute or until aromatic.
5. Pour the sautéed mixture in a food processor and add the beans and bread crumbs. Sprinkle with salt and ground black pepper, then pulse to combine well and the mixture holds together.
6. Shape the mixture into balls with a 2-ounce (57-g) cookie scoop, then arrange the balls on the baking sheet.
7. Bake in the preheated oven for 30 minutes or until lightly browned. Flip the balls halfway through the cooking time.
Make the Marinara
8. While baking the bean balls, heat the olive oil in a saucepan over medium-high heat until shimmering.
9. Add the garlic and basil and sauté for 2 minutes or until fragrant. Fold in the tomatoes and juice. Bring to a boil. Reduce the heat to low. Put the lid on and simmer for 15 minutes. Sprinkle with salt. Transfer the bean balls on a large plate and baste with marinara before serving.
Per Serving calories: 351 | fat: 16.4g | protein: 11.5g | carbs: 42.9g | fiber: 10.3g | sodium: 377mg

Wild Rice, Celery, and Cauliflower Pilaf

Prep Time: 10 minutes | **Cooking Time:** 45 minutes | **Servings:** 4

Ingredients
1 tablespoon olive oil, plus more for greasing the baking dish
1 cup wild rice
2 cups low-sodium chicken broth
1 sweet onion, chopped
2 stalks celery, chopped

1 teaspoon minced garlic
2 carrots, peeled, halved lengthwise, and sliced
½ cauliflower head, cut into small florets
1 teaspoon chopped fresh thyme
Sea salt, to taste

Directions
1. Preheat the oven to 350°F (180°C). Line a baking sheet with parchment paper and grease with olive oil.
2. Put the wild rice in a saucepan, then pour in the chicken broth. Bring to a boil. Reduce the heat to low and simmer for 30 minutes or until the rice is plump.
3. Meanwhile, heat the remaining olive oil in an oven-proof skillet over medium-high heat until shimmering.
4. Add the onion, celery, and garlic to the skillet and sauté for 3 minutes or until the onion is translucent.
5. Add the carrots and cauliflower to the skillet and sauté for 5 minutes. Turn off the heat and set aside.
6. Pour the cooked rice in the skillet with the vegetables. Sprinkle with thyme and salt.
7. Set the skillet in the preheated oven and bake for 15 minutes or until the vegetables are soft. Serve immediately.
Per Serving calories: 214 | fat: 3.9g | protein: 7.2g | carbs: 37.9g | fiber: 5.0g | sodium: 122mg

Bulgur Pilaf with Garbanzo

Prep Time: 5 minutes | **Cooking Time:** 20 minutes | **Servings:** 4 to 6

Ingredients
3 tablespoons extra-virgin olive oil
1 large onion, chopped
1 (1-pound / 454-g) can garbanzo beans, rinsed and drained

2 cups bulgur wheat, rinsed and drained
1½ teaspoons salt
½ teaspoon cinnamon
4 cups water

Directions
1. In a large pot over medium heat, heat the olive oil. Add the onion and cook for 5 minutes.
2. Add the garbanzo beans and cook for an additional 5 minutes.
3. Stir in the remaining .
4. Reduce the heat to low. Cover and cook for 10 minutes.
5. When done, fluff the pilaf with a fork. Cover and let sit for another 5 minutes before serving.
Per Serving
calories: 462 | fat: 13.0g | protein: 15.0g | carbs: 76.0g | fiber: 19.0g | sodium: 890mg

Mashed Beans with Cumin

Prep Time: 10 minutes | **Cooking Time:** 10 to 12 minutes | **Servings:** 4 to 6

Ingredients

1 tablespoon extra-virgin olive oil, plus extra for serving
4 garlic cloves, minced
1 teaspoon ground cumin
2 (15-ounce / 425-g) cans fava beans
3 tablespoons tahini

2 tablespoons lemon juice, plus lemon wedges for serving
Salt and pepper, to taste
1 tomato, cored and cut into ½-inch pieces
1 small onion, chopped finely
2 hard-cooked large eggs, chopped
2 tablespoons minced fresh parsley

Directions

1. Add the olive oil, garlic and cumin to a medium saucepan over medium heat. Cook for about 2 minutes, or until fragrant. Stir in the beans with their liquid and tahini. Bring to a simmer and cook for 8 to 10 minutes, or until the liquid thickens slightly.
2. Turn off the heat, mash the beans to a coarse consistency with a potato masher. Stir in the lemon juice and 1 teaspoon pepper. Season with salt and pepper.
3. Transfer the mashed beans to a serving dish. Top with the tomato, onion, eggs and parsley. Drizzle with the extra olive oil. Serve with the lemon wedges.

Per Serving

calories: 125 | fat: 8.6g | protein: 4.9g | carbs: 9.1g | fiber: 2.9g | sodium: 131mg

Quinoa with Baby Potatoes and Broccoli

Prep Time: 5 minutes | **Cooking Time:** 10 minutes | **Servings:** 4

Ingredients

2 tablespoons olive oil
1 cup baby potatoes, cut in half
1 cup broccoli florets

2 cups cooked quinoa
Zest of 1 lemon
Sea salt and freshly ground pepper, to taste

Directions

1. Heat the olive oil in a large skillet over medium heat until shimmering. Add the potatoes and cook for about 6 to 7 minutes, or until softened and golden brown. Add the broccoli and cook for about 3 minutes, or until tender.
2. Remove from the heat and add the quinoa and lemon zest. Season with salt and pepper to taste, then serve.

Per Serving

calories: 205 | fat: 8.6g | protein: 5.1g | carbs: 27.3g | fiber: 3.7g | sodium: 158mg

Turkish Canned Pinto Bean Salad

Prep Time: 10 minutes | **Cooking Time:** 3 minutes | **Servings:** 4 to 6

Ingredients

¼ cup extra-virgin olive oil, divided
3 garlic cloves, lightly crushed and peeled
2 (15-ounce / 425-g) cans pinto beans, rinsed 2 cups plus
1 tablespoon water
Salt and pepper, to taste
¼ cup tahini
3 tablespoons lemon juice

1 tablespoon ground dried Aleppo pepper, plus extra for serving
8 ounces (227 g) cherry tomatoes, halved
¼ red onion, sliced thinly
½ cup fresh parsley leaves
2 hard-cooked large eggs, quartered
1 tablespoon toasted sesame seeds

Directions

1. Add 1 tablespoon of the olive oil and garlic to a medium saucepan over medium heat. Cook for about 3 minutes, stirring constantly, or until the garlic turns golden but not brown.
2. Add the beans, 2 cups of the water and 1 teaspoon salt and bring to a simmer. Remove from the heat, cover and let sit for 20 minutes. Drain the beans and discard the garlic.
3. In a large bowl, whisk together the remaining 3 tablespoons of the oil, tahini, lemon juice, Aleppo, the remaining 1 tablespoon of the water and ¼ teaspoon salt. Stir in the beans, tomatoes, onion and parsley. Season with salt and pepper to taste.
4. Transfer to a serving platter and top with the eggs. Sprinkle with the sesame seeds and extra Aleppo before serving.

Per Serving calories: 402 | fat: 18.9g | protein: 16.2g | carbs: 44.4g | fiber: 11.2g | sodium: 456mg

Broccoli and Carrot Pasta Salad

Prep Time: 5 minutes | **Cooking Time:** 10 minutes | **Servings:** 2

Ingredients

8 ounces (227 g) whole-wheat pasta
2 cups broccoli florets
1 cup peeled and shredded carrots
¼ cup plain Greek yogurt

Juice of 1 lemon
1 teaspoon red pepper flakes
Sea salt and freshly ground pepper, to taste

Directions

1. Bring a large pot of lightly salted water to a boil. Add the pasta to the boiling water and cook until al dente, about 8 to 10 minutes. Drain the pasta and let rest for a few minutes.
2. When cooled, combine the pasta with the veggies, yogurt, lemon juice, and red pepper flakes in a large bowl, and stir thoroughly to combine.
3. Taste and season to taste with salt and pepper. Serve immediately.

Per Serving

calories: 428 | fat: 2.9g | protein: 15.9g | carbs: 84.6g | fiber: 11.7g | sodium: 642mg

Triple-Green Pasta with Cheese

Prep Time: 5 minutes | **Cooking Time:** 14 to 16 minutes | **Servings:** 4

Ingredients

8 ounces (227 g) uncooked penne
1 tablespoon extra-virgin olive oil
2 garlic cloves, minced
¼ teaspoon crushed red pepper
2 cups chopped fresh flat-
5 cups loosely packed baby spinach
¼ teaspoon ground nutmeg
¼ teaspoon kosher salt
¼ teaspoon freshly ground black pepper
⅓ cup Castelvetrano olives, pitted and sliced
⅓ cup grated Parmesan cheese
leaf parsley, including stems

Directions

1. In a large stockpot of salted water, cook the pasta for about 8 to 10 minutes. Drain the pasta and reserve ¼ cup of the cooking liquid.
2. Meanwhile, heat the olive oil in a large skillet over medium heat. Add the garlic and red pepper and cook for 30 seconds, stirring constantly.
3. Add the parsley and cook for 1 minute, stirring constantly. Add the spinach, nutmeg, salt, and pepper, and cook for 3 minutes, stirring occasionally, or until the spinach is wilted.
4. Add the cooked pasta and the reserved ¼ cup cooking liquid to the skillet. Stir in the olives and cook for about 2 minutes, or until most of the pasta water has been absorbed. Remove from the heat and stir in the cheese before serving.

Per Serving

calories: 262 | fat: 4.0g | protein: 15.0g | carbs: 51.0g | fiber: 13.0g | sodium: 1180mg

Lentil Risotto

Prep Time: 10 minutes | **Cooking Time:** 20 minutes | **Servings:** 2

Ingredients

½ tablespoon olive oil
½ medium onion, chopped
½ cup dry lentils, soaked overnight
½ celery stalk, chopped
1 sprig parsley, chopped
½ cup Arborio (short-grain Italian) rice
1 garlic clove, lightly mashed
2 cups vegetable stock

Directions

1. Press the Sauté button to heat your Instant Pot.
2. Add the oil and onion to the Instant Pot and sauté for 5 minutes.
3. Add the remaining to the Instant Pot, stirring well.
4. Secure the lid. Select the Manual mode and set the cooking time for 15 minutes at High Pressure.
5. Once cooking is complete, do a natural pressure release for 20 minutes, then release any remaining pressure. Carefully open the lid. Stir and serve hot.

Per Serving

calories: 261 | fat: 3.6g | protein: 10.6g | carbs: 47.1g | fiber: 8.4g | sodium: 247mg

Caprese Pasta with Roasted Asparagus

Prep Time: 5 minutes | **Cooking Time:** 25 minutes | **Servings:** 6

Ingredients

8 ounces (227 g) uncooked small pasta, like orecchiette (little ears) or farfalle (bow ties)
1½ pounds (680 g) fresh asparagus, ends trimmed and stalks chopped into 1-inch pieces
1½ cups grape tomatoes, halved
2 tablespoons extra-virgin olive oil
¼ teaspoon kosher salt
¼ teaspoon freshly ground black pepper
2 cups fresh Mozzarella, drained and cut into bite-size pieces (about 8 ounces / 227 g)
⅓ cup torn fresh basil leaves
2 tablespoons balsamic vinegar

Directions

1. Preheat the oven to 400ºF (205ºC).
2. In a large stockpot of salted water, cook the pasta for about 8 to 10 minutes. Drain and reserve about ¼ cup of the cooking liquid.
3. Meanwhile, in a large bowl, toss together the asparagus, tomatoes, oil, salt and pepper. Spread the mixture onto a large, rimmed baking sheet and bake in the oven for 15 minutes, stirring twice during cooking.
4. Remove the vegetables from the oven and add the cooked pasta to the baking sheet. Mix with a few tablespoons of cooking liquid to help the sauce become smoother and the saucy vegetables stick to the pasta.
5. Gently mix in the Mozzarella and basil. Drizzle with the balsamic vinegar. Serve from the baking sheet or pour the pasta into a large bowl.

Per Serving

calories: 147 | fat: 3.0g | protein: 16.0g | carbs: 17.0g | fiber: 5.0g | sodium: 420mg

Freekeh Pilaf with Dates and Pistachios

Prep Time: 10 minutes | **Cooking Time:** 10 minutes | **Servings:** 4 to 6

Ingredients

2 tablespoons extra-virgin olive oil, plus extra for drizzling
1 shallot, minced
1½ teaspoons grated fresh ginger
¼ teaspoon ground coriander
¼ teaspoon ground cumin
Salt and pepper, to taste

1¾ cups water
1½ cups cracked freekeh, rinsed
3 ounces (85 g) pitted dates, chopped
¼ cup shelled pistachios, toasted and coarsely chopped
1½ tablespoons lemon juice
¼ cup chopped fresh mint

Directions

1. Set the Instant Pot to Sauté mode and heat the olive oil until shimmering. Add the shallot, ginger, coriander, cumin, salt, and pepper to the pot and cook for about 2 minutes, or until the shallot is softened. Stir in the water and freekeh.
2. Secure the lid. Select the Manual mode and set the cooking time for 4 minutes at High Pressure. Once cooking is complete, do a quick pressure release. Carefully open the lid. Add the dates, pistachios and lemon juice and gently fluff the freekeh with a fork to combine. Season to taste with salt and pepper. Transfer to a serving dish and sprinkle with the mint. Serve drizzled with extra olive oil.

Per Serving calories: 280 | fat: 8.0g | protein: 8.0g | carbs: 46.0g | fiber: 9.0g | sodium: 200mg

Black-Eyed Pea and Vegetable Stew

Prep Time: 15 minutes | **Cooking Time:** 40 minutes | **Servings:** 2

Ingredients

½ cup black-eyed peas, soaked in water overnight
3 cups water, plus more as needed
1 large carrot, peeled and cut into ½-inch pieces (about ¾ cup)
1 large beet, peeled and cut into ½-inch pieces

¼ teaspoon turmeric
¼ teaspoon cayenne pepper
¼ teaspoon ground cumin seeds, toasted
¼ cup finely chopped parsley
¼ teaspoon salt (optional)
½ teaspoon fresh lime juice

Directions

1. Pour the black-eyed peas and water into a large pot, then cook over medium heat for 25 minutes. Add the carrot and beet to the pot and cook for 10 minutes more, adding more water as needed. Add the turmeric, cayenne pepper, cumin, and parsley to the pot and cook for another 6 minutes, or until the vegetables are softened.
2. Stir the mixture periodically. Season with salt, if desired.
3. Serve drizzled with the fresh lime juice.

Per Serving
calories: 89 | fat: 0.7g | protein: 4.1g | carbs: 16.6g | fiber: 4.5g | sodium: 367mg

Chickpea Salad with Tomatoes and Basil

Prep Time: 5 minutes | **Cooking Time:** 45 minutes | **Servings:** 2

Ingredients

1 cup dried chickpeas, rinsed
1 quart water, or enough to cover the chickpeas by 3 to 4 inches
1½ cups halved grape tomatoes

1 cup chopped fresh basil leaves
2 to 3 tablespoons balsamic vinegar
½ teaspoon garlic powder
½ teaspoon salt, or more to taste

Directions

1. In your Instant Pot, combine the chickpeas and water.
2. Secure the lid. Select the Manual mode and set the cooking time for 45 minutes at High Pressure.
3. Once cooking is complete, do a natural pressure release for 20 minutes, then release any remaining pressure. Carefully open the lid and drain the chickpeas. Refrigerate to cool (unless you want to serve this warm, which is good, too).
4. While the chickpeas cool, in a large bowl, stir together the basil, tomatoes, vinegar, garlic powder, and salt. Add the beans, stir to combine, and serve.

Per Serving
calories: 395 | fat: 6.0g | protein: 19.8g | carbs: 67.1g | fiber: 19.0g | sodium: 612mg

Mediterranean Lentils

Prep Time: 7 minutes | **Cooking Time:** 24 minutes | **Servings:** 2

Ingredients

1 tablespoon olive oil
1 small sweet or yellow onion, diced
1 garlic clove, diced
1 teaspoon dried oregano
½ teaspoon ground cumin
½ teaspoon dried parsley

½ teaspoon salt, plus more as needed
¼ teaspoon freshly ground black pepper, plus more as needed
1 tomato, diced
1 cup brown or green lentils
2½ cups vegetable stock
1 bay leaf

Directions

1. Set your Instant Pot to Sauté and heat the olive oil until it shimmers. Add the onion and cook for 3 to 4 minutes until soft. Turn off the Instant Pot and add the garlic, oregano, cumin, parsley, salt, and pepper. Cook until fragrant, about 1 minute.
2. Stir in the tomato, lentils, stock, and bay leaf.
3. Lock the lid. Select the Manual mode and set the cooking time for 18 minutes at High Pressure.
4. When the timer beeps, perform a natural pressure release for 10 minutes, then release any remaining pressure. Carefully open the lid. Remove and discard the bay leaf. Taste and season with more salt and pepper, as needed. If there's too much liquid remaining, select Sauté and cook until it evaporates. Serve warm.

Per Serving calories: 426 | fat: 8.1g | protein: 26.2g | carbs: 63.8g | fiber: 31.0g | sodium: 591mg

Roasted Ratatouille Pasta

Prep Time: 10 minutes | **Cooking Time:** 30 minutes | **Servings:** 2

Ingredients

1 small eggplant (about 8 ounces / 227 g)
1 small zucchini
1 portobello mushroom
1 Roma tomato, halved
½ medium sweet red pepper, seeded
½ teaspoon salt, plus additional for the pasta water
1 teaspoon Italian herb seasoning
1 tablespoon olive oil
2 cups farfalle pasta (about 8 ounces / 227 g)
2 tablespoons minced sun-dried tomatoes in olive oil with herbs
2 tablespoons prepared pesto

Directions

1. Slice the ends off the eggplant and zucchini. Cut them lengthwise into ½-inch slices. Place the eggplant, zucchini, mushroom, tomato, and red pepper in a large bowl and sprinkle with ½ teaspoon of salt. Using your hands, toss the vegetables well so that they're covered evenly with the salt. Let them rest for about 10 minutes.
2. While the vegetables are resting, preheat the oven to 400°F (205°C). Line a baking sheet with parchment paper.
3. When the oven is hot, drain off any liquid from the vegetables and pat them dry with a paper towel. Add the Italian herb seasoning and olive oil to the vegetables and toss well to coat both sides.
4. Lay the vegetables out in a single layer on the baking sheet. Roast them for 15 to 20 minutes, flipping them over after about 10 minutes or once they start to brown on the underside. When the vegetables are charred in spots, remove them from the oven.
5. While the vegetables are roasting, fill a large saucepan with water. Add salt and cook the pasta until al dente, about 8 to 10 minutes. Drain the pasta, reserving ½ cup of the pasta water. When cool enough to handle, cut the vegetables into large chunks (about 2 inches) and add them to the hot pasta. Stir in the sun-dried tomatoes and pesto and toss everything well. Serve immediately.

Per Serving calories: 613 | fat: 16.0g | protein: 23.1g | carbs: 108.5g | fiber: 23.0g | sodium: 775mg

Tomato Basil Pasta

Prep Time: 3 minutes | **Cooking Time:** 2 minutes | **Servings:** 2

Ingredients

2 cups dried campanelle or similar pasta
1¾ cups vegetable stock
½ teaspoon salt, plus more as needed
2 tomatoes, cut into large dices
1 or 2 pinches red pepper flakes
½ teaspoon garlic powder
½ teaspoon dried oregano
10 to 12 fresh sweet basil leaves
Freshly ground black pepper, to taste

Directions

1. In your Instant Pot, stir together the pasta, stock, and salt. Scatter the tomatoes on top (do not stir).
2. Secure the lid. Select the Manual mode and set the cooking time for 2 minutes at High Pressure.
3. Once cooking is complete, do a quick pressure release. Carefully open the lid.
4. Stir in the red pepper flakes, oregano, and garlic powder. If there's more than a few tablespoons of liquid in the bottom, select Sauté and cook for 2 to 3 minutes until it evaporates.
5. When ready to serve, chiffonade the basil and stir it in. Taste and season with more salt and pepper, as needed. Serve warm.

Per Serving
calories: 415 | fat: 2.0g | protein: 15.2g | carbs: 84.2g | fiber: 5.0g | sodium: 485mg

Pork and Spinach Spaghetti

Prep Time: 15 minutes | **Cooking Time:** 16 minutes | **Servings:** 4

Ingredients

2 tablespoons olive oil
½ cup onion, chopped
1 garlic clove, minced
1 pound (454 g) ground pork
2 cups water
1 (14-ounce / 397-g) can diced tomatoes, drained
½ cup sun-dried tomatoes
1 tablespoon dried oregano
1 teaspoon Italian seasoning
1 fresh jalapeño chile, stemmed, seeded, and minced
1 teaspoon salt
8 ounces (227 g) dried spaghetti, halved
1 cup spinach

Directions

1. Warm oil on Sauté. Add onion and garlic and cook for 2 minutes until softened. Stir in pork and cook for 5 minutes. Stir in jalapeño, water, sun-dried tomatoes, Italian seasoning, oregano, diced tomatoes, and salt with the chicken; mix spaghetti and press to submerge into the sauce.
2. Seal the lid and cook on High Pressure for 9 minutes. Release the pressure quickly. Stir in spinach, close lid again, and simmer on Keep Warm for 5 minutes until spinach is wilted.

Per Serving
calories: 621 | fat: 32.2g | protein: 29.1g | carbs: 53.9g | fiber: 5.9g | sodium: 738mg

Papaya, Jicama, and Peas Rice Bowl

Prep Time: 20 minutes | **Cooking Time:** 45 minutes | **Servings:** 4

Ingredients

Sauce:

Juice of ¼ lemon

2 teaspoons chopped fresh basil

1 tablespoon raw honey

1 tablespoon extra-virgin olive oil

Sea salt, to taste

Rice:

1½ cups wild rice

2 papayas, peeled, seeded, and diced

1 jicama, peeled and shredded

1 cup snow peas, julienned

2 cups shredded cabbage

1 scallion, white and green parts, chopped

Directions

1. Combine the for the sauce in a bowl. Stir to mix well. Set aside until ready to use.
2. Pour the wild rice in a saucepan, then pour in enough water to cover. Bring to a boil.
3. Reduce the heat to low, then simmer for 45 minutes or until the wild rice is soft and plump. Drain and transfer to a large serving bowl.
4. Top the rice with papayas, jicama, peas, cabbage, and scallion. Pour the sauce over and stir to mix well before serving.

Per Serving

calories: 446 | fat: 7.9g | protein: 13.1g | carbs: 85.8g | fiber: 16.0g | sodium: 70mg

Black Bean Chili with Mangoes

Prep Time: 10 minutes | **Cooking Time:** 10 minutes | **Servings:** 4

Ingredients

2 tablespoons coconut oil

1 onion, chopped

2 (15-ounce / 425-g) cans black beans, drained and rinsed

1 tablespoon chili powder

1 teaspoon sea salt

¼ teaspoon freshly ground black pepper

1 cup water

2 ripe mangoes, sliced thinly

¼ cup chopped fresh cilantro, divided

¼ cup sliced scallions, divided

Directions

1. Heat the coconut oil in a pot over high heat until melted.
2. Put the onion in the pot and sauté for 5 minutes or until translucent. Add the black beans to the pot. Sprinkle with chili powder, salt, and ground black pepper. Pour in the water. Stir to mix well.
3. Bring to a boil. Reduce the heat to low, then simmering for 5 minutes or until the beans are tender.
4. Turn off the heat and mix in the mangoes, then garnish with scallions and cilantro before serving.

Per Serving

calories: 430 | fat: 9.1g | protein: 20.2g | carbs: 71.9g | fiber: 22.0g | sodium: 608mg

Israeli Style Eggplant and Chickpea Salad

Prep Time: 5 minutes | **Cooking Time:** 20 minutes | **Servings:** 6

Ingredients

2 tablespoons freshly squeezed lemon juice

1 teaspoon ground cumin

¼ teaspoon sea salt

2 tablespoons olive oil, divided

1 (1-pound / 454-g) medium globe eggplant, stem removed, cut into flat cubes (about ½ inch thick)

2 tablespoons balsamic vinegar

1 (15-ounce / 425-g) can chickpeas, drained and rinsed

¼ cup chopped mint leaves

1 cup sliced sweet onion

1 garlic clove, finely minced

1 tablespoon sesame seeds, toasted

Directions

1. Preheat the oven to 550°F (288°C) or the highest level of your oven or broiler. Grease a baking sheet with 1 tablespoon of olive oil.
2. Combine the balsamic vinegar, lemon juice, cumin, salt, and 1 tablespoon of olive oil in a small bowl. Stir to mix well.
3. Arrange the eggplant cubes on the baking sheet, then brush with 2 tablespoons of the balsamic vinegar mixture on both sides.
4. Broil in the preheated oven for 8 minutes or until lightly browned. Flip the cubes halfway through the cooking time.
5. Meanwhile, combine the chickpeas, mint, onion, garlic, and sesame seeds in a large serving bowl. Drizzle with remaining balsamic vinegar mixture. Stir to mix well.
6. Remove the eggplant from the oven. Allow to cool for 5 minutes, then slice them into ½-inch strips on a clean work surface.
7. Add the eggplant strips in the serving bowl, then toss to combine well before serving.

Per Serving

calories: 125 | fat: 2.9g | protein: 5.2g | carbs: 20.9g | fiber: 6.0g | sodium: 222mg

Pesto Arborio Rice and Veggie Bowls

Prep Time: 10 minutes | **Cooking Time:** 1 minute |
Servings: 2

Ingredients

1 cup arborio rice, rinsed and drained
2 cups vegetable broth
Salt and black pepper to taste
1 potato, peeled, cubed
1 head broccoli, cut into small florets
1 bunch baby carrots, peeled
¼ cabbage, chopped
2 eggs
¼ cup pesto sauce
Lemon wedges, for serving

Directions

1. In the pot, mix broth, pepper, rice and salt. Set trivet to the inner pot on top of rice and add a steamer basket to the top of the trivet. Mix carrots, potato, eggs and broccoli in the steamer basket. Add pepper and salt for seasoning.
2. Seal the lid and cook for 1 minute on High Pressure. Quick release the pressure. Take away the trivet and steamer basket from the pot.
3. Set the eggs in a bowl of ice water. Then peel and halve the eggs. Use a fork to fluff rice.
4. Adjust the seasonings. In two bowls, equally divide rice, broccoli, eggs, carrots, sweet potatoes, and a dollop of pesto. Serve alongside a lemon wedge.

Per Serving calories: 858 | fat: 24.4g | protein: 26.4g | carbs: 136.2g | fiber: 14.1g | sodium: 985mg

Rice and Bean Stuffed Zucchini

Prep Time: 10 minutes | **Cooking Time:** 15 minutes |
Servings: 4

Ingredients

2 small zucchinis, halved lengthwise
½ cup cooked rice
½ cup canned white beans, drained and rinsed
½ cup chopped tomatoes
½ cup chopped toasted cashew nuts
½ cup grated Parmesan cheese
1 tablespoon olive oil
½ teaspoon salt
½ teaspoon freshly ground black pepper

Directions

1. Pour 1 cup of water in the instant pot and insert a trivet. Scoop out the pulp of zucchini and chop roughly.
2. In a bowl, mix the zucchini pulp, rice, tomatoes, cashew nuts, ¼ cup of Parmesan, olive oil, salt, and black pepper. Fill the zucchini boats with the mixture, and arrange the stuffed boats in a single layer on the trivet. Seal the lid and cook for 15 minutes on Steam on High. Do a quick release and serve.

Per Serving calories: 239 | fat: 14.7g | protein: 9.4g | carbs: 19.0g | fiber: 2.6g | sodium: 570mg

Chard and Mushroom Risotto

Prep Time: 15 minutes | **Cooking Time:** 20 minutes |
Servings: 4

Ingredients

3 tablespoons olive oil
1 onion, chopped
2 Swiss chard, stemmed and chopped
1 cup risotto rice
⅓ cup white wine
3 cups vegetable stock
½ teaspoon salt
½ cup mushrooms
4 tablespoons pumpkin seeds, toasted
⅓ cup grated Pecorino Romano cheese

Directions

1. Heat oil on Sauté, and cook onion and mushrooms for 5 minutes, stirring, until tender. Add the rice and cook for a minute. Stir in wine and cook for 2 to 3 minutes until almost evaporated.
2. Pour in stock and season with salt. Seal the lid and cook on High Pressure for 10 minutes.
3. Do a quick release. Stir in chard until wilted, mix in cheese to melt, and serve scattered with pumpkin seeds.

Per Serving calories: 420 | fat: 17.7g | protein: 11.8g | carbs: 54.9g | fiber: 4.9g | sodium: 927mg

Cheesy Tomato Linguine

Prep Time: 15 minutes | **Cooking Time:** 11 minutes |
Servings: 4

Ingredients

2 tablespoons olive oil
1 small onion, diced
2 garlic cloves, minced
1 cup cherry tomatoes, halved
1½ cups vegetable stock
¼ cup julienned basil leaves
1 teaspoon salt
½ teaspoon ground black pepper
¼ teaspoon red chili flakes
1 pound (454 g) Linguine noodles, halved
Fresh basil leaves for garnish
½ cup Parmigiano-Reggiano cheese, grated

Directions

1. Warm oil on Sauté. Add onion and Sauté for 2 minutes until soft. Mix garlic and tomatoes and sauté for 4 minutes. To the pot, add vegetable stock, salt, julienned basil, red chili flakes and pepper.
2. Add linguine to the tomato mixture until covered. Seal the lid and cook on High Pressure for 5 minutes.
3. Naturally release the pressure for 5 minutes. Stir the mixture to ensure it is broken down.
4. Divide into plates. Top with basil and Parmigiano-Reggiano cheese and serve.

Per Serving calories: 311 | fat: 11.3g | protein: 10.3g | carbs: 42.1g | fiber: 1.9g | sodium: 1210mg

Beef and Bean Stuffed Pasta Shells

Prep Time: 15 minutes | **Cooking Time:** 17 minutes | **Servings:** 4

Ingredients

2 tablespoons olive oil
1 pound (454 g) ground beef
1 pound (454 g) pasta shells
2 cups water
15 ounces (425 g) tomato sauce
1 (15-ounce / 425-g) can black beans, drained and rinsed
15 ounces (425 g) canned corn, drained (or 2 cups frozen corn)
10 ounces (283 g) red enchilada sauce
4 ounces (113 g) diced green chiles
1 cup shredded Mozzarella cheese
Salt and ground black pepper to taste
Additional cheese for topping
Finely chopped parsley for garnish

Directions

1. Heat oil on Sauté. Add ground beef and cook for 7 minutes until it starts to brown.
2. Mix in pasta, tomato sauce, enchilada sauce, black beans, water, corn, and green chiles and stir to coat well. Add more water if desired.
3. Seal the lid and cook on High Pressure for 10 minutes. Do a quick Pressure release. Into the pasta mixture, mix in Mozzarella cheese until melted; add black pepper and salt. Garnish with parsley to serve.

Per Serving

calories: 1006 | fat: 30.0g | protein: 53.3g | carbs: 138.9g | fiber: 24.4g | sodium: 1139mg
g Protein 23.7 g Cholesterol 55 mg

Pesto Chicken Pasta (Italian)

Prep Time: 10 minutes **Cooking Time:** 10 minutes
Servings: 6

Ingredients

1 lb. chicken breast, skinless, boneless, and diced
3 tbsp olive oil
1/4 cup heavy cream
3 1/2 cups water Pepper
6 oz basil pesto
1/2 cup parmesan cheese, shredded
1 tsp Italian seasoning
16 oz whole wheat pasta
Salt

Directions

1. Season chicken with Italian seasoning, pepper, and salt.
2. Add oil into the inner pot of instant pot and set the pot on sauté mode.
3. Add chicken to the pot and sauté until brown.
4. Add remaining except for parmesan cheese, heavy cream, and pesto and stir well.
5. Seal pot with lid and cook on high for 5 minutes.
6. Once done, release pressure using quick release. Remove lid.
7. Stir in parmesan cheese, heavy cream, and pesto and serve.

Nutrition: Calories 475 Fat 14.7 g Carbohydrates 57 g Sugar 2.8 g Protein 28.7 g Cholesterol 61 mg

Chicken and Spaghetti Ragù Bolognese

Prep Time: 15 minutes | **Cooking Time:** 42 minutes | **Servings:** 8

Ingredients

2 tablespoons olive oil
6 ounces (170 g) bacon, cubed
1 onion, minced
1 carrot, minced
1 celery stalk, minced
2 garlic cloves, crushed
¼ cup tomato paste
¼ teaspoon crushed red pepper flakes
1½ pounds (680 g) ground chicken
½ cup white wine
1 cup milk
1 cup chicken broth
Salt, to taste
1 pound (454 g) spaghetti

Directions

1. Warm oil on Sauté. Add bacon and fry for 5 minutes until crispy.
2. Add celery, carrot, garlic and onion and cook for 5 minutes until fragrant. Mix in red pepper flakes and tomato paste, and cook for 2 minutes. Break chicken into small pieces and place in the pot.
3. Cook for 10 minutes, as you stir, until browned. Pour in wine and simmer for 2 minutes. Add chicken broth and milk. Seal the lid and cook for 15 minutes on High Pressure. Release the pressure quickly.
4. Add the spaghetti and stir. Seal the lid, and cook on High Pressure for another 5 minutes.
5. Release the pressure quickly. Check the pasta for doneness. Taste, adjust the seasoning and serve hot.

Per Serving calories: 477 | fat: 20.6g | protein: 28.1g | carbs: 48.5g | fiber: 5.3g | sodium: 279mg

Italian Chicken Pasta (Italian)

Prep Time: 10 minutes **Cooking Time:** 9 minutes
Servings: 8

Ingredients

1 lb. chicken breast, skinless, boneless, and cut into chunks
1 tsp garlic, minced
1/2 cup cream cheese
2 tomatoes, diced
2 cups of water
1 cup mozzarella cheese, shredded
1 1/2 tsp Italian seasoning
1cup mushrooms, diced
1/2 onion, diced
16 oz whole wheat penne pasta Pepper, Salt

Directions

1. Add all except cheeses into the inner pot of instant pot and stir well.
2. Seal pot with lid and cook on high for 9 minutes.
3. Once done, allow to release pressure naturally for 5 minutes then release remaining using quick release. Remove lid.
4. Add cheeses and stir well and serve.

Nutrition: Calories 328 Fat 8.5 g Carbohydrates 42.7 g Sugar 1.4

48

Shrimp and Leek Spaghetti (Italian)

Prep Time: 10 minutes **Cooking Time:** 20 minutes
Servings: 4

Ingredients

2 cups leek, chopped	8 oz. spaghetti uncooked whole-grain
1/4 cup heavy cream	1 lb. raw medium shrimp peeled deveined
2 teaspoons lemon zest	1tablespoon garlic, chopped
1/2 teaspoon black pepper	2cups baby sweet peas, frozen, thawed
1 1/2 tablespoons olive oil divided	3/4 teaspoon kosher salt divided
2 tablespoons fresh lemon juice	2 tablespoons fresh dill chopped

Directions

1. Cook the pasta, drain and reserve ½ cup of the cooking liquid. Cover the cooked pasta and keep warm.
2. In the meantime, pat dries the shrimp with the paper towels, season with pepper, and ¼ teaspoon of salt.
3. Heat ½ of olive oil in a nonstick skillet over high heat, then add shrimp. Cook for about 3-4 minutes as you stir often until the shrimp is cooked through. Transfer the cooked shrimp into a plate and cover it to keep warm.
4. Reduce the heat to medium-high and add leek to the same skillet along with garlic, remaining ½ teaspoon of salt, and the remaining oil. Cook for about 2-3 minutes as you stir often until the leek has become slightly tender.
5. Add the peas to the skillet along with cream, lemon juice, lemon zest and the reserved ½ cup of the cooking liquid. Reduce the heat to medium and simmer for 2-3 minutes until the sauce has slightly thickened. Add in the shrimp and toss well until coated.
6. When through, divide the cooked pasta among the serving bowls and top with the shrimp and sauce evenly. Sprinkle with the chopped fresh dill. Serve immediately and enjoy!

Nutrition: Calories: 446 Fat: 13 g Carbs: 59 g Protein: 28 g

Garlic Shrimp Fettuccine (Italian)

Prep Time: 10 minutes **Cooking Time:** 15 minutes
Servings: 4 to 6

Ingredients

8 ounces (227 g) fettuccine pasta	3 tablespoons garlic, minced
1 pound (454 g) large shrimp, peeled and deveined	1/4 cup virgin olive oil
1/3 cup lemon juice	1 tablespoon lemon zest
1/2 teaspoon freshly ground black pepper	1/2 teaspoon salt

Directions

1. Bring a large pot of salted water to a boil. Add the fettuccine and cook for 8 minutes. Reserve ½ cup of the cooking liquid and drain the pasta.
2. In a large saucepan over medium heat, heat the olive oil. Add the garlic and sauté for 1 minute.
3. Add the shrimp to the saucepan and cook each side for 3 minutes. Remove the shrimp from the pan and set aside.
4. Add the remaining to the saucepan. Stir in the cooking liquid. Add the pasta and toss together to coat the pasta evenly.
5. Transfer the pasta to a serving dish and serve topped with the cooked shrimp.

Nutrition: calories: 615 fats: 17.0g protein: 33.0g carbs: 89.0g fiber: 4.0g sodium: 407mg

Asparagus Pasta (Italian)

Prep Time: 10 minutes **Cooking Time:** 25 minutes
Servings: 6

Ingredients

8 Oz. Farfalle Pasta, Uncooked	1½ Cups Asparagus, Fresh, Trimmed & Chopped into
1 Inch Pieces	1 Pint Grape Tomatoes,
2 tbsp. Balsamic Vinegar	Halved
2tbsp. Olive Oil	Salt & Black Pepper Taste
2 Cups Mozzarella, Fresh & Drained	
1/3 Cup Basil Leaves, Fresh & Torn	

Directions

1. Start by heating the oven to 400°F, and then get out a stockpot. Cook your pasta per package instructions, and reserve ¼ cup of pasta water.
2. Get out a bowl and toss the tomatoes, oil, asparagus, and season with salt and pepper. Spread this mixture on a baking sheet, and bake for fifteen minutes. Stir twice in this time.
3. Remove your vegetables from the oven, and then add the cooked pasta to your baking sheet. Mix with a few tbsp. of pasta water so that your sauce becomes smoother.
4. Mix in your basil and mozzarella, drizzling with balsamic vinegar. Serve warm.

Nutrition: Calories: 307 Protein: 18 g Fat: 14 g Carbs: 33 g

Chapter 6
Vegetable Recipes

Stuffed Portobello Mushrooms with Spinach

Prep Time: 5 minutes | **Cooking Time:** 20 minutes | **Servings:** 4

Ingredients

8 large portobello mushrooms, stems removed
3 teaspoons extra-virgin olive oil, divided
1 medium red bell pepper, diced
4 cups fresh spinach
¼ cup crumbled feta cheese

Directions

1. Preheat the oven to 450°F (235°C).
2. Using a spoon to scoop out the gills of the mushrooms and discard them. Brush the mushrooms with 2 teaspoons of olive oil.
3. Arrange the mushrooms (cap-side down) on a baking sheet. Roast in the preheated oven for 20 minutes.
4. Meantime, in a medium skillet, heat the remaining olive oil over medium heat until it shimmers.
5. Add the bell pepper and spinach and sauté for 8 to 10 minutes, stirring occasionally, or until the spinach is wilted.
6. Remove the mushrooms from the oven to a paper towel-lined plate. Using a spoon to stuff each mushroom with the bell pepper and spinach mixture. Scatter the feta cheese all over. Serve immediately.

Per Serving (2 mushrooms)
calories: 115 | fat: 5.9g | protein: 7.2g | carbs: 11.5g | fiber: 4.0g | sodium: 125mg

Chickpea Lettuce Wraps with Celery

Prep Time: 10 minutes | **Cooking Time:** 0 minutes | **Servings:** 4

Ingredients

1 (15-ounce / 425-g) can low-sodium chickpeas, drained and rinsed
1 celery stalk, thinly sliced
2 tablespoons finely chopped red onion
2 tablespoons unsalted tahini
3 tablespoons honey mustard
1 tablespoon capers, undrained
12 butter lettuce leaves

Directions

1. In a bowl, mash the chickpeas with a potato masher or the back of a fork until mostly smooth.
2. Add the celery, red onion, tahini, honey mustard, and capers to the bowl and stir until well incorporated.
3. For each serving, place three overlapping lettuce leaves on a plate and top with ¼ of the mashed chickpea filling, then roll up. Repeat with the remaining lettuce leaves and chickpea mixture.

Per Serving
calories: 182 | fat: 7.1g | protein: 10.3g | carbs: 19.6g | fiber: 3.0g | sodium: 171mg

Zoodles with Walnut Pesto

Prep Time: 10 minutes | **Cooking Time:** 10 minutes | **Servings:** 4

Ingredients

4 medium zucchinis, spiralized
¼ cup extra-virgin olive oil, divided
1 tbsp minced garlic, divided
½ teaspoon crushed red pepper
¼ teaspoon freshly ground black pepper, divided
¼ teaspoon kosher salt, divided
2 tablespoons grated Parmesan cheese, divided
1 cup packed fresh basil leaves
¾ cup walnut pieces, divided

Directions

1. In a large bowl, stir together the zoodles, 1 tablespoon of the olive oil, ½ teaspoon of the minced garlic, red pepper, ⅛ teaspoon of the black pepper and ⅛ teaspoon of the salt. Set aside.
2. Heat ½ tablespoon of the oil in a large skillet over medium-high heat. Add half of the zoodles to the skillet and cook for 5 minutes, stirring constantly. Transfer the cooked zoodles into a bowl. Repeat with another ½ tablespoon of the oil and the remaining zoodles. When done, add the cooked zoodles to the bowl.
3. Make the pesto: In a food processor, combine the remaining ½ teaspoon of the minced garlic, ⅛ teaspoon of the black pepper and ⅛ teaspoon of the salt, 1 tablespoon of the Parmesan, basil leaves and ¼ cup of the walnuts. Pulse until smooth and then slowly drizzle the remaining 2 tablespoons of the oil into the pesto. Pulse again until well combined.
4. Add the pesto to the zoodles along with the remaining 1 tablespoon of the Parmesan and the remaining ½ cup of the walnuts. Toss to coat well. Serve immediately.

Per Serving
calories: 166 | fat: 16.0g | protein: 4.0g | carbs: 3.0g | fiber: 2.0g | sodium: 307mg

Mushroom and Spinach Stuffed Peppers

Prep Time: 15 minutes | **Cooking Time:** 8 minutes | **Servings:** 7

Ingredients

7 mini sweet peppers
1 cup button mushrooms, minced
5 ounces (142 g) organic baby spinach
½ teaspoon fresh garlic
½ teaspoon coarse sea salt
¼ teaspoon cracked mixed pepper
2 tablespoons water
1 tablespoon olive oil
Organic Mozzarella cheese, diced

Directions

1. Put the sweet peppers and water in the instant pot and Sauté for 2 minutes.
2. Remove the peppers and put the olive oil into the pot.
3. Stir in the mushrooms, garlic, spices and spinach.
4. Cook on Sauté until the mixture is dry.
5. Stuff each sweet pepper with the cheese and spinach mixture.
6. Bake the stuffed peppers in an oven for 6 minutes at 400°F (205°C). Once done, serve hot.

Per Serving
calories: 81 | fat: 2.4g | protein: 4.1g | carbs: 13.2g | fiber: 2.4g | sodium: 217mg

Black Bean and Corn Tortilla Bowls

Prep Time: 10 minutes | **Cooking Time:** 8 minutes | **Servings:** 4

Ingredients

1½ cups vegetable broth
½ cup tomatoes, undrained diced
1 small onion, diced
2 garlic cloves, finely minced
1 teaspoon chili powder
1 teaspoon cumin
½ teaspoon paprika
½ teaspoon ground coriander
Salt and pepper to taste
½ cup carrots, diced
2 small potatoes, cubed
½ cup bell pepper, chopped
½ can black beans, drained and rinsed
1 cup frozen corn kernels
½ tablespoon lime juice
2 tablespoons cilantro for topping, chopped
Whole-wheat tortilla chips

Directions

1. Add the oil and all the vegetables into the instant pot and Sauté for 3 minutes.
2. Add all the spices, corn, lime juice, and broth, along with the beans, to the pot.
3. Seal the lid and cook on Manual setting at High Pressure for 5 minutes.
4. Once done, natural release the pressure when the timer goes off. Remove the lid.
5. To serve, put the prepared mixture into a bowl.
6. Top with tortilla chips and fresh cilantro. Serve.

Per Serving
calories: 183 | fat: 0.9g | protein: 7.1g | carbs: 39.8g | fiber: 8.3g | sodium: 387mg

Potato, Corn, and Spinach Medley

Prep Time: 10 minutes | **Cooking Time:** 10 minutes | **Servings:** 6

Ingredients

1 tablespoon olive oil
3 scallions, chopped
½ cup onion, chopped
2 large white potatoes, peeled and diced
1 tablespoon ginger, grated
3 cups frozen corn kernels
1 cup vegetable stock
1 tablespoon fish sauce
2 tablespoons light soy sauce
2 large cloves garlic, diced
⅓ teaspoon white pepper
1 teaspoon salt
3-4 handfuls baby spinach leaves
Juice of ½ lemon

Directions

1. Put the oil, ginger, garlic and onions in the instant pot and Sauté for 5 minutes. Add all the remaining except the spinach leaves and lime juice Secure the lid and cook on the Manual setting for 5 minutes at High Pressure. After the beep, Quick release the pressure and remove the lid.
2. Add the spinach and cook for 3 minutes on Sauté
3. Drizzle the lime juice over the dish and serve hot.

Per Serving
calories: 217 | fat: 3.4g | protein: 6.5g | carbs: 44.5g | fiber: 6.3g | sodium: 892mg

Mushroom and Potato Oat Burgers

Prep Time: 20 minutes | **Cooking Time:** 21 minutes | **Servings:** 5

Ingredients

½ cup minced onion
1 teaspoon grated fresh ginger
½ cup minced mushrooms
½ cup red lentils, rinsed
¾ sweet potato, peeled and diced
1 cup vegetable stock
2 tablespoons hemp seeds
2 tablespoons chopped cilantro
1 tablespoon curry powder
1 cup quick oats
Brown rice flour, optional
5 tomato slices
Lettuce leaves
5 whole-wheat buns
2 tablespoons chopped parsley

Directions

1. Add the oil, ginger, mushrooms and onion into the instant pot and Sauté for 5 minutes.
2. Stir in the lentils, stock, and the sweet potatoes.
3. Secure the lid and cook on the Manual function for 6 minutes at High Pressure. After the beep, natural release the pressure and remove the lid. Meanwhile, heat the oven to 375°F (190°C) and line a baking tray with parchment paper.
4. Mash the prepared lentil mixture with a potato masher.
5. Add the oats and the remaining spices. Put in some brown rice flour if the mixture is not thick enough.
6. Wet your hands and prepare 5 patties, using the mixture, and place them on the baking tray.
7. Bake the patties for 10 minutes in the preheated oven.
8. Slice the buns in half and stack each with a tomato slice, a vegetable patty and lettuce leaves. Serve and enjoy.

Per Serving calories: 266 | fat: 5.3g | protein: 14.5g | carbs: 48.7g | fiber: 9.6g | sodium: 276mg

Veggie-Stuffed Portabello Mushrooms

Prep Time: 5 minutes | **Cooking Time:** 24 to 25 minutes | **Servings:** 6

Ingredients

3 tablespoons extra-virgin olive oil, divided
1 cup diced onion
2 garlic cloves, minced
1 large zucchini, diced
3 cups chopped mushrooms
1 cup chopped tomato
1 teaspoon dried oregano
¼ teaspoon kosher salt
¼ teaspoon crushed red pepper
6 large portabello mushrooms, stems and gills removed
Cooking spray
4 ounces (113 g) fresh Mozzarella cheese, shredded

Directions

1. In a large skillet over medium heat, heat 2 tablespoons of the oil. Add the onion and sauté for 4 minutes. Stir in the garlic and sauté for 1 minute. Stir in the zucchini, mushrooms, tomato, oregano, salt and red pepper. Cook for 10 minutes, stirring constantly. Remove from the heat.
2. Meanwhile, heat a grill pan over medium-high heat.
3. Brush the remaining 1 tablespoon of the oil over the portabello mushroom caps. Place the mushrooms, bottom-side down, on the grill pan. Cover with a sheet of aluminum foil sprayed with nonstick cooking spray. Cook for 5 minutes. Flip the mushroom caps over, and spoon about ½ cup of the cooked vegetable mixture into each cap. Top each with about 2½ tablespoons of the Mozzarella.
4. Cover and grill for 4 to 5 minutes, or until the cheese is melted. Using a spatula, transfer the portabello mushrooms to a plate. Let cool for about 5 minutes before serving.

Per Serving

calories: 111 | fat: 4.0g | protein: 11.0g | carbs: 11.0g | fiber: 4.0g | sodium: 314mg

Cauliflower and Broccoli Bowls

Prep Time: 5 minutes | **Cooking Time:** 7 minutes | **Servings:** 3

Ingredients

½ medium onion, diced
2 teaspoons olive oil
1 garlic clove, minced
½ cup tomato paste
½ pound (227 g) frozen cauliflower
½ pound (227 g) broccoli florets
½ cup vegetable broth
½ teaspoon paprika
¼ teaspoon dried thyme
2 pinches sea salt

Directions

1. Add the oil, onion and garlic into the instant pot and Sauté for 2 minutes. Add the broth, tomato paste, cauliflower, broccoli, and all the spices, to the pot. Secure the lid. Cook on the Manual setting at with pressure for 5 minutes.
2. After the beep, Quick release the pressure and remove the lid. Stir well and serve hot.

Per Serving

calories: 109 | fat: 3.8g | protein: 6.1g | carbs: 16.7g | fiber: 6.1g | sodium: 265mg

Stir-Fried Eggplant

Prep Time: 25 minutes | **Cooking Time:** 15 minutes | **Servings:** 2

Ingredients

1 cup water, plus more as needed
½ cup chopped red onion
1 tablespoon finely chopped garlic
1 tablespoon dried Italian herb seasoning
1 teaspoon ground cumin
1 small eggplant (about 8 ounces / 227 g), peeled and cut into ½-inch cubes
1 medium carrot, sliced
2 cups green beans, cut into 1-inch pieces
2 ribs celery, sliced
1 cup corn kernels
2 tablespoons almond butter
2 medium tomatoes, chopped

Directions

1. Heat 1 tablespoon of water in a large soup pot over medium-high heat until it sputters.
2. Cook the onion for 2 minutes, adding a little more water as needed.
3. Add the garlic, Italian seasoning, cumin, and eggplant and stir-fry for 2 to 3 minutes, adding a little more water as needed.
4. Add the carrot, green beans, celery, corn kernels, and ½ cup of water and stir well. Reduce the heat to medium, cover, and cook for 8 to 10 minutes, stirring occasionally, or until the vegetables are tender.
5. Meanwhile, in a bowl, stir together the almond butter and ½ cup of water. Remove the vegetables from the heat and stir in the almond butter mixture and chopped tomatoes. Cool for a few minutes before serving.

Per Serving

calories: 176 | fat: 5.5g | protein: 5.8g | carbs: 25.4g | fiber: 8.6g | sodium: 198mg

Radish and Cabbage Congee

Prep Time: 5 minutes | **Cooking Time:** 20 minutes | **Servings:** 3

Ingredients

1 cup carrots, diced
½ cup radish, diced
6 cups vegetable broth
Salt, to taste
1½ cups short grain rice, rinsed
1 tablespoon grated fresh ginger
4 cups cabbage, shredded
Green onions for garnishing, chopped

Directions

1. Add all the , except the cabbage and green onions, into the instant pot.
2. Select the Porridge function and cook on the default time and settings.
3. After the beep, Quick release the pressure and remove the lid Stir in the shredded cabbage and cover with the lid.
4. Serve after 10 minutes with chopped green onions on top.

Per Serving calories: 438 | fat: 0.8g | protein: 8.7g | carbs: 98.4g | fiber: 6.7g | sodium: 1218mg

Rice, Corn, and Bean Stuffed Peppers

Prep Time: 15 minutes | **Cooking Time:** 15 minutes | **Servings:** 4

Ingredients

- 4 large bell peppers
- 2 cups cooked white rice
- 1 medium onion, peeled and diced
- 3 small Roma tomatoes, diced
- ¼ cup marinara sauce
- 1 cup corn kernels (cut from the cob is preferred)
- ¼ cup sliced black olives
- ¼ cup canned cannellini beans, rinsed and drained
- ¼ cup canned black beans, rinsed and drained
- 1 teaspoon sea salt
- 1 teaspoon garlic powder
- ½ cup vegetable broth
- 2 tablespoons grated Parmesan cheese

Directions

1. Cut off the bell pepper tops as close to the tops as possible. Hollow out and discard seeds. Poke a few small holes in the bottom of the peppers to allow drippings to drain.
2. In a medium bowl, combine remaining except for broth and Parmesan cheese. Stuff equal amounts of mixture into each of the bell peppers.
3. Place trivet into the Instant Pot and pour in the broth. Set the peppers upright on the trivet. Lock lid.
4. Press the Manual button and adjust time to 15 minutes. When timer beeps, let pressure release naturally until float valve drops and then unlock lid.
5. Serve immediately and garnish with Parmesan cheese.

Per Serving calories: 265 | fat: 3.0g | protein: 8.1g | carbs: 53.1g | fiber: 8.0g | sodium: 834mg

Carrot and Turnip Purée

Prep Time: 10 minutes | **Cooking Time:** 10 minutes | **Servings:** 6

Ingredients

- 2 tablespoons olive oil, divided
- 3 large turnips, peeled and quartered
- 4 large carrots, peeled and cut into 2-inch pieces
- 2 cups vegetable broth
- 1 teaspoon salt
- ½ teaspoon ground nutmeg
- 2 tablespoons sour cream

Directions

1. Press the Sauté button on Instant Pot. Heat 1 tablespoon olive oil. Toss turnips and carrots in oil for 1 minute. Add broth. Lock lid. Press the Manual button and adjust time to 8 minutes. When timer beeps, quick release pressure until float valve drops and then unlock lid.
2. Drain vegetables and reserve liquid; set liquid aside. Add 2 tablespoons of reserved liquid plus remaining to vegetables in the Instant Pot.
3. Use an immersion blender to blend until desired smoothness. If too thick, add more liquid 1 tablespoon at a time. Serve warm.

Per Serving calories: 95 | fat: 5.2g | protein: 1.4g | carbs: 11.8g | fiber: 3.0g | sodium: 669mg

Brussels Sprouts Linguine

Prep Time: 5 minutes | **Cooking Time:** 25 minutes | **Servings:** 4

Ingredients

- 8 ounces (227 g) whole-wheat linguine
- ⅓ cup plus 2 tablespoons extra-virgin olive oil, divided
- 1 medium sweet onion, diced
- 2 to 3 garlic cloves, smashed
- 8 ounces (227 g) Brussels sprouts, chopped
- ½ cup chicken stock
- ⅓ cup dry white wine
- ½ cup shredded Parmesan cheese
- 1 lemon, quartered

Directions

1. Bring a large pot of water to a boil and cook the pasta for about 5 minutes, or until al dente. Drain the pasta and reserve 1 cup of the pasta water. Mix the cooked pasta with 2 tablespoons of the olive oil. Set aside.
2. In a large skillet, heat the remaining ⅓ cup of the olive oil over medium heat. Add the onion to the skillet and sauté for about 4 minutes, or until tender. Add the smashed garlic cloves and sauté for 1 minute, or until fragrant.
3. Stir in the Brussels sprouts and cook covered for 10 minutes. Pour in the chicken stock to prevent burning. Once the Brussels sprouts have wilted and are fork-tender, add white wine and cook for about 5 minutes, or until reduced.
4. Add the pasta to the skillet and add the pasta water as needed.
5. Top with the Parmesan cheese and squeeze the lemon over the dish right before eating.

Per Serving

calories: 502 | fat: 31.0g | protein: 15.0g | carbs: 50.0g | fiber: 9.0g | sodium: 246mg

Baby Kale and Cabbage Salad

Prep Time: 10 minutes | **Cooking Time:** 0 minutes | **Servings:** 6

Ingredients

- 2 bunches baby kale, thinly sliced
- ½ head green savoy cabbage, cored and thinly sliced
- 1 medium red bell pepper, thinly sliced
- 1 garlic clove, thinly sliced

Dressing:
- Juice of 1 lemon
- ¼ cup apple cider vinegar
- 1 teaspoon ground cumin
- ¼ teaspoon smoked paprika
- 1 cup toasted peanuts

Directions

1. In a large mixing bowl, toss together the kale and cabbage.
2. Make the dressing: Whisk together the lemon juice, vinegar, cumin and paprika in a small bowl.
3. Pour the dressing over the greens and gently massage with your hands. Add the pepper, garlic and peanuts to the mixing bowl. Toss to combine. Serve immediately.

Per Serving calories: 199 | fat: 12.0g | protein: 10.0g | carbs: 17.0g | fiber: 5.0g | sodium: 46mg

Peanut and Coconut Stuffed Eggplants

Prep Time: 15 minutes | **Cooking Time:** 9 minutes | **Servings:** 4

Ingredients

1 tablespoon coriander seeds
½ teaspoon cumin seeds
½ teaspoon mustard seeds
2 to 3 tablespoons chickpea flour
2 tablespoons chopped peanuts
2 tablespoons coconut shreds
1-inch ginger, chopped
2 cloves garlic, chopped
1 hot green chili, chopped
½ teaspoon ground cardamom

A pinch of cinnamon
⅓ to ½ teaspoon cayenne
½ teaspoon turmeric
½ teaspoon raw sugar
½ to ¾ teaspoon salt
1 teaspoon lemon juice
Water as needed
4 baby eggplants
Fresh Cilantro for garnishing

Directions

1. Add the coriander, mustard seeds and cumin in the instant pot.
2. Roast on Sauté function for 2 minutes.
3. Add the chickpea flour, nuts and coconut shred to the pot, and roast for 2 minutes.
4. Blend this mixture in a blender, then transfer to a medium-sized bowl. Roughly blend the ginger, garlic, raw sugar, chili, and all the spices in a blender.
5. Add the water and lemon juice to make a paste. Combine it with the dry flour mixture.
6. Cut the eggplants from one side and stuff with the spice mixture. Add 1 cup of water to the instant pot and place the stuffed eggplants inside.
7. Sprinkle some salt on top and secure the lid.
8. Cook on Manual for 5 minutes at High Pressure, then quick release the steam. Remove the lid and garnish with fresh cilantro, then serve hot.

Per Serving calories: 207 | fat: 4.9g | protein: 7.9g | carbs: 39.6g | fiber: 18.3g | sodium: 315mg

Cauliflower with Sweet Potato

Prep Time: 15 minutes | **Cooking Time:** 8 minutes | **Servings:** 8

Ingredients

1 small onion
4 tomatoes
4 garlic cloves, chopped
2-inch ginger, chopped
2 teaspoons olive oil
1 teaspoon turmeric
2 teaspoons ground cumin
Salt, to taste

1 teaspoon paprika
2 medium sweet potatoes, cubed small
2 small cauliflowers, diced
2 tablespoons fresh cilantro for topping, chopped

Directions

1. Blend the tomatoes, garlic, ginger and onion in a blender.
2. Add the oil and cumin in the instant pot and Sauté for 1 minute.
3. Stir in the blended mixture and the remaining spices.
4. Add the sweet potatoes and cook for 5 minutes on Sauté
5. Add the cauliflower chunks and secure the lid.
6. Cook on Manual for 2 minutes at High Pressure.
7. Once done, Quick release the pressure and remove the lid.
8. Stir and serve with cilantro on top.

Per Serving

calories: 76 | fat: 1.6g | protein: 2.7g | carbs: 14.4g | fiber: 3.4g | sodium: 55mg

Sweet Potato and Tomato Curry

Prep Time: 5 minutes | **Cooking Time:** 8 minutes | **Servings:** 8

Ingredients

2 large brown onions, finely diced
4 tablespoons olive oil
4 teaspoons salt
4 large garlic cloves, diced
1 red chili, sliced
4 tablespoons cilantro, chopped
4 teaspoons ground cumin

2 teaspoons ground coriander
2 teaspoons paprika
2 pounds (907 g) sweet potato, diced
4 cups chopped, tinned tomatoes
2 cups water
2 cups vegetable stock
Lemon juice and cilantro (garnish)

Directions

1. Put the oil and onions into the instant pot and Sauté for 5 minutes.
2. Stir in the remaining and secure the lid.
3. Cook on Manual function for 3 minutes at High Pressure.
4. Once done, Quick release the pressure and remove the lid.
5. Garnish with cilantro and lemon juice.
6. Serve.

Per Serving

calories: 224 | fat: 8.0g | protein: 4.6g | carbs: 35.9g | fiber: 7.5g | sodium: 1385mg

Zoodles with Beet Pesto

Prep Time: 10 minutes | **Cooking Time:** 50 minutes | **Servings:** 2

Ingredients

1 medium red beet, peeled, chopped
½ cup walnut pieces
½ cup crumbled goat cheese
squeezed lemon juice

2 tablespoons plus 2 teaspoons extra-virgin olive oil, divided
¼ teaspoon salt
4 small zucchinis, spiralized
3 garlic cloves
2 tablespoons freshly

Directions

1. Preheat the oven to 375°F (190°C).
2. Wrap the chopped beet in a piece of aluminum foil and seal well.
3. Roast in the preheated oven for 30 to 40 minutes until tender.
4. Meanwhile, heat a skillet over medium-high heat until hot. Add the walnuts and toast for 5 to 7 minutes, or until fragrant and lightly browned.
5. Remove the cooked beets from the oven and place in a food processor. Add the toasted walnuts, goat cheese, garlic, lemon juice, 2 tablespoons of olive oil, and salt. Pulse until smoothly blended. Set aside.
6. Heat the remaining 2 teaspoons of olive oil in a large skillet over medium heat. Add the zucchini and toss to coat in the oil. Cook for 2 to 3 minutes, stirring gently, or until the zucchini is softened. Transfer the zucchini to a serving plate and toss with the beet pesto, then serve.

Per Serving

calories: 423 | fat: 38.8g | protein: 8.0g | carbs: 17.1g | fiber: 6.0g | sodium: 338mg

Cauliflower Hash with Carrots

Prep Time: 10 minutes | **Cooking Time:** 10 minutes | **Servings:** 4

Ingredients

3 tablespoons extra-virgin olive oil
1 large onion, chopped
1 tablespoon minced garlic

2 cups diced carrots
4 cups cauliflower florets
½ teaspoon ground cumin
1 teaspoon salt

Directions

1. In a large skillet, heat the olive oil over medium heat.
2. Add the onion and garlic and sauté for 1 minute. Stir in the carrots and stir-fry for 3 minutes.
3. Add the cauliflower florets, cumin, and salt and toss to combine.
4. Cover and cook for 3 minutes until lightly browned. Stir well and cook, uncovered, for 3 to 4 minutes, until softened.
5. Remove from the heat and serve warm.

Per Serving

calories: 158 | fat: 10.8g | protein: 3.1g | carbs: 14.9g | fiber: 5.1g | sodium: 656mg

Fried Eggplant Rolls

Prep Time: 20 minutes | **Cooking Time:** 10 minutes | **Servings:** 4 to 6

Ingredients

1 large eggplants, trimmed and cut lengthwise into ¼-inch-thick slices
1 teaspoon salt
1 cup ricotta cheese
Olive oil spray

4 ounces (113 g) goat cheese, shredded
¼ cup finely chopped fresh basil
½ teaspoon freshly ground black pepper

Directions

1. Add the eggplant slices to a colander and season with salt. Set aside for 15 to 20 minutes.
2. Mix together the ricotta and goat cheese, basil, and black pepper in a large bowl and stir to combine. Set aside.
3. Dry the eggplant slices with paper towels and lightly mist them with olive oil spray.
4. Heat a large skillet over medium heat and lightly spray it with olive oil spray.
5. Arrange the eggplant slices in the skillet and fry each side for 3 minutes until golden brown.
6. Remove from the heat to a paper towel-lined plate and rest for 5 minutes.
7. Make the eggplant rolls: Lay the eggplant slices on a flat work surface and top each slice with a tablespoon of the prepared cheese mixture. Roll them up and serve immediately.

Per Serving

calories: 254 | fat: 14.9g | protein: 15.3g | carbs: 18.6g | fiber: 7.1g | sodium: 745mg

Zoodles

Prep Time: 10 minutes | **Cooking Time:** 5 minutes | **Servings:** 2

Ingredients

2 tablespoons avocado oil
2 medium zucchini, spiralized

¼ teaspoon salt
Freshly ground black pepper

Directions

1. Heat the avocado oil in a large skillet over medium heat until it shimmers.
2. Add the zucchini noodles, salt, and black pepper to the skillet and toss to coat. Cook for 1 to 2 minutes, stirring constantly, until tender.
3. Serve warm.

Per Serving

calories: 128 | fat: 14.0g | protein: 0.3g | carbs: 0.3g | fiber: 0.1g | sodium: 291mg

Roasted Veggies and Brown Rice Bowl

Prep Time: 15 minutes | **Cooking Time:** 20 minutes | **Servings:** 4

Ingredients

2 cups cauliflower florets
2 cups broccoli florets
1 (15-ounce / 425-g) can chickpeas, drained and rinsed
1 cup carrot slices (about 1 inch thick)
2 to 3 tablespoons extra-virgin olive oil, divided
Salt and freshly ground black pepper, to taste
Nonstick cooking spray
2 cups cooked brown rice
2 to 3 tablespoons sesame seeds, for garnish
Dressing:
3 to 4 tablespoons tahini
2 tablespoons honey
1 lemon, juiced
1 garlic clove, minced
Salt and freshly ground black pepper, to taste

Directions

1. Preheat the oven to 400°F (205°C). Spritz two baking sheets with nonstick cooking spray.
2. Spread the cauliflower and broccoli on the first baking sheet and the second with the chickpeas and carrot slices.
3. Drizzle each sheet with half of the olive oil and sprinkle with salt and pepper. Toss to coat well.
4. Roast the chickpeas and carrot slices in the preheated oven for 10 minutes, leaving the carrots tender but crisp, and the cauliflower and broccoli for 20 minutes until fork-tender. Stir them once halfway through the cooking time.
5. Meanwhile, make the dressing: Whisk together the tahini, honey, lemon juice, garlic, salt, and pepper in a small bowl.
6. Divide the cooked brown rice among four bowls. Top each bowl evenly with roasted vegetables and dressing. Sprinkle the sesame seeds on top for garnish before serving.

Per Serving

calories: 453 | fat: 17.8g | protein: 12.1g | carbs: 61.8g | fiber: 11.2g | sodium: 60mg

Garlicky Zucchini Cubes with Mint

Prep Time: 5 minutes | **Cooking Time:** 10 minutes | **Servings:** 4

Ingredients

3 large green zucchini, cut into ½-inch cubes
3 tablespoons extra-virgin olive oil
1 large onion, chopped
3 cloves garlic, minced
1 teaspoon salt
1 teaspoon dried mint

Directions

1. Heat the olive oil in a large skillet over medium heat.
2. Add the onion and garlic and sauté for 3 minutes, stirring constantly, or until softened.
3. Stir in the zucchini cubes and salt and cook for 5 minutes, or until the zucchini is browned and tender.
4. Add the mint to the skillet and toss to combine, then continue cooking for 2 minutes. Serve warm.

Per Serving calories: 146 | fat: 10.6g | protein: 4.2g | carbs: 11.8g | fiber: 3.0g | sodium: 606mg

Zucchini and Artichokes Bowl with Farro

Prep Time: 15 minutes | **Cooking Time:** 10 minutes | **Servings:** 4 to 6

Ingredients

⅓ cup extra-virgin olive oil
⅓ cup chopped red onions
½ cup chopped red bell pepper
2 garlic cloves, minced
1 cup zucchini, cut into ½-inch-thick slices
½ cup coarsely chopped artichokes
½ cup canned chickpeas, drained and rinsed
3 cups cooked farro
Salt and freshly ground black pepper, to taste
½ cup crumbled feta cheese, for serving (optional)
¼ cup sliced olives, for serving (optional)
2 tablespoons fresh basil, chiffonade, for serving (optional)
3 tablespoons balsamic vinegar, for serving (optional)

Directions

1. Heat the olive oil in a large skillet over medium heat until it shimmers. Add the onions, bell pepper, and garlic and sauté for 5 minutes, stirring occasionally, until softened.
2. Stir in the zucchini slices, artichokes, and chickpeas and sauté for about 5 minutes until slightly tender.
3. Add the cooked farro and toss to combine until heated through. Sprinkle the salt and pepper to season.
4. Divide the mixture into bowls. Top each bowl evenly with feta cheese, olive slices, and basil and sprinkle with the balsamic vinegar, if desired.

Per Serving calories: 366 | fat: 19.9g | protein: 9.3g | carbs: 50.7g | fiber: 9.0g | sodium: 86mg

Wilted Dandelion Greens with Sweet Onion

Prep Time: 15 minutes | **Cooking Time:** 15 minutes | **Servings:** 4

Ingredients

1 tablespoon extra-virgin olive oil
1 Vidalia onion, thinly sliced
½ cup low-sodium vegetable broth
2 bunches dandelion greens, roughly chopped
Freshly ground black pepper, to taste
2 garlic cloves, minced

Directions

1. Heat the olive oil in a large skillet over low heat.
2. Add the garlic and onion and cook for 2 to 3 minutes, stirring occasionally, or until the onion is translucent.
3. Fold in the vegetable broth and dandelion greens and cook for 5 to 7 minutes until wilted, stirring frequently.
4. Sprinkle with the black pepper and serve on a plate while warm.

Per Serving

calories: 81 | fat: 3.9g | protein: 3.2g | carbs: 10.8g | fiber: 4.0g | sodium: 72mg

Cheesy Sweet Potato Burgers

Prep Time: 10 minutes | **Cooking Time:** 19 to 20 mins | **Servings:** 4

Ingredients

1 large sweet potato (about 8 ounces / 227 g)
2 tablespoons extra-virgin olive oil, divided
1 cup chopped onion
1 large egg
½ cup crumbled

1 garlic clove
1 cup old-fashioned rolled oats
1 tablespoon dried oregano
1 tablespoon balsamic vinegar
¼ teaspoon kosher salt
Gorgonzola cheese

Directions

1. Using a fork, pierce the sweet potato all over and microwave on high for 4 to 5 minutes, until softened in the center. Cool slightly before slicing in half.
2. Meanwhile, in a large skillet over medium-high heat, heat 1 tablespoon of the olive oil. Add the onion and sauté for 5 minutes.
3. Spoon the sweet potato flesh out of the skin and put the flesh in a food processor. Add the cooked onion, egg, garlic, oats, oregano, vinegar and salt. Pulse until smooth. Add the cheese and pulse four times to barely combine.
4. Form the mixture into four burgers. Place the burgers on a plate, and press to flatten each to about ¾-inch thick.
5. Wipe out the skillet with a paper towel. Heat the remaining 1 tablespoon of the oil over medium-high heat for about 2 minutes. Add the burgers to the hot oil, then reduce the heat to medium. Cook the burgers for 5 minutes per side.
6. Transfer the burgers to a plate and serve.

Per Serving

calories: 290 | fat: 12.0g | protein: 12.0g | carbs: 43.0g | fiber: 8.0g | sodium: 566mg

Quick Steamed Broccoli

Prep Time: 5 minutes | **Cooking Time:** 0 minutes | **Servings:** 2

Ingredients

¼ cup water
3 cups broccoli florets

Salt and ground black pepper, to taste

Directions

1. Pour the water into the Instant Pot and insert a steamer basket. Place the broccoli florets in the basket.
2. Secure the lid. Select the Manual mode and set the cooking time for 0 minutes at High Pressure.
3. Once cooking is complete, do a quick pressure release. Carefully open the lid.
4. Transfer the broccoli florets to a bowl with cold water to keep bright green color.
5. Season the broccoli with salt and pepper to taste, then serve.

Per Serving

calories: 16 | fat: 0.2g | protein: 1.9g | carbs: 1.7g | fiber: 1.6g | sodium: 292mg

Eggplant and Zucchini Gratin

Prep Time: 10 minutes | **Cooking Time:** 19 minutes | **Servings:** 6

Ingredients

2 large zucchinis, finely chopped
1 large eggplant, finely chopped
¼ teaspoon kosher salt
¼ teaspoon freshly ground black pepper
3 tablespoons extra-virgin olive oil, divided
¼ cup fresh basil leaves

¾ cup unsweetened almond milk
1 tablespoon all-purpose flour
⅓ cup plus
2 tablespoons grated Parmesan cheese, divided
1 cup chopped tomato
1 cup diced fresh Mozzarella

Directions

1. Preheat the oven to 425°F (220°C).
2. In a large bowl, toss together the zucchini, eggplant, salt and pepper.
3. In a large skillet over medium-high heat, heat 1 tablespoon of the oil. Add half of the veggie mixture to the skillet. Stir a few times, then cover and cook for about 4 minutes, stirring occasionally. Pour the cooked veggies into a baking dish. Place the skillet back on the heat, add 1 tablespoon of the oil and repeat with the remaining veggies. Add the veggies to the baking dish.
4. Meanwhile, heat the milk in the microwave for 1 minute. Set aside.
5. Place a medium saucepan over medium heat. Add the remaining 1 tablespoon of the oil and flour to the saucepan. Whisk together until well blended.
6. Slowly pour the warm milk into the saucepan, whisking the entire time. Continue to whisk frequently until the mixture thickens a bit. Add ⅓ cup of the Parmesan cheese and whisk until melted. Pour the cheese sauce over the vegetables in the baking dish and mix well.
7. Fold in the tomatoes and Mozzarella cheese. Roast in the oven for 10 minutes, or until the gratin is almost set and not runny.
8. Top with the fresh basil leaves and the remaining 2 tablespoons of the Parmesan cheese before serving.

Per Serving

calories: 122 | fat: 5.0g | protein: 10.0g | carbs: 11.0g | fiber: 4.0g | sodium: 364mg

Asparagus with Feta (Greek)

Prep Time: 10 minutes **Cooking Time:** 5 minutes
Servings: 4

Ingredients

1 cup feta cheese, cubed	1-pound asparagus spears
1 tablespoon olive oil	end trimmed
1 cup of water	Salt and freshly ground
1 lemon	black pepper, to taste

Directions

1. Add water into a pot and set trivet over the water
2. Place steamer basket on the trivet
3. Place the asparagus into the steamer basket
4. Close the lid
5. Cook for 1 minute on high pressure
6. Release the pressure quickly
7. Take a bowl and add olive oil into it
8. Toss in asparagus until well-coated
9. Season with pepper and salt
10. Serve with feta cheese and lemon
11. Enjoy!

Nutrition: Calories: 170 Fat: 18g Carbohydrates: 2g Protein: 3g

Rosemary Sweet Potato Medallions (Spanish)

Prep Time: 10 minutes
Cooking Time: 18 minutes
Servings: 4

Ingredients

4 sweet potatoes	2 tablespoons coconut oil
1 tablespoon rosemary	1 teaspoon garlic powder
1 cup of water	Salt, to taste

Directions

1. Add water and place steamer rack over the water
2. Using a fork, prick sweet potatoes all over
3. Then set on a steamer rack
4. Close the lid and cook for 12 minutes on High pressure
5. Release the pressure quickly
6. Cut the sweet potatoes into ½ inch
7. Melt the coconut oil on Sauté mode
8. Add in the medallions
9. Cook each side for 2 to 3 minutes until browned
10. Season with salt and garlic powder
11. Add rosemary on top
12. Serve and enjoy!

Nutrition: Calories: 291 Fat: 10g Carbohydrates: 30g Protein: 5g

Garlic Eggplant Slices (Spanish)

Prep Time: 5 minutes **Cooking Time:** 25 minutes
Servings: 4

Ingredients

1 egg	1 tablespoon water
½ cup whole wheat bread crumbs	½ teaspoon dried oregano
½ teaspoon salt	1 teaspoon garlic powder
1 medium eggplant, sliced into ¼-inch-thick rounds	½ teaspoon paprika
	1 tablespoon olive oil

Directions

1. Preheat the air fryer to 360°F (182°C).
2. In a medium shallow bowl, beat together the egg and water until frothy.
3. In a separate medium shallow bowl, mix together bread crumbs, garlic powder, oregano, salt, and paprika.
4. Dip each eggplant slice into the egg mixture, then into the bread crumb mixture, coating the outside with crumbs. Place the slices in a single layer in the bottom of the air fryer basket.
5. Drizzle the tops of the eggplant slices with the olive oil, then fry for 15 minutes. Turn each slice and cook for an additional 10 minutes.

Nutrition: calories: 137 | fat: 5g | protein: 5g | carbs: 19g | fiber: 5g | sodium: 409mg

Delicious Tomato Broth (Spanish)

Prep Time: 10 minutes **Cooking Time:** 15 minutes
Servings: 2

Ingredients

14 oz can fire-roasted tomatoes	½ tsp dried basil
½ cup heavy cream	Salt
1 cup cheddar cheese,	½ cup parmesan cheese, grated
1 ½ cups vegetable stock	¼ cup zucchini, grated
½ tsp dried oregano Pepper	

Directions

1. Add tomatoes, stock, zucchini, oregano, basil, pepper, and salt into the instant pot and stir well.
2. Seal pot and cook on high pressure for 5 minutes.
3. Release pressure using quick release. Remove lid.
4. Set pot on sauté mode. Add heavy cream, parmesan cheese, and cheddar cheese and stir well and cook until cheese is melted.
5. Serve and enjoy.

Nutrition: 460 Calories 35g Fat 24g Protein

Chapter 7
Poultry Recipes & Meats Recipes

Herbed-Mustard-Coated Pork Tenderloin
Prep Time: 10 minutes | **Cooking Time:** 15 minutes | **Servings:** 4

Ingredients

3 tablespoons fresh rosemary leaves
¼ cup Dijon mustard
½ cup fresh parsley leaves
6 garlic cloves
½ teaspoon sea salt
¼ teaspoon freshly ground black pepper
1 tablespoon extra-virgin olive oil
1 (1½-pound / 680-g) pork tenderloin

Directions
1. Preheat the oven to 400ºF (205ºC).
2. Put all the , except for the pork tenderloin, in a food processor. Pulse until it has a thick consistency.
3. Put the pork tenderloin on a baking sheet, then rub with the mixture to coat well.
4. Put the sheet in the preheated oven and bake for 15 minutes or until the internal temperature of the pork reaches at least 165ºF (74ºC). Flip the tenderloin halfway through the cooking time.
5. Transfer the cooked pork tenderloin to a large plate and allow to cool for 5 minutes before serving.

Per Serving calories: 363 | fat: 18.1g | protein: 2.2g | carbs: 4.9g | fiber: 2.0g | sodium: 514mg

Grilled Pork Chops
Prep Time: 20 minutes | **Cooking Time:** 10 minutes | **Servings:** 4

Ingredients

¼ cup extra-virgin olive oil
2 tablespoons fresh thyme leaves
1 teaspoon smoked paprika
1 teaspoon salt
4 pork loin chops, ½-inch-thick

Directions
1. In a small bowl, mix together the olive oil, thyme, paprika, and salt. Put the pork chops in a plastic zip-top bag or a bowl and coat them with the spice mix. Let them marinate for 15 minutes.
2. Preheat the grill to high heat. Cook the pork chops for 4 minutes on each side until cooked through. Serve warm.

Per Serving calories: 282 | fat: 23.0g | protein: 21.0g | carbs: 1.0g | fiber: 0g | sodium: 832mg

Macadamia Pork
Prep Time: 10 minutes | **Cooking Time:** 10 minutes | **Servings:** 4

Ingredients

1 (1-pound / 454-g) pork tenderloin, cut into ½-inch slices and pounded thin
1 teaspoon sea salt, divided
1 tablespoon extra-virgin olive oil
¼ teaspoon freshly ground black pepper, divided
½ cup macadamia nuts
1 cup unsweetened coconut milk

Directions
1. Preheat the oven to 400ºF (205ºC).
2. On a clean work surface, rub the pork with ½ teaspoon of the salt and ⅛ teaspoon of the ground black pepper. Set aside. Ground the macadamia nuts in a food processor, then combine with remaining salt and black pepper in a bowl. Stir to mix well and set aside.
3. Combine the coconut milk and olive oil in a separate bowl. Stir to mix well. Dredge the pork chops into the bowl of coconut milk mixture, then dunk into the bowl of macadamia nut mixture to coat well. Shake the excess off.
4. Put the well-coated pork chops on a baking sheet, then bake for 10 minutes or until the internal temperature of the pork reaches at least 165ºF (74ºC). Transfer the pork chops to a serving plate and serve immediately.

Per Serving calories: 436 | fat: 32.8g | protein: 33.1g | carbs: 5.9g | fiber: 3.0g | sodium: 310mg

Beef, Tomato, and Lentils Stew
Prep Time: 10 minutes | **Cooking Time:** 10 minutes | **Servings:** 4

Ingredients

1 tablespoon extra-virgin olive oil
1 onion, chopped
1 (14-ounce / 397-g) can chopped tomatoes with garlic and basil, drained
1 (14-ounce / 397-g) can lentils, drained
½ teaspoon sea salt
⅛ tbsp. freshly ground black pepper
1 pound (454 g) extra-lean ground beef

Directions
1. Heat the olive oil in a pot over medium-high heat until shimmering.
2. Add the beef and onion to the pot and sauté for 5 minutes or until the beef is lightly browned.
3. Add the remaining. Bring to a boil. Reduce the heat to medium and cook for 4 more minutes or until the lentils are tender. Keep stirring during the cooking.
4. Pour them in a large serving bowl and serve immediately.

Per Serving calories: 460 | fat: 14.8g | protein: 44.2g | carbs: 36.9g | fiber: 17.0g | sodium: 320mg

Gyro Burgers with Tahini Sauce

Prep Time: 15 minutes | **Cooking Time:** 10 minutes | **Servings:** 4

Ingredients

2 tablespoons extra-virgin olive oil
1 tablespoon dried oregano
1¼ teaspoons garlic powder, divided
1 teaspoon ground cumin
½ teaspoon freshly ground black pepper
¼ teaspoon kosher or sea salt
1 pound (454 g) beef flank steak, top round steak, or lamb leg steak, center cut, about 1 inch thick

1 medium green bell pepper, halved and seeded
2 tablespoons tahini or peanut butter
1 tablespoon hot water (optional)
½ cup plain Greek yogurt
1 tablespoon freshly squeezed lemon juice
1 cup thinly sliced red onion
4 (6-inch) whole-wheat pita breads, warmed
Nonstick cooking spray

Directions

1. Set an oven rack about 4 inches below the broiler element. Preheat the oven broiler to high. Line a large, rimmed baking sheet with aluminum foil. Place a wire cooling rack on the foil, and spray the rack with nonstick cooking spray. Set aside.
2. In a small bowl, whisk together the olive oil, oregano, 1 teaspoon of garlic powder, cumin, pepper, and salt. Rub the oil mixture on all sides of the steak, reserving 1 teaspoon of the mixture. Place the steak on the prepared rack. Rub the remaining oil mixture on the bell pepper, and place on the rack, cut-side down. Press the pepper with the heel of your hand to flatten.
3. Broil for 5 minutes. Flip the steak and the pepper pieces, and broil for 2 to 5 minutes more, until the pepper is charred and the internal temperature of the meat measures 145°F (63°C) on a meat thermometer. Put the pepper and steak on a cutting board to rest for 5 minutes.
4. Meanwhile, in a small bowl, whisk the tahini until smooth (adding 1 tablespoon of hot water if your tahini is sticky). Add the remaining ¼ teaspoon of garlic powder and the yogurt and lemon juice, and whisk thoroughly.
5. Slice the steak crosswise into ¼-inch-thick strips. Slice the bell pepper into strips. Divide the steak, bell pepper, and onion among the warm pita breads. Drizzle with tahini sauce and serve.

Per Serving

calories: 348 | fat: 15.0g | protein: 33.0g | carbs: 20.0g | fiber: 3.0g | sodium: 530mg

Quick Chicken Salad Wraps

Prep Time: 15 minutes | **Cooking Time:** 0 minutes | **Servings:** 2

Ingredients

Tzatziki Sauce:
½ cup plain Greek yogurt
1 tablespoon freshly squeezed lemon juice
Pinch garlic powder
1 teaspoon dried dill
Salt and freshly ground black pepper, to taste
¼ cup pitted black olives
1 scallion, chopped

Salad Wraps:
2 (8-inch) whole-grain pita bread
1 cup shredded chicken meat
2 cups mixed greens
2 roasted red bell peppers, thinly sliced
½ English cucumber, peeled if desired and thinly sliced

Directions

1. Make the tzatziki sauce: In a bowl, whisk together the yogurt, lemon juice, garlic powder, dill, salt, and pepper until creamy and smooth.
2. Make the salad wraps: Place the pita bread on a clean work surface and spoon ¼ cup of the tzatziki sauce onto each piece of pita bread, spreading it all over. Top with the shredded chicken, mixed greens, red pepper slices, cucumber slices, black olives, finished by chopped scallion.
3. Roll the salad wraps and enjoy.

Per Serving

calories: 428 | fat: 10.6g | protein: 31.1g | carbs: 50.9g | fiber: 6.0g | sodium: 675mg

Sautéed Ground Turkey with Brown Rice

Prep Time: 20 minutes | **Cooking Time:** 45 minutes | **Servings:** 2

Ingredients

1 tablespoon olive oil
½ medium onion, minced
2 garlic cloves, minced
8 ounces (227 g) ground turkey breast
½ cup chopped roasted red peppers, (about 2 jarred peppers)

¼ cup sun-dried tomatoes, minced
1¼ cups low-sodium chicken stock
½ cup brown rice
1 tbsp dried oregano Salt, to taste
2 cups lightly packed baby spinach

Directions

1. In a skillet, heat the olive oil over medium heat. Sauté the onion for 5 minutes, stirring occasionally.
2. Stir in the garlic and sauté for 30 seconds more until fragrant.
3. Add the turkey breast and cook for about 7 minutes, breaking apart with a wooden spoon, until the turkey is no longer pink.
4. Stir in the roasted red peppers, tomatoes, chicken stock, brown rice, and oregano and bring to a boil.
5. When the mixture starts to boil, cover, and reduce the heat to medium- low. Bring to a simmer until the rice is tender, stirring occasionally, about 30 minutes. Sprinkle with the salt.
6. Add the baby spinach and keep stirring until wilted.
7. Remove from the heat and serve warm.

Per Serving

calories: 445 | fat: 16.8g | protein: 30.2g | carbs: 48.9g | fiber: 5.1g | sodium: 662mg

Roasted Chicken Thighs With Basmati Rice

Prep Time: 15 minutes | **Cooking Time:** 50 to 55 mins | Servings: 2

Ingredients

Chicken:
½ teaspoon cumin
½ teaspoon cinnamon
½ teaspoon paprika
¼ teaspoon ginger powder
¼ teaspoon garlic powder
¼ teaspoon coriander
¼ teaspoon salt
⅛ teaspoon cayenne pepper
¼ teaspoon salt

10 ounces (284 g) boneless, skinless chicken thighs (about 4 pieces)
Rice:
1 tablespoon olive oil
½ small onion, minced
½ cup basmati rice 2 pinches saffron
1 cup low-sodium chicken stock

Directions

Make the Chicken

1. Preheat the oven to 350°F (180°C).
2. Combine the cumin, cinnamon, paprika, ginger powder, garlic powder, coriander, salt, and cayenne pepper in a small bowl. Using your hands to rub the spice mixture all over the chicken thighs.
3. Transfer the chicken thighs to a baking dish. Roast in the preheated oven for 35 to 40 minutes, or until the internal temperature reaches 165°F (74°C) on a meat thermometer.

Make the Rice

4. Meanwhile, heat the olive oil in a skillet over medium-high heat. Sauté the onion for 5 minutes until fragrant, stirring occasionally.
5. Stir in the basmati rice, saffron, chicken stock, and salt. Reduce the heat to low, cover, and bring to a simmer for 15 minutes, until light and fluffy. Remove the chicken from the oven to a plate and serve with the rice.

Per Serving calories: 400 | fat: 9.6g | protein: 37.2g | carbs: 40.7g | fiber: 2.1g | sodium: 714mg

Roasted Pork Meat (Spanish)

Prep Time: 5 minutes **Cooking Time:** 55 minutes
Servings: 6

Ingredients

3 pounds of roast pork	1 tablespoon vegetable
Salt and pepper	oil
1 sliced onion	2 cups of water

Directions

1. Pour vegetable oil into the pot. Brown the pork on both sides in medium pressure over medium heat and then remove from the pot.
2. Pour the water into the pot. Put the pork on the rack of the pot. Season with salt, pepper and sliced onions.
3. Close and secure the lid. Place the pressure regulator on the vent tube and cook 55 minutes once the pressure regulator begins to rock slowly. Let the pressure decrease on its own.

Nutrition: Calories: 483, Carbohydrates: 0g, Fat: 27g, Protein: 53g, Cholesterol: 171mg,

Yogurt Chicken Breasts

Prep Time: 10 minutes | **Cooking Time:** 10 minutes | Servings: 4

Ingredients

1 pound (454 g) boneless, skinless chicken breasts, cut into 2-inch strips
1 tablespoon extra-virgin olive oil
Yogurt Sauce:
½ cup plain Greek yogurt
2 tablespoons water

Pinch saffron (3 or 4 threads)
3 garlic cloves, minced
½ onion, chopped
2 tablespoons chopped fresh cilantro
Juice of ½ lemon
½ teaspoon salt

Directions

1. Make the yogurt sauce: Place the yogurt, water, saffron, garlic, onion, cilantro, lemon juice, and salt in a blender, and pulse until completely mixed.
2. Transfer the yogurt sauce to a large bowl, along with the chicken strips. Toss to coat well.
3. Cover with plastic wrap and marinate in the refrigerator for at least 1 hour, or up to overnight.
4. When ready to cook, heat the olive oil in a large skillet over medium heat.
5. Add the chicken strips to the skillet, discarding any excess marinade. Cook each side for 5 minutes, or until cooked through.
6. Let the chicken cool for 5 minutes before serving.

Per Serving
calories: 154 | fat: 4.8g | protein: 26.3g | carbs: 2.9g | fiber: 0g | sodium: 500mg

Lemon Beef (Spanish)

Prep Time: 10 mins **Cooking Time:** 6 hours
Servings: 4

Ingredients

1 lb. beef chuck roast	1 garlic clove, crushed
1 teaspoon chili powder	2 cups lemon-lime soda
1/2 teaspoon salt	1 fresh lime juice

Directions

1. Place beef chuck roast into the slow cooker.
2. Season roast with garlic, chili powder, and salt.
3. Pour lemon-lime soda over the roast.
4. Cover slow cooker with lid and cook on low for 6 hours. Shred the meat using fork.
5. Add lime juice over shredded roast and serve.

Nutrition: Calories 355 Fat 16.8 g Carbohydrates 14 g Sugar 11.3 g Protein 35.5 g Cholesterol 120 mg

Greek Chicken Salad (Greek)

Prep Time: 10 minutes **Cooking Time:** 5 minutes
Servings: 1

Ingredients

1 cup cooked chicken, shredded
1/4 cup cucumber, diced
1 tablespoon sour cream
Pepper

1 teaspoon vinegar
2 teaspoon fresh basil, chopped
Salt

Directions

1. Add all into the medium bowl and mix well to combine.
2. Season with pepper and salt. Place in refrigerator for 10 minutes.
3. Serve and enjoy.

Nutrition: Calories 243 Fat 6.8 g Carbohydrates 1.6 g Sugar 0.5 g Protein 41.2g Cholesterol 113 mg

Seasoned Pork Chops (Spanish)

Prep Time: 10 minutes **Cooking Time:** 4 hours
Servings: 4

Ingredients

4 pork chops
1/4 cup olive oil
1 tablespoon poultry seasoning

2 garlic cloves, minced
1 cup chicken broth
Pepper and salt

Directions

1. In a bowl, whisk together olive oil, poultry seasoning, garlic, broth, pepper, and salt.
2. Pour olive oil mixture into the slow cooker then place pork chops to the crock pot.
3. Cover and cook on high for 4 hours.
4. Serve and enjoy.

Nutrition: Calories 386 Fat 32.9 g Carbohydrates 3 g Sugar 1 g Protein 20 g Cholesterol 70 mg

Beef Stroganoff (Spanish)

Prep Time: 10 minutes **Cooking Time:** 8 hours
Servings: 2

Ingredients

1/2 lb. beef stew meat
10 oz mushroom soup
1/2 cup sour cream oz mushrooms

homemade
1 medium onion chopped sliced
Pepper and salt

Directions

1. Add all except sour cream into the crock pot and mix well. Cover and cook on low for 8 hours.
2. Add sour cream and stir well.
3. Serve and enjoy.

Nutrition: Calories 470 Fat 25 g Carbohydrates 8.6 g Sugar 3 g Protein 49 g Cholesterol 108 mg

Greek Turkey Burgers (Greek)

Prep Time: 10 minutes **Cooking Time:** 15 minutes
Servings: 4

Ingredients

1/3 cup feta cheese, crumbled
7 ounces roasted red bell peppers, sliced
¾ cup mint, chopped
1 cup red onion, sliced
4 Iceberg salad leaves

1 egg white
1 teaspoon dill
½ cup breadcrumbs
4 whole-wheat buns
2 tablespoons lemon juice
Canola oil as needed
1 pound ground turkey

Directions

1. In a mixing bowl, beat the egg whites. Add the mint, breadcrumbs, onions, feta cheese, lemon juice, dill and turkey; combine well.
2. Form 4 patties from the mixture.
3. Over medium stove flame, heat the oil in a skillet or saucepan (preferably of medium size).
4. Add the patties and cook them until evenly brown on both sides.
5. Serve the patties in the buns topping them with roasted peppers and iceberg leaves.

Nutrition: Calories 362 Fat 13gCarbohydrates 38gFiber 4gProtein 33g

Mediterranean Chicken (Greek)

Prep Time: 10 minutes **Cooking Time:** 10 minutes
Servings: 6

Ingredients

2 lb. chicken breast fillet, sliced into strips
sugar
1 1/2 tbsp dried oregano
6 garlic cloves, chopped

Wine mixture (1/4 cup white wine mixed with 3 tablespoons red wine)
2 tablespoons light brown

Directions

Pour in the wine mixture to the Instant Pot.
2.Stir in the rest
3.Toss the chicken to coat evenly.
4.Seal the pot.
5.Set it to high pressure.
6.Cook for 10 minutes.
7.Release the pressure naturally.

Nutrition: Calories 304 Total Fat 11.3g Saturated Fat 3.1g Cholesterol 135mg Sodium 131mg Total Carbohydrate 4.2g Dietary Fiber 0.2g Total Sugars 3g Protein 44g Potassium 390mg

Tender Chicken Quesadilla (Spanish)

Prep Time: 10 minutes **Cooking Time:** 20 minutes
Servings: 4

Ingredients

bread tortillas
2teaspoons olive oil
6 oz chicken breast, skinless, boneless, sliced
1/3 cup Cheddar cheese, shredded

1teaspoon butter
1 teaspoon Taco seasoning
1 bell pepper, cut on the wedges

Directions

1. Pour 1 teaspoon of olive oil in the skillet and add chicken.
2. Sprinkle the meat with Taco seasoning and mix up well.
3. Roast chicken for 10 minutes over the medium heat. Stir it from time to time.
4. Then transfer the cooked chicken in the plate.
5. Add remaining olive oil in the skillet.
6. Then add bell pepper and roast it for 5 minutes. Stir it all the time.
7. Mix up together bell pepper with chicken.
8. Toss butter in the skillet and melt it.
9. Put 1 tortilla in the skillet.
10. Put Cheddar cheese on the tortilla and flatten it.
11. Then add chicken-pepper mixture and cover it with the second tortilla. Roast the quesadilla for 2 minutes from each side.
12. Cut the cooked meal on the halves and transfer in the serving plates.

Nutrition: Calories 167, Fat 8.2 g, Fiber 0.8 g, Carbs 16.4 g, Protein 24.2 g

Crack Chicken (Greek)

Prep Time: 10 minutes **Cooking Time:** 30 minutes
Servings: 4

Ingredients

4 chicken thighs, skinless, boneless
1 tablespoon cream cheese
1 teaspoon paprika
1 tablespoon butter
½ teaspoon garlic powder
1teaspoon olive oil

½ teaspoon salt
1 teaspoon ground black pepper
¼ cup Cheddar cheese, shredded
1 tbsp fresh dill, chopped
½ teaspoon ground nutmeg

Directions

1. Grease the baking dish with butter. Then heat up olive oil in the skillet. Meanwhile, rub the chicken thighs with ground nutmeg, garlic powder, paprika, and salt. Add ground black pepper.
2. Roast the chicken thighs in the hot oil over the high heat for 2 minutes from each side.
3. Then transfer the chicken thighs in the prepared baking dish.
4. Mix up together Cheddar cheese, cream cheese, and dill.
5. Top every chicken thigh with cheese mixture and bake for 25 minutes at 365F.

Nutrition: Calories 79, Fat 7.3 g, Fiber 0.1, Carbs 1 g, Protein 2.4 g

Chicken Bacon Salad (Italian)

Prep Time: 10 minutes **Cooking Time:** 5 minutes
Servings: 3

Ingredients

1cups cooked chicken, shredded
1 cup celery, chopped
/4 cup mayonnaise
Salt

1/2 cup sour cream
1 cup cheddar cheese, shredded
1/2 cup bacon, crumbles
3 green onions, sliced
1/4 cup onion, chopped
Pepper

Directions

1. Add all ingredients into the large bowl and mix until well combined.
2. Serve and enjoy.

Nutrition: Calories 482 Fat 31.3 g Carbohydrates 9.9 g Sugar 2.7 g Protein 39.6 g Cholesterol 137 mg

Green Salsa Chicken (Italian)

Prep Time: 10 minutes **Cooking Time:** 3 hours
Servings: 6

Ingredients

1 lb. chicken breasts, skinless and boneless
Salt

15 oz green salsa Pepper

Directions

1. Add all ingredients into the crock pot.
2. Cover and cook on high for 3 hours.
3. Shred the chicken using fork.
4. Serve and enjoy.

Nutrition: Calories 166 Fat 6 g Carbohydrates 3 g Sugar 1.4 g Protein 22 g Cholesterol 67 mg

Chicken Chili (Greek)

Prep Time: 10 minutes **Cooking Time:** 6 hours
Servings: 4

Ingredients

1 lb. chicken breasts, skinless and boneless
1 jalapeno pepper, chopped
1 poblano pepper, chopped
12 oz can green chilies
1 teaspoon dried oregano
1/2 cup dried chives

14 oz can tomato, diced
2 cups of water
1/2 teaspoon paprika
1/2 teaspoon dried sage
1/2 teaspoon cumin
1 teaspoon sea salt

Directions

1. Add all ingredients into the crockpot and stir well.
2. Cover and cook on low for 6 hours.
3. Shred the chicken using a fork.
4. Stir well and serve.

Nutrition: Calories 265 Fat 8.9 g Carbohydrates 11.1 g Sugar 4.2 g Protein 34.9 g Cholesterol 101 mg

Parsley-Dijon Chicken and Potatoes

Prep Time: 5 minutes | **Cooking Time:** 22 minutes | **Servings:** 6

Ingredients

1 tablespoon extra-virgin olive oil

1½ pounds (680 g) boneless, skinless chicken thighs, cut into 1-inch cubes, patted dry

1½ pounds (680 g) Yukon Gold potatoes, unpeeled, cut into ½-inch cubes

2 garlic cloves, minced

¼ cup dry white wine

1 cup low-sodium or no-salt-added chicken broth

1 tablespoon Dijon mustard

¼ teaspoon freshly ground black pepper

¼ teaspoon kosher or sea salt

1 cup chopped fresh flat-leaf (Italian) parsley, including stems

1 tablespoon freshly squeezed lemon juice

Directions

1. In a large skillet over medium-high heat, heat the oil. Add the chicken and cook for 5 minutes, stirring only after the chicken has browned on one side. Remove the chicken and reserve on a plate.
2. Add the potatoes to the skillet and cook for 5 minutes, stirring only after the potatoes have become golden and crispy on one side. Push the potatoes to the side of the skillet, add the garlic, and cook, stirring constantly, for 1 minute. Add the wine and cook for 1 minute, until nearly evaporated.
3. Add the chicken broth, mustard, salt, pepper, and reserved chicken. Turn the heat to high and bring to a boil. Once boiling, cover, reduce the heat to medium-low, and cook for 10 to 12 minutes, until the potatoes are tender and the internal temperature of the chicken measures 165ºF (74ºC) on a meat thermometer and any juices run clear. During the last minute of cooking, stir in the parsley. Remove from the heat, stir in the lemon juice, and serve.

Per Serving calories: 324 | fat: 9.0g | protein: 16.0g | carbs: 45.0g | fiber: 5.0g | sodium: 560mg

Potato Lamb and Olive Stew

Prep Time: 20 mins | **Cooking Time:** 3 hours 42 mins | **Servings:** 10

Ingredients

4 tablespoons almond flour

¾ cup low-sodium chicken stock

1¼ pounds (567 g) small potatoes, halved

3 cloves garlic, minced

4 large shallots, cut into ½-inch wedges

3 sprigs fresh rosemary

1 tablespoon lemon zest

Coarse sea salt and black pepper, to taste

3½ pounds (1.6 kg) lamb shanks, fat trimmed and cut crosswise into 1½-inch pieces

2 tablespoons extra-virgin olive oil

½ cup dry white wine

1 cup pitted green olives, halved

2 tablespoons lemon juice

Directions

1. Combine 1 tablespoon of almond flour with chicken stock in a bowl. Stir to mix well. Put the flour mixture, potatoes, garlic, shallots, rosemary, and lemon zest in the slow cooker. Sprinkle with salt and black pepper. Stir to mix well. Set aside.
2. Combine the remaining almond flour with salt and black pepper in a large bowl, then dunk the lamb shanks in the flour and toss to coat.
3. Heat the olive oil in a nonstick skillet over medium-high heat until shimmering.
4. Add the well-coated lamb and cook for 10 minutes or until golden brown. Flip the lamb pieces halfway through the cooking time. Transfer the cooked lamb to the slow cooker.
5. Pour the wine in the same skillet, then cook for 2 minutes or until it reduces in half. Pour the wine in the slow cooker.
6. Put the slow cooker lid on and cook on high for 3 hours and 30 minutes or until the lamb is very tender.
7. In the last 20 minutes of the cooking, open the lid and fold in the olive halves to cook.
8. Pour the stew on a large plate, let them sit for 5 minutes, then skim any fat remains over the face of the liquid.
9. Drizzle with lemon juice and sprinkle with salt and pepper. Serve warm.

Per Serving

calories: 309 | fat: 10.3g | protein: 36.9g | carbs: 16.1g | fiber: 2.2g | sodium: 239mg

Chapter 8
Fish Recipes & Seafood Recipes

Avocado Shrimp Ceviche
Prep Time: 15 minutes | **Cooking Time:** 0 minutes | **Servings:** 4

Ingredients
1 pound (454 g) fresh shrimp, peeled, deveined, and cut in half lengthwise
1 small red or yellow bell pepper, cut into ½-inch chunks
½ small red onion, cut into thin slivers
½ English cucumber, peeled and cut into ½-inch chunks
¼ cup chopped fresh cilantro
½ cup extra-virgin olive oil
⅓ cup freshly squeezed lime juice
2 tablespoons freshly squeezed clementine juice
2 tablespoons freshly squeezed lemon juice
1 teaspoon salt
½ teaspoon freshly ground black pepper
2 ripe avocados, peeled, pitted, and cut into ½-inch chunks

Directions
1. Place the shrimp, bell pepper, red onion, cucumber, and cilantro in a large bowl and toss to combine.
2. In a separate bowl, stir together the olive oil, lime, clementine, and lemon juice, salt, and black pepper until smooth. Pour the mixture into the bowl of shrimp and vegetable mixture and toss until they are completely coated.
3. Cover the bowl with plastic wrap and transfer to the refrigerator to marinate for at least 2 hours, or up to 8 hours.
4. When ready, stir in the avocado chunks and toss to incorporate. Serve immediately.

Per Serving
calories: 496 | fat: 39.5g | protein: 25.3g | carbs: 13.8g | fiber: 6.0g | sodium: 755mg

Cioppino (Seafood Tomato Stew)
Prep Time: 10 minutes | **Cooking Time:** 20 minutes | **Servings:** 2

Ingredients
2 tablespoons olive oil
½ small onion, diced
½ green pepper, diced
2 teaspoons dried basil
2 teaspoons dried oregano
½ cup dry white wine
1 (14.5-ounce / 411-g) can diced tomatoes with basil
1 (8-ounce / 227-g) can no-salt-added tomato sauce
1 (6.5-ounce / 184-g) can minced clams with their juice
8 ounces (227 g) peeled, deveined raw shrimp
4 ounces (113 g) any white fish (a thick piece works best)
3 tablespoons fresh parsley
Salt and freshly ground black pepper, to taste

Directions
1. In a Dutch oven, heat the olive oil over medium heat.
2. Sauté the onion and green pepper for 5 minutes, or until tender. Stir in the basil, oregano, wine, diced tomatoes, and tomato sauce and bring to a boil.
3. Once boiling, reduce the heat to low and bring to a simmer for 5 minutes.
4. Add the clams, shrimp, and fish and cook for about 10 minutes, or until the shrimp are pink and cooked through.
5. Scatter with the parsley and add the salt and black pepper to taste. Remove from the heat and serve warm.

Per Serving calories: 221 | fat: 7.7g | protein: 23.1g | carbs: 10.9g | fiber: 4.2g | sodium: 720mg

Slow Cooker Salmon in Foil
Prep Time: 5 minutes | **Cooking Time:** 2 hours | **Servings:** 2

Ingredients
2 (6-ounce / 170-g) salmon fillets
1 tablespoon olive oil
2 cloves garlic, minced
½ tablespoon lime juice
1 teaspoon finely chopped fresh parsley
¼ teaspoon black pepper

Directions
1. Spread a length of foil onto a work surface and place the salmon fillets in the middle. Mix together the olive oil, garlic, lime juice, parsley, and black pepper in a small bowl. Brush the mixture over the fillets. Fold the foil over and crimp the sides to make a packet.
2. Place the packet into the slow cooker, cover, and cook on High for 2 hours, or until the fish flakes easily with a fork.
3. Serve hot.

Per Serving calories: 446 | fat: 20.7g | protein: 65.4g | carbs: 1.5g | fiber: 0.2g | sodium: 240mg

Honey-Mustard Roasted Salmon

Prep Time: 5 minutes | **Cooking Time:** 15 to 20 minutes | **Servings:** 4

Ingredients
2 tablespoons whole-grain mustard
2 garlic cloves, minced
1 tablespoon honey
¼ teaspoon salt
¼ teaspoon freshly ground black pepper
1 pound (454 g) salmon fillet
Nonstick cooking spray

Directions
1. Preheat the oven to 425°F (220°C). Coat a baking sheet with nonstick cooking spray.
2. Stir together the mustard, garlic, honey, salt, and pepper in a small bowl.
3. Arrange the salmon fillet, skin-side down, on the coated baking sheet. Spread the mustard mixture evenly over the salmon fillet.
4. Roast in the preheated oven for 15 to 20 minutes, or until it flakes apart easily and reaches an internal temperature of 145°F (63°C).Serve hot.

Per Serving
calories: 185 | fat: 7.0g | protein: 23.2g | carbs: 5.8g | fiber: 0g | sodium: 311mg

Baked Fish with Pistachio Crust

Prep Time: 10 minutes | **Cooking Time:** 15 to 20 minutes | **Servings:** 4

Ingredients
½ cup extra-virgin olive oil, divided
1 pound (454 g) flaky white fish (such as cod, haddock, or halibut), skin removed
½ cup shelled finely chopped pistachios
½ cup ground flaxseed
Zest and juice of 1 lemon, divided
1 teaspoon ground cumin
1 teaspoon ground allspice
½ teaspoon salt
¼ teaspoon freshly ground black pepper

Directions
1. Preheat the oven to 400°F (205°C).
2. Line a baking sheet with parchment paper or aluminum foil and drizzle 2 tablespoons of olive oil over the sheet, spreading to evenly coat the bottom.
3. Cut the fish into 4 equal pieces and place on the prepared baking sheet. In a small bowl, combine the pistachios, flaxseed, lemon zest, cumin, allspice, salt, and pepper. Drizzle in ¼ cup of olive oil and stir well.
4. Divide the nut mixture evenly on top of the fish pieces. Drizzle the lemon juice and remaining 2 tablespoons of olive oil over the fish and bake until cooked through, 15 to 20 minutes, depending on the thickness of the fish.
5. Cool for 5 minutes before serving.

Per Serving
calories: 509 | fat: 41.0g | protein: 26.0g | carbs: 9.0g | fiber: 6.0g | sodium: 331mg

Sole Piccata with Capers

Prep Time: 10 minutes | **Cooking Time:** 17 minutes | **Servings:** 4

Ingredients
1 teaspoon extra-virgin olive oil
4 (5-ounce / 142-g) sole fillets, patted dry
3 tablespoons almond butter
2 teaspoons minced garlic
2 tablespoons all-purpose flour
2 cups low-sodium chicken broth
Juice and zest of ½ lemon
2 tablespoons capers

Directions
1. Place a large skillet over medium-high heat and add the olive oil.
2. Sear the sole fillets until the fish flakes easily when tested with a fork, about 4 minutes on each side. Transfer the fish to a plate and set aside.
3. Return the skillet to the stove and add the butter.
4. Sauté the garlic until translucent, about 3 minutes.
5. Whisk in the flour to make a thick paste and cook, stirring constantly, until the mixture is golden brown, about 2 minutes.
6. Whisk in the chicken broth, lemon juice and zest.
7. Cook for about 4 minutes until the sauce is thickened.
8. Stir in the capers and serve the sauce over the fish.

Per Serving
calories: 271 | fat:13.0g | protein: 30.0g | carbs: 7.0g | fiber: 0g | sodium: 413mg

Haddock with Cucumber Sauce

Prep Time: 10 minutes | **Cooking Time:** 10 minutes | **Servings:** 4

Ingredients
¼ cup plain Greek yogurt
½ scallion, white and green parts, finely chopped
½ English cucumber, grated, liquid squeezed out
2 tbsp chopped fresh mint
1 teaspoon honey
Sea salt and freshly ground black pepper, to taste
4 (5-ounce / 142-g) haddock fillets, patted dry
Nonstick cooking spray

Directions
1. In a small bowl, stir together the yogurt, cucumber, scallion, mint, honey, and a pinch of salt. Set aside.
2. Season the fillets lightly with salt and pepper.
3. Place a large skillet over medium-high heat and spray lightly with cooking spray.
4. Cook the haddock, turning once, until it is just cooked through, about 5 minutes per side.
5. Remove the fish from the heat and transfer to plates.
6. Serve topped with the cucumber sauce.

Per Serving
calories: 164 | fat: 2.0g | protein: 27.0g | carbs: 4.0g | fiber: 0g | sodium: 104mg

Catfish and Shrimp Jambalaya

Prep Time: 20 minutes | **Cooking Time:** 4 hours 45 minutes
Servings: 4

Ingredients

4 ounces (113 g) catfish (cut into 1-inch cubes)
4 ounces (113 g) shrimp (peeled and deveined)
1 tablespoon olive oil
2 bacon slices, chopped
1¼ cups vegetable broth
¾ cup sliced celery stalk
¼ teaspoon minced garlic
½ cup chopped onion
1 cup canned diced tomatoes
1 cup uncooked long-grain white rice
½ tablespoon Cajun seasoning
¼ teaspoon dried thyme
¼ teaspoon cayenne pepper
½ teaspoon dried oregano
Salt and freshly ground black pepper, to taste

Directions

1. Select the Sauté function on your Instant Pot and add the oil into it.
2. Put the onion, garlic, celery, and bacon to the pot and cook for 10 minutes.
3. Add all the remaining to the pot except seafood.
4. Stir well, then secure the cooker lid.
5. Select the Slow Cook function on a medium mode.
6. Keep the pressure release handle on venting position. Cook for 4 hours.
7. Once done, remove the lid and add the seafood to the gravy.
8. Secure the lid again, keep the pressure handle in the venting position.
9. Cook for another 45 minutes then serve.

Per Serving calories: 437 | fat: 13.1g | protein: 21.3g | carbs: 56.7g | fiber: 2.6g | sodium: 502mg

Mahi-Mahi Meal

Prep Time: 15 minutes | **Cooking Time:** 7 minutes |
Servings: 4

Ingredients

1½ cups water
4 (4-ounce / 113-g) mahi-mahi fillets
Salt and freshly ground black pepper, to taste
4 garlic cloves, minced
4 tablespoons fresh lime juice
4 tablespoons erythritol
2 teaspoons red pepper flakes, crushed

Directions

1. Sprinkle some salt and pepper over Mahi-Mahi fillets for seasoning. In a separate bowl add all the remaining & mix well.
2. Add the water to the Instant pot and place the trivet in it.
3. Arrange the seasoned fillets over the trivet in a single layer.
4. Pour the prepared sauce on top of each fillet.
5. Cover and secure the lid.
6. Set the Steam function on your cooker for 5 minutes.
7. Once it beeps, do a quick release then remove the lid.
8. Serve the steaming hot Mahi-Mahi and enjoy.

Per Serving calories: 228 | fat: 1.4g | protein: 38.0g | carbs: 14.2g | fiber: 0.1g | sodium: 182mg

Salmon and Potato Casserole

Prep Time: 20 minutes | **Cooking Time:** 8 hours |
Servings: 4

Ingredients

½ tablespoon olive oil
8 ounces (227 g) cream of mushroom soup
¼ cup water
3 medium potatoes (peeled and sliced)
3 tablespoons flour
1 (1-pound / 454-g) can salmon (drained and flaked)
½ cup chopped scallion
¼ teaspoon ground nutmeg
Salt and freshly ground black pepper, to taste

Directions

1. Pour mushroom soup and water in a separate bowl and mix them well.
2. Add the olive oil to the Instant Pot and grease it lightly.
3. Place half of the potatoes in the pot and sprinkle salt, pepper, and half of the flour over it.
4. Now add a layer of half of the salmon over potatoes, then a layer of half of the scallions.
5. Repeat these layers and pour mushroom soup mix on top.
6. Top it with nutmeg evenly.
7. Secure the lid and set its pressure release handle to the venting position.
8. Select the Slow Cook function with Medium heat on your Instant Pot.
9. Let it cook for 8 hours then serve.

Per Serving
calories: 388 | fat: 11.6g | protein: 34.6g | carbs: 37.2g | fiber: 4.4g | sodium: 842mg

Lemony Salmon

Prep Time: 10 minutes | **Cooking Time:** 3 minutes |
Servings: 3

Ingredients

1 cup water
3 lemon slices
1 (5-ounce / 142-g) salmon fillet
1 teaspoon fresh lemon juice
Salt and ground black pepper, to taste
Fresh cilantro to garnish

Directions

1. Add the water to the Instant pot and place a trivet inside.
2. In a shallow bowl, place the salmon fillet. Sprinkle salt and pepper over it.
3. Squeeze some lemon juice on top then place a lemon slice over the salmon fillet.
4. Cover the lid and lock it. Set its pressure release handle to Sealing position.
5. Use Steam function on your cooker for 3 minutes to cook.
6. After the beep, do a Quick release and release the pressure.
7. Remove the lid, then serve with the lemon slice and fresh cilantro on top.

Per Serving
calories: 161 | fat: 5.0g | protein: 26.6g | carbs: 0.7g | fiber: 0.2g | sodium: 119mg

Cod Curry

Prep Time: 5 minutes | **Cooking Time:** 12 minutes | **Servings:** 8

Ingredients

3 pounds (1.4 kg) cod fillets, cut into bite-sized pieces
2 tablespoons olive oil
4 curry leaves
4 medium onions, chopped
2 tablespoons fresh ginger, grated finely
4 garlic cloves, minced
4 tablespoons curry powder
2 tbsp fresh lemon juice
4 teaspoons ground cumin
4 teaspoons ground coriander
2 teaspoons red chili powder
1 teaspoon ground turmeric
4 cups unsweetened coconut milk
2½ cups tomatoes, chopped
2 Serrano peppers, seeded and chopped

Directions

1. Add the oil to the Instant Pot and select Sauté function for cooking. Add the curry leaves and cook for 30 seconds. Stir the onion, garlic, and ginger into the pot and cook 5 minutes. Add all the spices to the mixture and cook for another 1½ minutes. Hit Cancel then add the coconut milk, Serrano pepper, tomatoes, and fish to the pot.
2. Secure the lid and select the Manual settings with Low Pressure and 5 minutes cooking time. After the beep, do a Quick release and remove the lid. Drizzle lemon juice over the curry then stir. Serve immediately.

Per Serving

calories: 424 | fat: 29.1g | protein: 30.2g | carbs: 14.4g | fiber: 3.8g | sodium: 559mg

Spiced Citrus Sole

Prep Time: 10 minutes | **Cooking Time:** 10 minutes | **Servings:** 4

Ingredients

1 teaspoon garlic powder
1 teaspoon chili powder
½ teaspoon lemon zest
½ teaspoon lime zest
¼ teaspoon smoked paprika
¼ teaspoon freshly ground black pepper Pinch sea salt
4 (6-ounce / 170-g) sole fillets, patted dry
1 tablespoon extra-virgin olive oil
2 teaspoons freshly squeezed lime juice

Directions

1. Preheat the oven to 450°F (235°C). Line a baking sheet with aluminum foil and set aside.
2. Mix together the garlic powder, chili powder, lemon zest, lime zest, paprika, pepper, and salt in a small bowl until well combined. Arrange the sole fillets on the prepared baking sheet and rub the spice mixture all over the fillets until well coated. Drizzle the olive oil and lime juice over the fillets.
3. Bake in the preheated oven for about 8 minutes until flaky.
4. Remove from the heat to a plate and serve.

Per Serving

calories: 183 | fat: 5.0g | protein: 32.1g | carbs: 0g | fiber: 0g | sodium: 136mg

Shrimps with Northern Beans

Prep Time: 10 minutes | **Cooking Time:** 25 minutes | **Servings:** 3

Ingredients

1½ tablespoons olive oil
1 medium onion, chopped
½ small green bell pepper, seeded and chopped
½ celery stalk, chopped
1 garlic clove, minced
1 tablespoon fresh parsley, chopped
½ teaspoon red pepper flakes, crushed
½ teaspoon cayenne pepper
½ pound (227 g) great northern beans, rinsed, soaked, and drained
1 cup chicken broth
1 bay leaf
½ pound (227 g) medium shrimp, peeled and deveined

Directions

1. Select the Sauté function on your Instant pot, then add the oil, onion, celery, bell pepper and cook for 5 minutes.
2. Now add the parsley, garlic, spices, and bay leaf to the pot and cook for another 2 minutes. Pour in the chicken broth then add the beans to it. Secure the cooker lid.
3. Select the Manual function for 15 minutes with medium pressure. After the beep, do a Natural release for 10 minutes and remove the lid. Add the shrimp to the beans and cook them together on the Manual function for 2 minutes at High Pressure. Do a Quick release, keep it aside for 10 minutes, then remove the lid. Serve hot.

Per Serving calories: 405 | fat: 9.1g | protein: 29.1g | carbs: 53.1g | fiber: 16.4g | sodium: 702mg

Mussels with Onions

Prep Time: 10 minutes | **Cooking Time:** 7 minutes | **Servings:** 8

Ingredients

2 tablespoons olive oil
2 medium yellow onions, chopped
1 teaspoon dried rosemary, crushed
2 garlic cloves, minced
2 cups chicken broth
4 pounds (1.8 kg) mussels, cleaned and debearded
¼ cup fresh lemon juice
Salt and ground black pepper as needed

Directions

1. Put the oil to the Instant Pot and select the Sauté function for cooking. Add the onions and cook for 5 minutes with occasional stirring.
2. Add the rosemary and garlic to the pot. Stir and cook for 1 minute. Pour the chicken broth and lemon juice into the cooker, sprinkle some salt and black pepper over it.
3. Place the trivet inside the cooker and arrange the mussels over it.
4. Select the Manual function at Low Pressure for 1 minute.
5. Secure the lid and let the mussels cook.
6. After the beep, do a Quick release then remove the lid.
7. Serve the mussels with its steaming hot soup in a bowl.

Per Serving calories: 249 | fat: 8.8g | protein: 28.5g | carbs: 11.9g | fiber: 0.5g | sodium: 844mg

Spicy Haddock Stew

Prep Time: 15 minutes | **Cooking Time:** 35 minutes | **Servings:** 6

Ingredients

¼ cup coconut oil	1 cup coconut milk
1 tablespoon minced garlic	1 cup low-sodium chicken
1 onion, chopped	broth
2 celery stalks, chopped	¼ teaspoon red pepper
½ fennel bulb, thinly sliced	flakes
1 carrot, diced	12 ounces (340 g) haddock,
1 sweet potato, diced	cut into 1-inch chunks
1 (15-ounce / 425-g) can	2 tablespoons chopped
low-sodium diced tomatoes	fresh cilantro, for garnish

Directions

1. In a large saucepan, heat the coconut oil over medium-high heat.
2. Add the garlic, onion, and celery and sauté for about 4 minutes, stirring occasionally, or until they are tender.
3. Stir in the fennel bulb, carrot, and sweet potato and sauté for 4 minutes more.
4. Add the diced tomatoes, coconut milk, chicken broth, and red pepper flakes and stir to incorporate, then bring the mixture to a boil.
5. Once it starts to boil, reduce the heat to low, and bring to a simmer for about 15 minutes, or until the vegetables are fork-tender.
6. Add the haddock chunks and continue simmering for about 10 minutes, or until the fish is cooked through.
7. Sprinkle the cilantro on top for garnish before serving.

Per Serving

calories: 276 | fat: 20.9g | protein: 14.2g | carbs: 6.8g | fiber: 3.0g | sodium: 226mg

Balsamic-Honey Glazed Salmon

Prep Time: 2 minutes | **Cooking Time:** 8 minutes | **Servings:** 4

Ingredients

½ cup balsamic vinegar	Sea salt and freshly ground
1 tablespoon honey	pepper, to taste
4 (8-ounce / 227-g) salmon fillets	1 tablespoon olive oil

Directions

1. Heat a skillet over medium-high heat. Combine the vinegar and honey in a small bowl.
2. Season the salmon fillets with the sea salt and freshly ground pepper; brush with the honey-balsamic glaze.
3. Add olive oil to the skillet, and sear the salmon fillets, cooking for 3 to 4 minutes on each side until lightly browned and medium rare in the center.
4. Let sit for 5 minutes before serving.

Per Serving calories: 454 | fat: 17.3g | protein: 65.3g | carbs: 9.7g | fiber: 0g | sodium: 246mg

Canned Sardine Donburi (Rice Bowl)

Prep Time: 10 mins | **Cooking Time:** 40 to 50 mins | **Servings:** 4 to 6

Ingredients

4 cups water	3 scallions, sliced thin
2 cups brown rice, rinsed	1-inch piece fresh ginger,
well	grated
½ teaspoon salt	4 tablespoons sesame oil
3 (4-ounce / 113-g) cans	
sardines packed in water,	
drained	

Directions

1. Place the water, brown rice, and salt to a large saucepan and stir to combine. Allow the mixture to boil over high heat.
2. Once boiling, reduce the heat to low, and cook covered for 45 to 50 minutes, or until the rice is tender.
3. Meanwhile, roughly mash the sardines with a fork in a medium bowl.
4. When the rice is done, stir in the mashed sardines, scallions, and ginger.
5. Divide the mixture into four bowls. Top each bowl with a drizzle of sesame oil. Serve warm.

Per Serving

calories: 603 | fat: 23.6g | protein: 25.2g | carbs: 73.8g | fiber: 4.0g | sodium: 498mg

Orange Flavored Scallops

Prep Time: 10 minutes | **Cooking Time:** 10 minutes | **Servings:** 4

Ingredients

2 pounds (907 g) sea	1 tablespoon minced garlic
scallops, patted dry	¼ cup freshly squeezed
Sea salt and freshly ground	orange juice
black pepper, to taste	1 teaspoon orange zest
2 tablespoons extra-virgin	2 teaspoons chopped fresh
olive oil	thyme, for garnish

Directions

1. In a bowl, lightly season the scallops with salt and pepper. Set aside.
2. Heat the olive oil in a large skillet over medium-high heat until it shimmers.
3. Add the garlic and sauté for about 3 minutes, or until fragrant.
4. Stir in the seasoned scallops and sear each side for about 4 minutes, or until the scallops are browned.
5. Remove the scallops from the heat to a plate and set aside.
6. Add the orange juice and zest to the skillet, scraping up brown bits from bottom of skillet.
7. Drizzle the sauce over the scallops and garnish with the thyme before serving.

Per Serving

calories: 266 | fat: 7.6g | protein: 38.1g | carbs: 7.9g | fiber: 0g | sodium: 360mg

Teriyaki Salmon

Prep Time: 10 minutes | **Cooking Time:** 8 minutes | **Servings:** 4

Ingredients

4 (8-ounce / 227-g) thick salmon fillets.
1 cup soy sauce
2 cups water
½ cup mirin
2 tablespoons sesame oil

4 teaspoons sesame seeds
2 cloves garlic, minced
2 tablespoons freshly grated ginger
4 tablespoons brown sugar
1 tablespoon corn starch
4 green onions, minced

Directions

1. Add the soy sauce, sesame oil, sesame seeds, mirin, ginger, water, garlic, green onions, and brown sugar to a small bowl. Mix them well. In a shallow dish place the salmon fillets and pour half of the prepared mixture over the fillets. Let it marinate for 30 minutes in a refrigerator.
2. Pour 1 cup of water into the insert of your Instant pot and place trivet inside it. Arrange the marinated salmon fillets over the trivet and secure the lid.
3. Select the Manual settings with High Pressure and 8 minutes cooking time. Meanwhile, take a skillet and add the remaining marinade mixture in it.
4. Let it cook for 2 minutes, then add the corn starch mixed with water. Stir well and cook for 1 minute.
5. Check the pressure cooker, do a Quick release if it is done.
6. Transfer the fillets to a serving platter and pour the sesame mixture over it. Garnish with chopped green chilies then serve hot.

Per Serving calories: 622 | fat: 28.6g | protein: 51.3g | carbs: 29.6g | fiber: 2.0g | sodium: 1086mg

Coconut Tangy Cod Curry

Prep Time: 5 minutes | **Cooking Time:** 3 minutes | **Servings:** 6

1 (28-ounce / 794-g) can coconut milk
Juice of 2 lemons
2 tablespoons red curry paste
2 teaspoons fish sauce
2 teaspoons honey
4 teaspoons Sriracha
4 cloves garlic, minced

2 teaspoons ground turmeric
2 teaspoons ground ginger
1 teaspoon sea salt
1 teaspoon white pepper
2 pounds (907 g) codfish, cut into 1-inch cubes
½ cup chopped fresh cilantro, for garnish
4 lime wedges, for garnish

Directions

1. Add all the , except the cod cubes and garnish, to a large bowl and whisk them well. Arrange the cod cube at the base of the Instant Pot and pour the coconut milk mixture over it. Secure the lid and hit the Manual key, select High Pressure with 3 minutes cooking time.
2. After the beep, do a Quick release then remove the lid.
3. Garnish with fresh cilantro and lemon wedges then serve.

Per Serving calories: 396 | fat: 29.1g | protein: 26.6g | carbs: 11.4g | fiber: 2.0g | sodium: 1024mg

Shrimps with Broccoli

Prep Time: 5 minutes | **Cooking Time:** 10 minutes | **Servings:** 2

Ingredients

2 teaspoons vegetable oil
2 tablespoons corn starch
1 cup broccoli florets
¼ cup chicken broth
8 ounces (227 g) large shrimp, peeled and deveined
¼ cup soy sauce

¼ cup water
¼ cup sliced carrots
3 tablespoons rice vinegar
2 teaspoons sesame oil
1 tablespoon chili garlic sauce
Coriander leaves to garnish
Boiled rice or noodles, for serving

Directions

1. Add 1 tablespoon of corn starch and shrimp to a bowl. Mix them well then set it aside.
2. In a small bowl, mix the remaining corn starch, chicken broth, carrots, chili garlic sauce, rice vinegar and soy sauce together. Keep the mixture aside.
3. Select the Sauté function on your Instant pot, add the sesame oil and broccoli florets to the pot and sauté for 5 minutes. Add the water to the broccoli, cover the lid and cook for 5 minutes. Stir in shrimp and vegetable oil to the broccoli, sauté it for 5 minutes. Garnish with coriander leaves on top. Serve with rice or noodles.

Per Serving calories: 300 | fat: 16.5g | protein: 19.6g | carbs: 17.1g | fiber: 2.2g | sodium: 1241mg

Mahi-Mahi and Tomato Bowls

Prep Time: 5 minutes | **Cooking Time:** 14 minutes | **Servings:** 3

Ingredients

3 (4-ounce / 113-g) mahi-mahi fillets
1½ tablespoons olive oil
½ yellow onion, sliced
½ teaspoon dried oregano

1 tablespoon fresh lemon juice
Salt and freshly ground black pepper, to taste
1 (14-ounce / 397-g) can sugar-free diced tomatoes

Directions

1. Add the olive oil to the Instant Pot. Select the Sauté function on it. Add all the ingredient to the pot except the fillets. Cook them for 10 minutes. Press the Cancel key, then add the mahi-mahi fillets to the sauce.
2. Cover the fillets with sauce by using a spoon.
3. Secure the lid and set the Manual function at High Pressure for 4 minutes. After the beep, do a Quick release then remove the lid. Serve the fillets with their sauce, poured on top.

Per Serving calories: 265 | fat: 8.6g | protein: 39.1g | carbs: 7.0g | fiber: 3.1g | sodium: 393mg

Lemon Grilled Shrimp

Prep Time: 20 minutes | **Cooking Time:** 4 to 6 minutes | **Servings:** 4

Ingredients

2 tablespoons garlic, minced
3 tablespoons fresh Italian parsley, finely chopped
¼ cup extra-virgin olive oil
½ cup lemon juice
1 teaspoon salt
2 pounds (907 g) jumbo shrimp (21 to 25), peeled and deveined
Special Equipment:
4 wooden skewers, soaked in water for at least 30 minutes

Directions

1. Whisk together the garlic, parsley, olive oil, lemon juice, and salt in a large bowl.
2. Add the shrimp to the bowl and toss well, making sure the shrimp are coated in the marinade. Set aside to sit for 15 minutes.
3. When ready, skewer the shrimps by piercing through the center. You can place about 5 to 6 shrimps on each skewer.
4. Preheat the grill to high heat.
5. Grill the shrimp for 4 to 6 minutes, flipping the shrimp halfway through, or until the shrimp are pink on the outside and opaque in the center. Serve hot.

Per Serving

calories: 401 | fat: 17.8g | protein: 56.9g | carbs: 3.9g | fiber: 0g | sodium: 1223mg

Garlic Shrimp with Mushrooms

Prep Time: 10 minutes | **Cooking Time:** 15 minutes | **Servings:** 4

Ingredients

1 pound (454 g) fresh shrimp, peeled, deveined, and patted dry
1 teaspoon salt
1 cup extra-virgin olive oil
8 large garlic cloves, thinly sliced
4 ounces (113 g) sliced mushrooms (shiitake, baby bella, or button)
½ teaspoon red pepper flakes
¼ cup chopped fresh flat-leaf Italian parsley

Directions

1. In a bowl, season the shrimp with salt. Set aside.
2. Heat the olive oil in a large skillet over medium-low heat.
3. Add the garlic and cook for 3 to 4 minutes until fragrant, stirring occasionally.
4. Sauté the mushrooms for 5 minutes, or until they start to exude their juices. Stir in the shrimp and sprinkle with red pepper flakes and sauté for 3 to 4 minutes more, or until the shrimp start to turn pink.
5. Remove the skillet from the heat and add the parsley. Stir to combine and serve warm.

Per Serving

calories: 619 | fat: 55.5g | protein: 24.1g | carbs: 3.7g | fiber: 0g | sodium: 735mg

Lemony Shrimp with Orzo Salad

Prep Time: 10 minutes | **Cooking Time:** 22 minutes | **Servings:** 4

Ingredients

1 cup orzo
1 hothouse cucumber, deseeded and chopped
½ cup finely diced red onion
2 tablespoons extra-virgin olive oil
2 pounds (907 g) shrimp, peeled and deveined
3 lemons, juiced
Salt and freshly ground black pepper, to taste
¾ cup crumbled feta cheese
2 tablespoons dried dill
1 cup chopped fresh flat-leaf parsley

Directions

1. Bring a large pot of water to a boil. Add the orzo and cook covered for 15 to 18 minutes, or until the orzo is tender. Transfer to a colander to drain and set aside to cool.
2. Mix the cucumber and red onion in a bowl. Set aside.
3. Heat the olive oil in a medium skillet over medium heat until it shimmers.
4. Reduce the heat, add the shrimp, and cook each side for 2 minutes until cooked through.
5. Add the cooked shrimp to the bowl of cucumber and red onion. Mix in the cooked orzo and lemon juice and toss to combine. Sprinkle with salt and pepper. Scatter the top with the feta cheese and dill. Garnish with the parsley and serve immediately.

Per Serving

calories: 565 | fat: 17.8g | protein: 63.3g | carbs: 43.9g | fiber: 4.1g | sodium: 2225mg

Spicy Grilled Shrimp with Lemon Wedges

Prep Time: 15 minutes | **Cooking Time:** 6 minutes | **Servings:** 6

Ingredients

1 large clove garlic, crushed
1 teaspoon coarse salt
1 teaspoon paprika
½ teaspoon cayenne pepper
2 teaspoons lemon juice
2 tablespoons plus 1 teaspoon olive oil, divided
2 pounds (907 g) large shrimp, peeled and deveined
8 wedges lemon, for garnish

Directions

1. Preheat the grill to medium heat.
2. Stir together the garlic, salt, paprika, cayenne pepper, lemon juice, and 2 tablespoons of olive oil in a small bowl until a paste forms. Add the shrimp and toss until well coated.
3. Grease the grill grates lightly with remaining 1 teaspoon of olive oil.
4. Grill the shrimp for 4 to 6 minutes, flipping the shrimp halfway through, or until the shrimp is totally pink and opaque.
5. Garnish the shrimp with lemon wedges and serve hot.

Per Serving

calories: 163 | fat: 5.8g | protein: 25.2g | carbs: 2.8g | fiber: 0.4g | sodium: 585mg

Easy Seafood French Stew (Italian)

Prep Time: 10 minutes **Cooking Time:** 45 minutes
Servings: 12

Ingredients

Pepper and Salt
1lb. shrimp, peeled and deveined
1 large lobster
1/2 lb. mussels
2tablespoon garlic, chopped
3cups tomatoes, peeled, seeded, and chopped
1 cup white wine Water
1 cup leeks, julienned
8 peppercorns
3 cloves garlic Salt and pepper

1/2 lb. littleneck clams
2lbs. assorted small whole fresh fish, scaled and cleaned
2 tbsp parsleys fine chopped
Juice and zest of one orange
Pinch of Saffron Stew
1 cup fennel, julienned
1 lb. fish bones
2 sprigs thyme
1 bay leaf
1/2 cup chopped celery
1/2 cup chopped onion
2 tablespoon olive oil

Directions

1. Do the stew: Heat oil in a large saucepan. Sauté the celery and onions for 3 minutes. Season with pepper and salt. Stir in the garlic and cook for about a minute. Add the thyme, peppercorns, and bay leaves. Stir in the wine, water and fish bones. Let it boil then before reducing to a simmer. Take the pan off the fire and strain broth into another container.
2. For the Bouillabaisse: Bring the strained broth to a simmer and stir in the parsley, leeks, orange juice, orange zest, garlic, fennel, tomatoes and saffron. Sprinkle with pepper and salt. Stir in the lobsters and fish. Let it simmer for eight minutes before stirring in the clams, mussels and shrimps. For six minutes, allow to cook while covered before seasoning again with pepper and salt.
3. Assemble in a shallow dish all the seafood and pour the broth over it.

Nutrition: Calories: 348; Carbs: 20.0g; Protein: 31.8g; Fat: 15.2g

Fresh and No-Cook Oysters (Spanish)

Prep Time: 10 minutes **Cooking Time:** 5 minutes
Servings: 4

Ingredients

1 lemons

24 medium oysters tabasco sauce

Directions

1. If you are a newbie when it comes to eating oysters, then I suggest that you blanch the oysters before eating.
2. For some, eating oysters raw is a great way to enjoy this dish because of the consistency and juiciness of raw oysters. Plus, adding lemon juice prior to eating the raw oysters cooks it a bit. So, to blanch oysters, bring a big pot of water to a rolling boil. Add oysters in batches of 6-10 pieces. Leave on boiling pot of water between 3-5 minutes and remove oysters right away. To eat oysters, squeeze lemon juice on oyster on shell, add tabasco as desired and eat.

Nutrition: Calories: 247; Protein: 29g; Fat: 7g; Carbs: 17g

Creamy Bacon-Fish Chowder (Greek)

Prep Time: 10 minutes **Cooking Time:** 30 minutes
Servings: 8

Ingredients

1 1/2 lbs. cod
1 medium carrot, coarsely chopped
1 large onion, chopped
31/2 cups baking potato, peeled and cubed 3 slices uncooked bacon
4bay leaves
4 1/2 cups water

1 1/2 teaspoon dried thyme
1 tablespoon butter, cut into small pieces
1 teaspoon salt, divided
3/4 teaspoon freshly ground black pepper, divided
4 cups 2% reduced-fat milk

Directions

1. In a large skillet, add the water and bay leaves and let it simmer. Add the fish. Cover and let it simmer some more until the flesh flakes easily with fork. Remove the fish from the skillet and cut into large pieces. Set aside the cooking liquid. Place Dutch oven in medium heat and cook the bacon until crisp. Remove the bacon and reserve the bacon drippings. Crush the bacon and set aside.
2. Stir potato, onion and carrot in the pan with the bacon drippings, cook over medium heat for 10 minutes. Add the cooking liquid, bay leaves, 1/2 teaspoon salt, 1/4 teaspoon pepper and thyme, let it boil. Lower the heat and let simmer for 10 minutes. Add the milk and butter, simmer until the potatoes becomes tender, but do not boil. Add the fish, 1/2 teaspoon salt, 1/2 teaspoon pepper. Remove the bay leaves. Serve sprinkled with the crushed bacon.

Nutrition: Calories: 400; Carbs: 34.5g; Protein: 20.8g; Fat: 19.7g

Simple Cod Piccata (Italian)

Prep Time: 10 minutes **Cooking Time:** 15 minutes
Servings: 3

Ingredients

¼ cup capers, drained
¾ cup chicken stock
1/3 cup almond flour
2tablespoon fresh parsley, chopped
2 tablespoon grapeseed oil

½ teaspoon salt
1-pound cod fillets, patted dry
3tablespoon extra-virgin oil
3 tablespoon lemon juice

Directions

1. In a bowl, combine the almond flour and salt.
2. Dredge the fish in the almond flour to coat. Set aside.
3. Heat a little bit of olive oil to coat a large skillet. Heat the skillet over medium high heat. Add grapeseed oil. Cook the cod for 3 minutes on each side to brown. Remove from the plate and place on a paper towel- lined plate.
4. In a saucepan, mix together the chicken stock, capers and lemon juice. Simmer to reduce the sauce to half. Add the remaining grapeseed oil.
5. Drizzle the fried cod with the sauce and sprinkle with parsley.

Nutrition: Calories: 277.1; Fat: 28.3 g; Protein: 1.9 g; Carbs: 3.7 g

Mediterranean Grilled Sea Bass

Prep Time: 20 minutes | **Cooking Time:** 20 minutes | **Servings:** 6

Ingredients

¼ teaspoon onion powder
¼ teaspoon garlic powder
¼ teaspoon paprika
Lemon pepper and sea salt to taste
2 pounds (907 g) sea bass

3 tablespoons extra-virgin olive oil, divided
2 large cloves garlic, chopped
1 tablespoon chopped Italian flat leaf parsley

Directions

1. Preheat the grill to high heat.
2. Place the onion powder, garlic powder, paprika, lemon pepper, and sea salt in a large bowl and stir to combine.
3. Dredge the fish in the spice mixture, turning until well coated.
4. Heat 2 tablespoon of olive oil in a small skillet. Add the garlic and parsley and cook for 1 to 2 minutes, stirring occasionally. Remove the skillet from the heat and set aside. Brush the grill grates lightly with remaining 1 tablespoon olive oil.
5. Grill the fish for about 7 minutes. Flip the fish and drizzle with the garlic mixture and cook for an additional 7 minutes, or until the fish flakes when pressed lightly with a fork. Serve hot.

Per Serving calories: 200 | fat: 10.3g | protein: 26.9g | carbs: 0.6g | fiber: 0.1g | sodium: 105mg

Asian-Inspired Tuna Lettuce Wraps

Prep Time: 10 minutes | **Cooking Time:** 0 minutes | **Servings:** 2

Ingredients

⅓ cup almond butter
1 tablespoon freshly squeezed lemon juice
1 teaspoon low-sodium soy sauce
1 teaspoon curry powder
½ teaspoon sriracha, or to taste

½ cup canned water chestnuts, drained and chopped
2 (2.6-ounce / 74-g) package tuna packed in water, drained
2 large butter lettuce leaves

Directions

1. Stir together the almond butter, lemon juice, soy sauce, curry powder, sriracha in a medium bowl until well mixed. Add the water chestnuts and tuna and stir until well incorporated.
2. Place 2 butter lettuce leaves on a flat work surface, spoon half of the tuna mixture onto each leaf and roll up into a wrap. Serve immediately.

Per Serving
calories: 270 | fat: 13.9g | protein: 19.1g | carbs: 18.5g | fiber: 3.0g | sodium: 626mg

Braised Branzino with Wine Sauce

Prep Time: 15 minutes | **Cooking Time:** 15 minutes | **Servings:** 2 to 3

Ingredients

Sauce:
¾ cup dry white wine
2 tablespoons white wine vinegar
2 tablespoons cornstarch
1 tablespoon honey
Fish:
1 large branzino, butterflied and patted dry
2 tablespoons onion powder

2 tablespoons paprika
½ tablespoon salt
6 tablespoons extra-virgin olive oil, divided
4 garlic cloves, thinly sliced
4 scallions, both green and white parts, thinly sliced
1 large tomato, cut into ¼-inch cubes
4 kalamata olives, pitted and chopped

Directions

1. Make the sauce: Mix together the white wine, vinegar, cornstarch, and honey in a bowl and keep stirring until the honey has dissolved. Set aside.
2. Make the fish: Place the fish on a clean work surface, skin-side down. Sprinkle the onion powder, paprika, and salt to season. Drizzle 2 tablespoons of olive oil all over the fish.
3. Heat 2 tablespoons of olive oil in a large skillet over high heat until it shimmers.
4. Add the fish, skin-side up, to the skillet and brown for about 2 minutes. Carefully flip the fish and cook for another 3 minutes. Remove from the heat to a plate and set aside.
5. Add the remaining 2 tablespoons olive oil to the skillet and swirl to coat. Stir in the garlic cloves, scallions, tomato, and kalamata olives and sauté for 5 minutes. Pour in the prepared sauce and stir to combine.
6. Return the fish (skin-side down) to the skillet, flipping to coat in the sauce. Reduce the heat to medium-low, and cook for an additional 5 minutes until cooked through.
7. Using a slotted spoon, transfer the fish to a plate and serve warm.

Per Serving calories: 1059 | fat: 71.9g | protein: 46.2g | carbs: 55.8g | fiber: 5.1g | sodium: 2807mg

Chapter 9
Fruits and Desserts

Rice Pudding with Roasted Orange

Prep Time: 10 minutes | **Cooking Time:** 19 to 20 minutes | **Servings:** 6

Ingredients

2 medium oranges
2 teaspoons extra-virgin olive oil
⅛ teaspoon kosher salt
2 large eggs
2 cups unsweetened almond milk
1 cup orange juice
1 cup uncooked instant brown rice
¼ cup honey
½ tbsp ground cinnamon
1 teaspoon vanilla extract
Cooking spray

Directions

1. Preheat the oven to 450ºF (235ºC). Spritz a large, rimmed baking sheet with cooking spray. Set aside.
2. Slice the unpeeled oranges into ¼-inch rounds. Brush with the oil and sprinkle with salt. Place the slices on the baking sheet and roast for 4 minutes. Flip the slices and roast for 4 more minutes, or until they begin to brown. Remove from the oven and set aside.
3. Crack the eggs into a medium bowl. In a medium saucepan, whisk together the milk, orange juice, rice, honey and cinnamon. Bring to a boil over medium-high heat, stirring constantly. Reduce the heat to medium- low and simmer for 10 minutes, stirring occasionally.
4. Using a measuring cup, scoop out ½ cup of the hot rice mixture and whisk it into the eggs. While constantly stirring the mixture in the pan, slowly pour the egg mixture back into the saucepan.
5. Cook on low heat for 1 to 2 minutes, or until thickened, stirring constantly. Remove from the heat and stir in the vanilla. Let the pudding stand for a few minutes for the rice to soften. The rice will be cooked but slightly chewy. For softer rice, let stand for another half hour. Top with the roasted oranges. Serve warm or at room temperature.

Per Serving
calories: 204 | fat: 6.0g | protein: 5.0g | carbs: 34.0g | fiber: 1.0g | sodium: 148mg

Crispy Sesame Cookies

Prep Time: 5 minutes | **Cooking Time:** 8 to 10 minutes | **Servings:** 14 to 16

Ingredients

1 cup hulled sesame seeds
1 cup sugar
8 tablespoons almond butter
2 large eggs
1¼ cups flour

Directions

1. Preheat the oven to 350ºF (180ºC).
2. Toast the sesame seeds on a baking sheet for 3 minutes. Set aside and let cool. Using a mixer, whisk together the sugar and butter. Add the eggs one at a time until well blended. Add the flour and toasted sesame seeds and mix until well blended. Drop spoonfuls of cookie dough onto a baking sheet and form them into round balls, about 1-inch in diameter, similar to a walnut.
3. Put in the oven and bake for 5 to 7 minutes, or until golden brown. Let the cookies cool for 5 minutes before serving.

Per Serving calories: 218 | fat: 12.0g | protein: 4.0g | carbs: 25.0g | fiber: 2.0g | sodium: 58mg

Watermelon and Blueberry Salad

Prep Time: 5 minutes | **Cooking Time:** 0 minutes | **Servings:** 6 to 8

Ingredients

1 medium watermelon
1 cup fresh blueberries
⅓ cup honey
2 tablespoons lemon juice
2 tablespoons finely chopped fresh mint leaves

Directions

1. Cut the watermelon into 1-inch cubes. Put them in a bowl.
2. Evenly distribute the blueberries over the watermelon.
3. In a separate bowl, whisk together the honey, lemon juice and mint. Drizzle the mint dressing over the watermelon and blueberries. Serve cold.

Per Serving calories: 238 | fat: 1.0g | protein: 4.0g | carbs: 61.0g | fiber: 3.0g | sodium: 11mg

Cherry Walnut Brownies

Prep Time: 10 minutes | **Cooking Time:** 20 minutes | **Servings:** 9

Ingredients

2 large eggs
½ cup 2% plain Greek yogurt
½ cup sugar ⅓ cup honey
¼ cup extra-virgin olive oil
1 teaspoon vanilla extract
½ cup whole-wheat pastry flour
⅓ cup unsweetened dark chocolate cocoa powder
¼ teaspoon baking powder
¼ teaspoon salt
⅓ cup chopped walnuts
9 fresh cherries, stemmed and pitted
Cooking spray

Directions

1. Preheat the oven to 375ºF (190ºC) and set the rack in the middle of the oven. Spritz a square baking pan with cooking spray. In a large bowl, whisk together the eggs, yogurt, sugar, honey, oil and vanilla.
   In a medium bowl, stir together the flour, cocoa powder, baking powder and salt. Add the flour mixture to the egg mixture and whisk until all the dry are incorporated. Fold in the walnuts.
2. Pour the batter into the prepared pan. Push the cherries into the batter, three to a row in three rows, so one will be at the center of each brownie once you cut them into squares. Bake the brownies for 20 minutes, or until just set. Remove from the oven and place on a rack to cool for 5 minutes. Cut into nine squares and serve.

Per Serving
calories: 154 | fat: 6.0g | protein: 3.0g | carbs: 24.0g | fiber: 2.0g | sodium: 125mg

Mint Banana Chocolate Sorbet

Prep Time: 4 hours 5 minutes | **Cooking Time:** 0 minutes | **Servings:** 1

Ingredients

1 frozen banana
1 tablespoon almond butter
2 tbsp minced fresh mint
2 to 3 tbsp dark chocolate chips (60% cocoa or higher)
2 to 3 tbsp goji (optional)

Directions

1. Put the banana, butter, and mint in a food processor. Pulse to purée until creamy and smooth.
2. Add the chocolate and goji, then pulse for several more times to combine well. Pour the mixture in a bowl or a ramekin, then freeze for at least 4 hours before serving chilled.

Per Serving calories: 213 | fat: 9.8g | protein: 3.1g | carbs: 2.9g | fiber: 4.0g | sodium: 155mg

Pecan and Carrot Cake

Prep Time: 15 minutes | **Cooking Time:** 45 minutes | **Servings:** 12

Ingredients

½ cup coconut oil, at room temperature, plus more for greasing the baking dish
2 teaspoons pure vanilla extract
¼ cup pure maple syrup
6 eggs
½ cup coconut flour
1 teaspoon baking powder
1 teaspoon baking soda
½ teaspoon ground nutmeg
1 teaspoon ground cinnamon
⅛ teaspoon sea salt
½ cup chopped pecans
3 cups finely grated carrots

Directions

1. Preheat the oven to 350ºF (180ºC). Grease a 13-by-9-inch baking dish with coconut oil.
2. Combine the vanilla extract, maple syrup, and ½ cup of coconut oil in a large bowl. Stir to mix well.
3. Break the eggs in the bowl and whisk to combine well. Set aside. Combine the coconut flour, baking powder, baking soda, nutmeg, cinnamon, and salt in a separate bowl. Stir to mix well. Make a well in the center of the flour mixture, then pour the egg mixture into the well. Stir to combine well. Add the pecans and carrots to the bowl and toss to mix well. Pour the mixture in the single layer on the baking dish. Bake in the preheated oven for 45 minutes or until puffed and the cake spring back when lightly press with your fingers. Remove the cake from the oven. Allow to cool for at least 15 minutes, then serve.

Per Serving calories: 255 | fat: 21.2g | protein: 5.1g | carbs: 12.8g | fiber: 2.0g | sodium: 202mg

Raspberry Yogurt Basted Cantaloupe

Prep Time: 15 minutes | **Cooking Time:** 0 minutes | **Servings:** 6

Ingredients

2 cups fresh raspberries, mashed
1 cup plain coconut yogurt
½ teaspoon vanilla extract
1 cantaloupe, peeled and sliced
½ cup toasted coconut flakes

Directions

1. Combine the mashed raspberries with yogurt and vanilla extract in a small bowl. Stir to mix well.
2. Place the cantaloupe slices on a platter, then top with raspberry mixture and spread with toasted coconut.
3. Serve immediately.

Per Serving calories: 75 | fat: 4.1g | protein: 1.2g | carbs: 10.9g | fiber: 6.0g | sodium: 36mg

Honey Baked Cinnamon Apples

Prep Time: 5 minutes | **Cooking Time:** 20 minutes | **Servings:** 2

Ingredients

1 teaspoon extra-virgin olive oil
4 firm apples, peeled, cored, and sliced
½ teaspoon salt
1½ teaspoons ground cinnamon, divided
2 tablespoons unsweetened almond milk
2 tablespoons honey

Directions

1. Preheat the oven to 375ºF (190ºC). Coat a small casserole dish with the olive oil.
2. Toss the apple slices with the salt and ½ teaspoon of the cinnamon in a medium bowl. Spread the apples in the prepared casserole dish and bake in the preheated oven for 20 minutes. Meanwhile, in a small saucepan, heat the milk, honey, and remaining 1 teaspoon of cinnamon over medium heat, stirring frequently. When it reaches a simmer, remove the pan from the heat and cover to keep warm. Divide the apple slices between 2 plates and pour the sauce over the apples. Serve warm.

Per Serving
calories: 310 | fat: 3.4g | protein: 1.7g | carbs: 68.5g | fiber: 12.6g | sodium: 593mg

Strawberries with Balsamic Vinegar

Prep Time: 5 minutes | **Cooking Time:** 0 minutes | **Servings:** 2

Ingredients

2 cups strawberries, hulled and sliced
2 tablespoons sugar
2 tbsp balsamic vinegar

Directions

1. Place the sliced strawberries in a bowl, sprinkle with the sugar, and drizzle lightly with the balsamic vinegar.
2. Toss to combine well and allow to sit for about 10 minutes before serving.

Per Serving calories: 92 | fat: 0.4g | protein: 1.0g | carbs: 21.7g | fiber: 2.9g | sodium: 5mg

Frozen Mango Raspberry Delight

Prep Time: 5 minutes | **Cooking Time:** 0 minutes | **Servings:** 2

Ingredients

3 cups frozen raspberries
1 mango, peeled and pitted
1 peach, peeled and pitted
1 teaspoon honey

Directions

1. Place all the into a blender and purée, adding some water as needed.
2. Put in the freezer for 10 minutes to firm up if desired. Serve chilled or at room temperature.

Per Serving
calories: 276 | fat: 2.1g | protein: 4.5g | carbs: 60.3g | fiber: 17.5g | sodium: 4mg

Grilled Stone Fruit with Honey

Prep Time: 8 minutes | **Cooking Time:** 6 minutes | **Servings:** 2

Ingredients

3 apricots, halved and pitted
2 plums, halved and pitted
2 peaches, halved and pitted
½ cup low-fat ricotta cheese
2 tablespoons honey
Cooking spray

Directions

1. Preheat the grill to medium heat. Spray the grill grates with cooking spray.
2. Arrange the fruit, cut side down, on the grill, and cook for 2 to 3 minutes per side, or until lightly charred and softened.
3. Serve warm with a sprinkle of cheese and a drizzle of honey.

Per Serving
calories: 298 | fat: 7.8g | protein: 11.9g | carbs: 45.2g | fiber: 4.3g | sodium: 259mg

Mascarpone Baked Pears

Prep Time: 10 minutes | **Cooking Time:** 20 minutes | **Servings:** 2

Ingredients

2 ripe pears, peeled
1 tablespoon plus 2 teaspoons honey, divided
1 teaspoon vanilla, divided
¼ teaspoon ground coriander
¼ teaspoon ginger
¼ cup minced walnuts
¼ cup mascarpone cheese
Pinch salt
Cooking spray

Directions

1. Preheat the oven to 350ºF (180ºC). Spray a small baking dish with cooking spray.
2. Slice the pears in half lengthwise. Using a spoon, scoop out the core from each piece. Put the pears, cut side up, in the baking dish.
3. Whisk together 1 tablespoon of honey, ½ teaspoon of vanilla, ginger, and coriander in a small bowl. Pour this mixture evenly over the pear halves.
4. Scatter the walnuts over the pear halves.
5. Bake in the preheated oven for 20 minutes, or until the pears are golden and you're able to pierce them easily with a knife.
6. Meanwhile, combine the mascarpone cheese with the remaining 2 teaspoons of honey, ½ teaspoon of vanilla, and a pinch of salt. Stir to combine well.
7. Divide the mascarpone among the warm pear halves and serve.

Per Serving
calories: 308 | fat: 16.0g | protein: 4.1g | carbs: 42.7g | fiber: 6.0g | sodium: 88mg

Walnut and Date Balls

Prep Time: 5 minutes | **Cooking Time:** 8 to 10 minutes | **Servings:** 6 to 8

Ingredients

1 cup walnuts
1 cup unsweetened shredded coconut
14 medjool dates, pitted
8 tablespoons almond butter

Directions

1. Preheat the oven to 350°F (180°C).
2. Put the walnuts on a baking sheet and toast in the oven for 5 minutes.
3. Put the shredded coconut on a clean baking sheet. Toast for about 3 to 5 minutes, or until it turns golden brown. Once done, remove it from the oven and put it in a shallow bowl.
4. In a food processor, process the toasted walnuts until they have a medium chop. Transfer the chopped walnuts into a medium bowl.
5. Add the dates and butter to the food processor and blend until the dates become a thick paste. Pour the chopped walnuts into the food processor with the dates and pulse just until the mixture is combined, about 5 to 7 pulses.
6. Remove the mixture from the food processor and scrape it into a large bowl. To make the balls, spoon 1 to 2 tablespoons of the date mixture into the palm of your hand and roll around between your hands until you form a ball. Put the ball on a clean, lined baking sheet. Repeat until all the mixture is formed into balls.
7. Roll each ball in the toasted coconut until the outside of the ball is coated. Put the ball back on the baking sheet and repeat.
8. Put all the balls into the refrigerator for 20 minutes before serving. Store any leftovers in the refrigerator in an airtight container.

Per Serving

calories: 489 | fat: 35.0g | protein: 5.0g | carbs: 48.0g | fiber: 7.0g | sodium: 114mg

Coconut Blueberries with Brown Rice

Prep Time: 55 minutes | **Cooking Time:** 10 minutes | **Servings:** 4

Ingredients

1 cup fresh blueberries
2 cups unsweetened coconut milk
1 teaspoon ground ginger
¼ cup maple syrup
Sea salt, to taste
2 cups cooked brown rice

Directions

1. Put all the , except for the brown rice, in a pot. Stir to combine well.
2. Cook over medium-high heat for 7 minutes or until the blueberries are tender.
3. Pour in the brown rice and cook for 3 more minute or until the rice is soft. Stir constantly.
4. Serve immediately.

Per Serving

calories: 470 | fat: 24.8g | protein: 6.2g | carbs: 60.1g | fiber: 5.0g | sodium: 75mg

Banana, Cranberry, and Oat Bars

Prep Time: 15 minutes | **Cooking Time:** 40 minutes | Makes 16 bars

Ingredients

2 tablespoon extra-virgin olive oil
2 medium ripe bananas, mashed
½ cup almond butter
½ cup maple syrup
⅓ cup dried cranberries
1½ cups old-fashioned rolled oats
¼ cup oat flour
¼ cup ground flaxseed
¼ teaspoon ground cloves
½ cup shredded coconut
½ teaspoon ground cinnamon
1 teaspoon vanilla extract

Directions

1. Preheat the oven to 400°F (205°C). Line a 8-inch square pan with parchment paper, then grease with olive oil.
2. Combine the mashed bananas, almond butter, and maple syrup in a bowl. Stir to mix well.
3. Mix in the remaining and stir to mix well until thick and sticky.
4. Spread the mixture evenly on the square pan with a spatula, then bake in the preheated oven for 40 minutes or until a toothpick inserted in the center comes out clean.
5. Remove them from the oven and slice into 16 bars to serve.

Per Serving calories: 145 | fat: 7.2g | protein: 3.1g | carbs: 18.9g | fiber: 2.0g | sodium: 3mg

Chocolate and Avocado Mousse

Prep Time: 40 minutes | **Cooking Time:** 5 minutes | **Servings:** 4 to 6

Ingredients

8 ounces (227 g) dark chocolate (60% cocoa or higher), chopped
¼ cup unsweetened coconut milk
2 tablespoons coconut oil
2 ripe avocados, deseeded
¼ cup raw honey
Sea salt, to taste

Directions

1. Put the chocolate in a saucepan. Pour in the coconut milk and add the coconut oil.
2. Cook for 3 minutes or until the chocolate and coconut oil melt. Stir constantly.
3. Put the avocado in a food processor, then drizzle with honey and melted chocolate. Pulse to combine until smooth.
4. Pour the mixture in a serving bowl, then sprinkle with salt. Refrigerate to chill for 30 minutes and serve.

Per Serving

calories: 654 | fat: 46.8g | protein: 7.2g | carbs: 55.9g | fiber: 9.0g | sodium: 112mg

Sweet Spiced Pumpkin Pudding

Prep Time: 2 hours 10 minutes | **Cooking Time:** 0 minutes
Servings: 6

Ingredients

1 cup pure pumpkin purée
2 cups unsweetened coconut milk
1 teaspoon ground cinnamon
¼ teaspoon ground nutmeg
½ teaspoon ground ginger
Pinch cloves
¼ cup pure maple syrup
2 tablespoons chopped pecans, for garnish

Directions

1. Combine all the , except for the chopped pecans, in a large bowl. Stir to mix well.
2. Wrap the bowl in plastic and refrigerate for at least 2 hours.
3. Remove the bowl from the refrigerator and discard the plastic. Spread the pudding with pecans and serve chilled.

Per Serving

calories: 249 | fat: 21.1g | protein: 2.8g | carbs: 17.2g | fiber: 3.0g | sodium: 46mg

Mango and Coconut Frozen Pie

Prep Time: 1 hour 10 minutes | **Cooking Time:** 0 minutes |
Servings: 8

Ingredients

Crust:
1 cup cashews
½ cup rolled oats
1 cup soft pitted dates
1 cup unsweetened coconut milk

Filling:
2 large mangoes, peeled and chopped
½ cup unsweetened shredded coconut
½ cup water

Directions

1. Combine the for the crust in a food processor. Pulse to combine well.
2. Pour the mixture in an 8-inch springform pan, then press to coat the bottom. Set aside.
3. Combine the for the filling in the food processor, then pulse to purée until smooth.
4. Pour the filling over the crust, then use a spatula to spread the filling evenly. Put the pan in the freeze for 30 minutes.
5. Remove the pan from the freezer and allow to sit for 15 minutes under room temperature before serving.

Per Serving (1 slice)

calories: 426 | fat: 28.2g | protein: 8.1g | carbs: 14.9g | fiber: 6.0g | sodium: 174mg

Mini Nuts and Fruits Crumble

Prep Time: 15 minutes | **Cooking Time:** 15 minutes |
Servings: 6

Ingredients

Topping:
¼ cup coarsely chopped hazelnuts
1 cup coarsely chopped walnuts
1 teaspoon ground cinnamon
Sea salt, to taste
1 tablespoon melted coconut oil

Filling:
6 fresh figs, quartered
2 nectarines, pitted and sliced
1 cup fresh blueberries
2 teaspoons lemon zest
½ cup raw honey
1 teaspoon vanilla extract

Directions

Make the Topping
1. Combine the for the topping in a bowl. Stir to mix well. Set aside until ready to use.

Make the Filling:
2. Preheat the oven to 375°F (190°C).
3. Combine the for the fillings in a bowl. Stir to mix well.
4. Divide the filling in six ramekins, then divide and top with nut topping. Bake in the preheated oven for 15 minutes or until the topping is lightly browned and the filling is frothy.
5. Serve immediately.

Per Serving

calories: 336 | fat: 18.8g | protein: 6.3g | carbs: 41.9g | fiber: 6.0g | sodium: 31mg

Cozy Superfood Hot Chocolate

Prep Time: 5 minutes | **Cooking Time:** 8 minutes |
Servings: 2

Ingredients

2 cups unsweetened almond milk
1 tablespoon avocado oil
1 tablespoon collagen protein powder
2 teaspoons coconut sugar
2 tablespoons cocoa powder
1 teaspoon ground cinnamon
1 teaspoon ground ginger
1 teaspoon vanilla extract
½ teaspoon ground turmeric
Dash salt
Dash cayenne pepper

Directions

1. In a small saucepan over medium heat, warm the almond milk and avocado oil for about 7 minutes, stirring frequently.
2. Fold in the protein powder, which will only properly dissolve in a heated liquid. Stir in the coconut sugar and cocoa powder until melted and dissolved.
3. Carefully transfer the warm liquid into a blender, along with the cinnamon, ginger, vanilla, turmeric, salt, and cayenne pepper (if desired). Blend for 15 seconds until frothy. Serve immediately.

Per Serving

calories: 217 | fat: 11.0g | protein: 11.2g | carbs: 14.8g | fiber: 6.0g | sodium: 202mg

Chapter 10
Sauces Recipes, Dips Recipes, & Dressings Recipes

Creamy Cucumber Dip

Prep Time: 10 minutes | **Cooking Time:** 0 minutes | **Servings:** 6

Ingredients

1 medium cucumber, peeled and grated
¼ teaspoon salt
1 cup plain Greek yogurt
2 garlic cloves, minced
1 tablespoon extra-virgin olive oil
1 tablespoon freshly squeezed lemon juice
¼ teaspoon freshly ground black pepper

Directions

1. Place the grated cucumber in a colander set over a bowl and season with salt. Allow the cucumber to stand for 10 minutes. Using your hands, squeeze out as much liquid from the cucumber as possible. Transfer the grated cucumber to a medium bowl.
2. Add the yogurt, garlic, olive oil, lemon juice, and pepper to the bowl and stir until well blended.
3. Cover the bowl with plastic wrap and refrigerate for at least 2 hours to blend the flavors. Serve chilled.

Per Serving (¼ cup)

calories: 47 | fat: 2.8g | protein: 4.2g | carbs: 2.7g | fiber: 0g | sodium: 103mg

Italian Dressing

Prep Time: 5 minutes | **Cooking Time:** 0 minutes | **Servings:** 12

Ingredients

½ cup extra-virgin olive oil
¼ cup red wine vinegar
1 teaspoon dried Italian seasoning
1 teaspoon Dijon mustard
¼ teaspoon salt
¼ teaspoon freshly ground black pepper
1 garlic clove, minced

Directions

1. Place all the in a mason jar and cover. Shake vigorously for 1 minute until completely mixed.
2. Store in the refrigerator for up to 1 week.

Per Serving (1 tablespoon)

calories: 80 | fat: 8.6g | protein: 0g | carbs: 0g | fiber: 0g | sodium: 51mg

Ranch-Style Cauliflower Dressing

Prep Time: 10 minutes | **Cooking Time:** 0 minutes | **Servings:** 8

Ingredients

2 cups frozen cauliflower, thawed
½ cup unsweetened plain almond milk
2 tablespoons apple cider vinegar
2 tbsp extra-virgin olive oil
1 garlic clove, peeled
2 teaspoons finely chopped fresh parsley
2 teaspoons finely chopped scallions (both white and green parts)
1 teaspoon finely chopped fresh dill
½ teaspoon onion powder
½ teaspoon Dijon mustard
½ teaspoon salt
¼ teaspoon freshly ground black pepper

Directions

1. Place all the in a blender and pulse until creamy and smooth.
2. Serve immediately, or transfer to an airtight container to refrigerate for up to 3 days.

Per Serving (2 tablespoons)

calories: 41 | fat: 3.6g | protein: 1.0g | carbs: 1.9g | fiber: 1.1g | sodium: 148mg

Asian-Inspired Vinaigrette

Prep Time: 5 minutes | **Cooking Time:** 0 minutes | **Servings:** 2

Ingredients

¼ cup extra-virgin olive oil
3 tablespoons apple cider vinegar
1 garlic clove, minced
1 tablespoon peeled and grated fresh ginger
1 tablespoon chopped fresh cilantro
1 tablespoon freshly squeezed lime juice
½ teaspoon sriracha

Directions

1. Add all the in a small bowl and stir to mix well.
2. Serve immediately, or store covered in the refrigerator and shake before using.

Per Serving

calories: 251 | fat: 26.8g | protein: 0g | carbs: 1.8g | fiber: 0.7g | sodium: 3mg

Lemon-Tahini Sauce

Prep Time: 10 minutes | **Cooking Time:** 0 minutes | Makes 1 cup

Ingredients

½ cup tahini
1 garlic clove, minced
Juice and zest of 1 lemon
½ tbsp salt, plus more as needed
½ cup warm water, plus

Directions

1. Combine the tahini and garlic in a small bowl.
2. Add the lemon juice and zest and salt to the bowl and stir to mix well. Fold in the warm water and whisk until well combined and creamy. Feel free to add more warm water if you like a thinner consistency. Taste and add more salt as needed. Store the sauce in a sealed container in the refrigerator for up to 5 days.

Per Serving (¼ cup)
calories: 179 | fat: 15.5g | protein: 5.1g | carbs: 6.8g | fiber: 3.0g | sodium: 324mg

Peri-Peri Sauce

Prep Time: 10 minutes | **Cooking Time:** 5 minutes | **Servings:** 4

Ingredients

1 tomato, chopped
1 red onion, chopped
1 red bell pepper, deseeded and chopped
1 red chile, deseeded and chopped
4 garlic cloves, minced
2 tablespoons extra-virgin olive oil
Juice of 1 lemon
1 tablespoon dried oregano
1 tablespoon smoked paprika
1 teaspoon sea salt

Directions

1. Process all the in a food processor or a blender until smooth. Transfer the mixture to a small saucepan over medium-high heat and bring to a boil, stirring often.
2. Reduce the heat to medium and allow to simmer for 5 minutes until heated through. You can store the sauce in an airtight container in the refrigerator for up to 5 days.

Per Serving calories: 98 | fat: 6.5g | protein: 1.0g | carbs: 7.8g | fiber: 3.0g | sodium: 295mg

Garlic Lemon-Tahini Dressing

Prep Time: 5 minutes | **Cooking Time:** 0 minutes | **Servings:** 8 to 10

Ingredients

½ cup tahini
¼ cup extra-virgin olive oil
2 teaspoons salt
1 garlic clove, finely minced
¼ cup freshly squeezed lemon juice

Directions

1. In a glass mason jar with a lid, combine the tahini, olive oil, lemon juice, garlic, and salt. Cover and shake well until combined and creamy. Store in the refrigerator for up to 2 weeks.

Per Serving
calories: 121 | fat: 12.0g | protein: 2.0g | carbs: 3.0g | fiber: 1.0g | sodium: 479mg

Peanut Sauce with Honey

Prep Time: 5 minutes | **Cooking Time:** 0 minutes | **Servings:** 4

Ingredients

¼ cup peanut butter
1 tablespoon peeled and grated fresh ginger
1 tablespoon honey
1 tablespoon low-sodium soy sauce
1 garlic clove, minced
Juice of 1 lime
Pinch red pepper flakes

Directions

1. Whisk together all the in a small bowl until well incorporated. Transfer to an airtight container and refrigerate for up to 5 days.

Per Serving calories: 117 | fat: 7.6g | protein: 4.1g | carbs: 8.8g | fiber: 1.0g | sodium: 136mg

Cilantro-Tomato Salsa

Prep Time: 10 minutes | **Cooking Time:** 0 minutes | **Servings:** 6

Ingredients

2 or 3 medium, ripe tomatoes, diced
1 serrano pepper, seeded and minced
½ red onion, minced
¼ cup minced fresh cilantro
Juice of 1 lime
¼ teaspoon salt, plus more as needed

Directions

1. Place the tomatoes, serrano pepper, onion, cilantro, lime juice, and salt in a small bowl and mix well. Taste and add additional salt, if needed. Store in an airtight container in the refrigerator for up to 3 days.

Per Serving (¼ cup) calories: 17 | fat: 0g | protein: 1.0g | carbs: 3.9g | fiber: 1.0g | sodium: 83mg

Cheesy Pea Pesto

Prep Time: 5 minutes | **Cooking Time:** 0 minutes | **Servings:** 4

Ingredients

½ cup fresh green peas
½ cup grated Parmesan cheese
¼ cup extra-virgin olive oil
¼ cup pine nuts
¼ cup fresh basil leaves
2 garlic cloves, minced
¼ teaspoon sea salt

Directions

1. Add all the to a food processor or blender and pulse until the nuts are chopped finely.
2. Transfer to an airtight container and refrigerate for up to 2 days. You can also store it in ice cube trays in the freezer for up to 6 months.

Per Serving calories: 247 | fat: 22.8g | protein: 7.1g | carbs: 4.8g | fiber: 1.0g | sodium: 337mg

Guacamole

Prep Time: 10 minutes | **Cooking Time:** 0 minutes | **Servings:** 6

Ingredients

2 large avocados
¼ white onion, finely diced
1 small, firm tomato, finely diced
¼ cup finely chopped fresh cilantro

2 tablespoons freshly squeezed lime juice
¼ teaspoon salt
Freshly ground black pepper, to taste

Directions

1. Slice the avocados in half and remove the pits. Using a large spoon to scoop out the flesh and add to a medium bowl.
2. Mash the avocado flesh with the back of a fork, or until a uniform consistency is achieved. Add the onion, tomato, cilantro, lime juice, salt, and pepper to the bowl and stir to combine.
3. Serve immediately, or transfer to an airtight container and refrigerate until chilled.

Per Serving (¼ cup)

calories: 81 | fat: 6.8g | protein: 1.1g | carbs: 5.7g | fiber: 3.0g | sodium: 83mg

Lemon-Dill Cashew Dip

Prep Time: 10 minutes | **Cooking Time:** 0 minutes
Makes 1 cup

Ingredients

¾ cup cashews, soaked in water for at least 4 hours and drained well
¼ cup water

Juice and zest of 1 lemon
2 tbsp chopped fresh dill
¼ teaspoon salt, plus more as needed

Directions

1. Put the cashews, water, lemon juice and zest in a blender and blend until smooth.
2. Add the dill and salt to the blender and blend again.
3. Taste and adjust the seasoning, if needed.
4. Transfer to an airtight container and refrigerate for at least 1 hour to blend the flavors. Serve chilled.

Per Serving (1 tablespoon)

calories: 37 | fat: 2.9g | protein: 1.1g | carbs: 1.9g | fiber: 0g | sodium: 36mg

Homemade Blackened Seasoning

Prep Time: 10 minutes | **Cooking Time:** 0 minutes
Makes about ½ cup

Ingredients

2 tablespoons smoked paprika
2 tablespoons garlic powder
2 tablespoons onion powder
1 tablespoon sweet paprika

1 teaspoon dried dill
1 teaspoon freshly ground black pepper
½ tbsp ground mustard
¼ teaspoon celery seeds

Directions

1. Add all the to a small bowl and mix well.
2. Serve immediately, or transfer to an airtight container and store in a cool, dry and dark place for up to 3 months.

Per Serving (1 tablespoon)

calories: 22 | fat: 0.9g | protein: 1.0g | carbs: 4.7g | fiber: 1.0g | sodium: 2mg

Basil Pesto

Prep Time: 5 minutes | **Cooking Time:** 0 minutes
Makes 1 cup

Ingredients

2 cups packed fresh basil leaves
3 garlic cloves, peeled
½ cup freshly grated Parmesan cheese
½ cup extra-virgin olive oil

⅓ cup pine nuts
Kosher salt and freshly ground black pepper, to taste

Directions

1. Place all the , except for the salt and pepper, in a food processor. Pulse a few times until smoothly puréed. Season with salt and pepper to taste.
2. Store in an airtight container in the fridge for up to 2 weeks.

Per Serving

calories: 100 | fat: 10.2g | protein: 2.2g | carbs: 1.2g | fiber: 0g | sodium: 72mg

Orange-Garlic Dressing

Prep Time: 5 minutes | **Cooking Time:** 0 minutes | **Servings:** 2

Ingredients

¼ cup extra-virgin olive oil
1 orange, zested
2 tablespoons freshly squeezed orange juice
¾ teaspoon za'atar seasoning
1.

1 teaspoon garlic powder
½ teaspoon salt
¼ teaspoon Dijon mustard
Freshly ground black pepper, to taste

Directions

Whisk together all in a bowl until well combined. Serve immediately or refrigerate until ready to serve.

Per Serving calories: 287 | fat: 26.7g | protein: 1.2g | carbs: 12.0g | fiber: 2.1g | sodium: 592mg

Rhubarb Strawberry Crunch (Greek)

Prep Time: 15 minutes **Cooking Time:** 45 minutes
Servings: 18

Ingredients

1 cup of white sugar	3 tbsps. all-purpose flour
3 cups fresh strawberries, sliced	1 ½ cup flour
1 cup butter	3 cups rhubarb, cut into cubes
1 cup packed brown sugar	1 cup oatmeal

Directions

1. Preheat the oven to 190°C.
2. Combine the white sugar, 3 tbsps. of flour, strawberries, and rhubarb in a large bowl.
3. Place the mixture in a 9x13-inch baking dish.
4. Mix 1 ½ cups of flour, brown sugar, butter, and oats until a crumbly texture is obtained. You may want to use a blender for this.
5. Crumble the mixture of rhubarb and strawberry.
6. Bake for 45 minutes.

Nutrition: Calories: 253 Fat: 10.8 g. Protein: 2.3 g.

Vanilla Cream (Italian)

Prep Time: 2 hours **Cooking Time:** 10 minutes
Servings: 4

Ingredients

1 cup almond milk	1cup coconut cream
2tbsps. cinnamon powder	2 cups coconut sugar
1 tsp. vanilla extract	

Directions

1. Heat a pan with the almond milk over medium heat, add the rest of the , whisk, and cook for 10 minutes more.
2. Divide the mix into bowls, cool down, and keep in the fridge for 2 hours before serving.

Nutrition: Calories: 254 Fat: 7.5 g. Protein: 9.5 g.

Cocoa Almond Pudding (Spanish)

Prep Time: 10 minutes **Cooking Time:** 10 minutes
Servings: 4

Ingredients

2 tbsps. coconut sugar	2eggs, whisked
3 tbsps. coconut flour	2 tbsps. cocoa powder
½ tsp. vanilla extract	2 cups almond milk

Directions

1. Fill the milk in a pan, add the cocoa and the other, whisk, simmer over medium heat for 10 minutes, pour into small cups, and serve cold.

Nutrition: Calories: 385 Fat: 31.7 g. Protein: 7.3 g.

Nutmeg Cream (Greek)

Prep Time: 10 minutes **Cooking Time:** 0 minutes
Servings: 6

Ingredients

2cups almond milk	1 tsp. nutmeg, ground
2 tsps. vanilla extract	4 tsps. coconut sugar
1cup walnuts, chopped	

Directions

1. In a bowl, combine the milk with the nutmeg and the other, whisk well, divide into small cups and serve cold.

Nutrition: Calories: 243 Fat: 12.4 g. Protein: 9.7 g.

Vanilla Avocado Cream (Greek)

Prep Time: 70 minutes **Cooking Time:** 0 minutes
Servings: 4

Ingredients

1cups coconut cream	2 avocados, peeled, pitted, and mashed
2 tbsps. coconut sugar	
1tsp. vanilla extract	

Directions

1. Blend the cream with the avocados and the other , pulse well, divide into cups and keep in the fridge for 1 hour before serving.

Nutrition: Calories: 532 Fat: 48.2 g. Protein: 5.2 g.

Ice Cream Sandwich Dessert (Italian)

Prep Time: 20 minutes **Cooking Time:** 0 minute
Servings: 12

Ingredients

22 ice cream sandwiches	16 oz. container frozen whipped topping, thawed
1 (12 oz.) jar caramel ice cream	
1½ cups salted peanuts	

Directions

1. Cut a sandwich with ice in 2. Place a whole sandwich and a half sandwich on a short side of a 9x13-inch baking dish. Repeat this until the bottom is covered. Alternate the full sandwich, and the half sandwich.
2. Spread half of the whipped topping. Pour the caramel over it. Sprinkle with half the peanuts. Do layers with the rest of the ice cream sandwiches, whipped cream, and peanuts.
3. Cover and freeze for up to 2 months. Remove from the freezer 20 minutes before serving. Cut into squares.

Nutrition: Calories: 559 Fat: 28.8 g. Protein: 10 g.

Chocolate Matcha Balls (Greek)

Prep Time: 10 minutes **Cooking Time:** 5 minutes
Servings: 15

Ingredients

1tbsp unsweetened cocoa powder	½ cup pine nuts
½ cup almonds	3 tbsp oats, gluten-free
2tbsp matcha powder	1cup dates, pitted

Directions

1. Add oats, pine nuts, almonds, and dates into a food processor and process until well combined.
2. Place matcha powder in a small dish.
3. Make small balls from mixture and coat with matcha powder.
4. Enjoy or store in refrigerator until ready to eat.

Nutrition: Calories 88, Fat 4.9g, Carbohydrates 11.3g, Sugar 7.8g, Protein 1.9g, Cholesterol 0mg

Blueberries Bowls (Greek)

Prep Time: 10 minutes **Cooking Time:** 0 minutes
Servings: 4

Ingredients

1 tsp. vanilla extract	1 tsp. coconut sugar
2 cups blueberries	8 oz. Greek yogurt

Directions

1. Mix strawberries with the vanilla and the other , toss and serve cold.

Nutrition: Calories: 343 Fat: 13.4 g. Protein: 5.5 g.

Brownies (Greek)

Prep Time: 10 minutes **Cooking Time:** 25 minutes
Servings: 8

Ingredients

1 cup pecans, chopped	cup avocado oil
3 tbsps. coconut sugar	2 tbsps. cocoa powder
2 tsps. vanilla extract	3 eggs, whisked
½ tsp. baking powder	
Cooking spray	

Directions

1. In your food processor, combine the pecans with the coconut sugar and the other except for the cooking spray and pulse well.
2. Grease a square pan with the cooking spray, add the brownies mix, spread, introduce in the oven, bake at 350°F for 25 minutes, leave aside to cool down, slice, and serve.

Nutrition: Calories: 370 Fat: 14.3 g. Protein: 5.6 g.

Raspberries Cream Cheese Bowls (Italian)

Prep Time: 10 minutes **Cooking Time:** 25 minutes
Servings: 4

Ingredients

1tbsps. almond flour	1 cup coconut sugar
1 cup coconut cream	8 oz. cream cheese
3 cups raspberries	

Directions

1. In a bowl, the flour with the cream and the other , whisk, transfer to a round pan, cook at 360°F for 25 minutes, divide into bowls and serve.

Nutrition: Calories: 429 Fat: 36.3 g. Protein: 7.8 g.

Minty Coconut Cream (Spanish)

Prep Time: 4 minutes **Cooking Time:** 0 minutes
Servings: 2

Ingredients

1banana, peeled	2cups coconut flesh, shredded
3 tablespoons mint	½ avocado, pitted and peeled
1and ½ cups coconut water	
2 tablespoons stevia	

Directions

1. In a blender, combine the coconut with the banana and the rest of the , pulse well, divide into cups and serve cold.

Nutrition: Calories 193; Fat 5.4 g; Fiber 3.4 g; Carbs 7.6 g; Protein 3 g

Almond Honey Ricotta Spread (Greek)

Prep Time: 7 minutes **Cooking Time:** 0 minutes
Servings: 3

Ingredients

½ cup whole milk Ricotta	¼ cup orange zest
¼ cup almonds, sliced	½ tsp. honey
1/8 tsp. almond extract	Bread of your choice
1Peaches, sliced Hone to drizzle	

Directions

1. Take a medium bowl, and combine the almonds, almond extract, and Ricotta.
2. Once you have stirred it well, place it in a bowl to serve.
3. Sprinkle with the sliced almonds and drizzle some honey on the Ricotta.
4. Extent 1 tbsp. the spread to your choice of bread, top it with some honey and sliced peaches.

Nutrition: Calories: 199 Protein: 8.5 g. Fat: 12 g.

Chocolate Covered Strawberries (Greek)

Prep Time: 15 minutes **Cooking Time:** 0 minute
Servings: 24

Ingredients
16 oz. milk chocolate chips

2 tbsps. shortening

1 lb. fresh strawberries with leaves

Directions
1. In a bain-marie, melt the chocolate and shortening, occasionally stirring until smooth. Pierce the tops of the strawberries with toothpicks and immerse them in the chocolate mixture.
2. Turn the strawberries and put the toothpick in Styrofoam so that the chocolate cools.

Nutrition: Calories: 115 Fat: 7.3 g. Protein: 1.4 g.

Almonds and Oats Pudding (Greek)

Prep Time: 10 minutes **Cooking Time:** 15 minutes
Servings: 4

Ingredients
1 tablespoon lemon juice

Zest of 1 lime

½ cup oats

½ cup silver almonds, chopped

1and ½ cups almond milk

1 teaspoon almond extract

2tablespoons stevia

Directions
1. In a pan, combine the almond milk with the lime zest and the other , whisk, bring to a simmer and cook over medium heat for 15 minutes.
2. Divide the mix into bowls and serve cold.

Nutrition: Calories 174 Fat 12.1 Fiber 3.2 Carbs 3.9 Protein 4.8

Chocolate Cups (Greek)

Prep Time: 2 hours **Cooking Time:** 0 minutes
Servings: 6

Ingredients
½ cup avocado oil

1teaspoon matcha powder

3 tablespoons stevia

1 cup, chocolate, melted

Directions
1. In a bowl, mix the chocolate with the oil and the rest of the , whisk really well, divide into cups and keep in the freezer for 2 hours before serving.

Nutrition: Calories 174 Fat 9.1 Fiber 2.2 Carbs 3.9 Protein 2.8

Peach Sorbet (Spanish)

Prep Time: 2 hours **Cooking Time:** 10 minutes
Servings: 4

Ingredients
2 cups apple juice

1 cup stevia

2pounds peaches, pitted and quartered

2 tablespoons lemon zest, grated

Directions
1. Heat up a pan over medium heat, add the apple juice and the rest of the , simmer for 10 minutes, transfer to a blender, pulse, divide into cups and keep in the freezer for 2 hours before serving.

Nutrition: Calories 182; Fat 5.4 g; Fiber 3.4 g; Carbs 12 g; Protein 5.4 g

Cranberries and Pears Pie (Italian)

Prep Time: 10 minutes **Cooking Time:** 40 minutes
Servings: 4

Ingredients
1cup cranberries

1 cup rolled oats

1/3 cup almond flour

1 cup stevia

2cups pears, cubed

A drizzle of olive oil

¼ avocado oil

Directions
1. In a bowl, mix the cranberries with the pears and the other except the olive oil and the oats, and stir well.
2. Grease a cake pan with a drizzle of olive oil, pour the pears mix inside, sprinkle the oats all over and bake at 350° F for 40 minutes.
3.Cool the mix down, and serve.

Nutrition: Calories 172; Fat 3.4 g; Fiber 4.3 g; Carbs 11.5 g; Protein 4.5 g

Chia and Berries Smoothie Bowl (Spanish)

Prep Time: 5 minutes **Cooking Time:** 0 minutes
Servings: 2

1 and ½ cup almond milk

1 cup blackberries

1 and ½ tablespoons chia seeds

¼ cup strawberries, chopped

1 teaspoon cinnamon powder

Directions
1. In a blender, combine the blackberries with the strawberries and the rest of the , pulse well, divide into small bowls and serve cold.

Nutrition: Calories 182; Fat 3.4 g; Fiber 3.4 g; Carbs 8 g; Protein 3 g

Creamy Grapefruit and Tarragon Dressing

Prep Time: 5 minutes | **Cooking Time:** 0 minutes | **Servings:** 4 to 6

Ingredients

½ cup avocado oil mayonnaise
2 tablespoons Dijon mustard
1 teaspoon dried tarragon or 1 tablespoon chopped fresh tarragon

½ teaspoon salt
Zest and juice of ½ grapefruit
¼ teaspoon freshly ground black pepper
1 to 2 tablespoons water (optional)

Directions

1. In a large mason jar with a lid, combine the mayonnaise, Dijon, tarragon, grapefruit zest and juice, salt, and pepper and whisk well with a fork until smooth and creamy. If a thinner dressing is preferred, thin out with water.
2. Serve immediately or refrigerate until ready to serve.

Per Serving

calories: 86 | fat: 7.0g | protein: 1.0g | carbs: 6.0g | fiber: 0g | sodium: 390mg

Vinaigrette

Prep Time: 5 minutes | **Cooking Time:** 0 minutes
Makes 1 cup

Ingredients

½ cup extra-virgin olive oil
¼ cup red wine vinegar
1 tablespoon Dijon mustard
1 teaspoon dried rosemary

½ teaspoon salt
½ teaspoon freshly ground black pepper

Directions

1. In a cup or a mansion jar with a lid, combine the olive oil, vinegar, mustard, rosemary, salt, and pepper and shake until well combined. Serve chilled or at room temperature.

Per Serving

calories: 124 | fat: 14.0g | protein: 0g | carbs: 1.0g | fiber: 0g | sodium: 170mg

Ginger Teriyaki Sauce

Prep Time: 5 minutes | **Cooking Time:** 0 minutes | **Servings:** 2

Ingredients

¼ cup pineapple juice
¼ cup low-sodium soy sauce
2 tablespoons packed coconut sugar

1 tablespoon grated fresh ginger
1 tablespoon arrowroot powder or cornstarch
1 teaspoon garlic powder

Directions

1. Whisk the pineapple juice, soy sauce, coconut sugar, ginger, arrowroot powder, and garlic powder together in a small bowl.
2. Store in an airtight container in the fridge for up to 5 days.

Per Serving

calories: 37 | fat: 0.1g | protein: 1.1g | carbs: 12.0g | fiber: 0g | sodium: 881mg

Aioli

Prep Time: 5 minutes | **Cooking Time:** 0 minutes
Makes ½ cup

Ingredients

½ cup plain Greek yogurt
2 teaspoons Dijon mustard

½ teaspoon hot sauce
¼ teaspoon raw honey
Pinch salt

Directions

1. In a small bowl, whisk together the yogurt, mustard, hot sauce, honey, and salt.
2. Serve immediately or refrigerate in an airtight container for up to 3 days.

Per Serving calories: 47 | fat: 2.5g | protein: 2.1g | carbs: 3.5g | fiber: 0g | sodium: 231mg

Parsley Vinaigrette

Prep Time: 5 minutes | **Cooking Time:** 0 mins
Makes about ½ cup

Ingredients

½ cup lightly packed fresh parsley, finely chopped
⅓ cup extra-virgin olive oil

3 tablespoons red wine vinegar
1 garlic clove, minced
¼ teaspoon salt, plus additional as needed

Directions

1. Place all the in a mason jar and cover. Shake vigorously for 1 minute until completely mixed.
2. Taste and add additional salt as needed.
3. Serve immediately or serve chilled.

Per Serving (1 tablespoon)
calories: 92 | fat: 10.9g | protein: 0g | carbs: 0g | fiber: 0g | sodium: 75mg

Hot Pepper Sauce

Prep Time: 10 minutes | **Cooking Time:** 20 minutes
Makes 4 cups

Ingredients

1 red hot fresh chiles, deseeded
2 dried chiles
2 garlic cloves, peeled

½ small yellow onion, roughly chopped
2 cups water
2 cups white vinegar

Directions

1. Place all the except the vinegar in a medium saucepan over medium heat. Allow to simmer for 20 minutes until softened. Transfer the mixture to a food processor or blender. Stir in the vinegar and pulse until very smooth. Serve immediately or transfer to a sealed container and refrigerate for up to 3 months.

Per Serving (2 tablespoons) calories: 20 | fat: 1.2g | protein: 0.6g | carbs: 4.4g | fiber: 0.6g | sodium: 12mg

Bananas Foster (Greek)

Prep Time: 5 minutes **Cooking Time:** 6 minutes
Servings: 4

Ingredients

2/3 cup dark brown sugar

1 ½ tsp. vanilla extract

3 bananas, peeled and cut lengthwise and broad

3 ½ tbsp. rum

¼ cup butter

½ tsp. ground cinnamon

¼ cup nuts, coarsely chopped Vanilla ice cream

Directions

1. Melt the butter in a deep-frying pan over medium heat. Stir in the sugar, rum, vanilla, and cinnamon.
2. When the mixture starts to bubble, place the bananas and nuts in the pan. Bake until the bananas are hot, 1–2 minutes. Serve immediately with vanilla ice cream.

Nutrition: Calories: 534 Fat: 23.8 g. Protein: 4.6 g.

A Taste of Dessert (Italian)

Prep Time: 15 minutes
Cooking Time: 0 minutes
Servings: 2

Ingredients

1 tbsp. cilantro

1 mango, peeled, seeded, and chopped

1 tbsp. green onion

¼ cup bell pepper, chopped

2 tbsps. honey

Directions

1. Incorporate all.
2. Serve when all of them are well combined.

Nutrition: Calories: 21 Fat: 0.1 g. Protein: 0.3 g.

Fresh Cherry Treat (Greek)

Prep Time: 10 minutes **Cooking Time:** 10 minutes
Servings: 2

Ingredients

1 tbsp. honey

1 tbsp. almonds, crushed

12 oz. cherries

Directions

1. Preheat the oven to 350°F, and bake the cherries for 5 minutes.
2. Coat them with the honey, and serve with almonds on top.

Nutrition: Calories: 448 Fat: 36.4 g. Protein: 3.5 g.

Key Lime Pie (Italian)

Prep Time: 15 minutes **Cooking Time:** 8 minutes
Servings: 8

Ingredients

1 (9-inch) Prepared Graham Cracker crust

¾ cup lime juice

½ cup sour cream

3 cups sweetened condensed milk

1 tbsp. lime zest, grated

Directions

1. Preheat the oven to 175°C.
2. Combine the condensed milk, sour cream, lime juice, and lime zest in a medium bowl. Mix well and pour into the graham cracker crust.
3. Bake in the preheated oven for 5–8 minutes.
4. Cool the cake well before serving. Decorate with lime slices and whipped cream if desired.

Nutrition: Calories: 553 Fat: 20.5 g. Protein: 10.9 g.

Lemon Cream (Greek)

Prep Time: 1 hour **Cooking Time:** 10 minutes
Servings: 6

Ingredients

1 eggs, whisked

10 tbsps. avocado oil

1 cup heavy cream

Juice of 2 lemons

¼ cup stevia

Zest of 2 lemons, grated

Directions

1. In a pan, combine the cream with the lemon juice and the other , whisk well, cook for 10 minutes, divide into cups, and keep in the fridge for 1 hour before Servings

Nutrition: Calories: 200, Fat: 8.5g, Fiber: 4.5g, Carbs: 8.6g, Protein: 4.5g

Blueberries Stew (Spanish)

Prep Time: 10 minutes **Cooking Time:** 10 minutes
Servings: 4

Ingredients

2 cups blueberries

½ cups pure apple juice

3 tbsps. stevia

1 tsp. vanilla extract

Directions

1. In a pan, combine the blueberries with stevia and the other, bring to a simmer and cook over medium-low heat for 10 minutes.
2. Divide into cups and serve cold.

Nutrition: Calories: 192, Fat: 5.4g, Fiber: 3.4g, Carbs: 9.4g, Protein: 4.5g

Apricot Energy Bites (Greek)

Prep Time: 16 minutes **Cooking Time:** 0 minute
Servings: 10

Ingredients

1cup unsalted raw cashew nuts	¼ tsp. ground ginger
½ cup dried apricots	2 tbsps. dates, chopped
1 tsp. lemon zest	2¾ tbsp. unsweetened coconut, shredded
1 tsp. orange zest	¼ tsp. cinnamon Salt to taste

Directions

1. Grind the apricots, coconut, dates, and cashew nuts in a food processor.
2. Pulse until a crumbly mixture has formed.
3. Add the spices, salt, and citrus zest to the mixture.
4. Pulse it again to mix well.
5. Process the batter on HIGH till it sticks together.
6. Take a dish or a tray and line it with parchment paper.
7. Shape the balls in your palm, make around 20 balls.
8. Keep in the refrigerator. Serve as needed.

Nutrition: Calories: 102 Protein: 2 g. Fat: 6 g.

Cranberry Orange Cookies (Italian)

Prep Time: 20 minutes **Cooking Time:** 16 minutes
Servings: 24

Ingredients

1 cup soft butter	½ cup brown sugar
1tsp. orange peel, grated	2½ cups flour
2 tbsps. orange juice	1 cup white sugar
½ tsp. baking powder	½ tsp. salt
2 cups cranberries, chopped	½ cup walnuts, chopped (optional) For the icing:
1 egg	
½ tsp. orange peel, grated	1½ cup confectioner's sugar
3 tbsps. orange juice	

Directions

1. Preheat the oven to 190°C.
2. Blend the butter, white sugar, and brown sugar. Beat the egg until everything is well mixed. Mix 1 tsp. orange zest and 2 tbsps. of orange juice. Mix the flour, baking powder, and salt; stir in the orange mixture.
3. Mix the cranberries and, if used, the nuts until well distributed. Place the dough with a spoon on ungreased baking trays.
4. Bake in the preheated oven for 12–14 minutes. Cool on racks.
5. In a small bowl, mix icing . Spread over cooled cookies.

Nutrition: Calories: 110 Fat: 4.8 g. Protein: 1.1 g.

Rhubarb Cream (Greek)

Prep Time: 10 minutes **Cooking Time:** 14 minutes
Servings: 4

Ingredients

1/3 cup cream cheese	½ cup coconut cream
1lbs. rhubarb, roughly chopped	3 tbsps. coconut sugar

Directions

1. Blend the cream cheese with the cream and the other well.
2. Divide into small cups, introduce in the oven, and bake at 350ºF for 14 minutes.
3. Serve cold.

Nutrition: Calories: 360 Fat: 14.3 g. Protein: 5.2 g.

Dipped Sprouts (Italian)

Prep Time: 12 minutes **Cooking Time:** 10 minutes
Servings: 2

Ingredients

16 oz. Brussels sprouts	6 tbsps. raisins and nuts, crushed
4 tbsps. honey	

Directions

1. Boil water in a pot
2. Add the sprouts, and cook for 10 minutes until soft.
3. Glaze the sprouts in the honey and coat well. Add the nuts and raisins.

Nutrition: Calories: 221 Fat: 15.1 g. Protein: 5.3 g.

Healthy & Quick Energy Bites (Italian)

Prep Time: 10 minutes **Cooking Time:** 0 minutes
Servings: 20

Ingredients

2 cups cashew nuts	¼ tsp cinnamon
4 tbsp dates, chopped	1/3 cup unsweetened shredded coconut
1 tsp lemon zest	
¾ cup dried apricots	

Directions

1. Line baking tray with parchment paper and set aside.
2. Add all in a food processor and process until the mixture is crumbly and well combined.
3. Make small balls from mixture and place on a prepared baking tray.
4. Serve and enjoy.

Nutrition: Calories: 100, Fat 7.5g, Carbohydrates 7.2g, Sugar 2.8g, Protein 2.4g, Cholesterol 0mg

Cocoa Brownies (Greek)

Prep Time: 10 minutes **Cooking Time:** 20 minutes
Servings: 8

Ingredients

30 ounces canned lentils, rinsed and drained
½ teaspoon baking soda
1 tablespoon honey

1 banana, peeled and chopped
4 tablespoons almond butter
2 tablespoons cocoa powder
Cooking spray

Directions

1. In a food processor, combine the lentils with the honey and the other except the cooking spray and pulse well.
2. Pour this into a pan greased with cooking spray, spread evenly, introduce in the oven at 375° F and bake for 20 minutes.
3. Cut the brownies and serve cold.

Nutrition: Calories 200; Fat 4.5 g; Fiber 2.4 g; Carbs 8.7 g; Protein 4.3 g

Chocolate Chip Banana Dessert (Italian)

Prep Time: 20 minutes **Cooking Time:** 20 minutes
Servings: 24

Ingredients

2/3 cup white sugar
3/4 cup butter
1 cup banana puree
13/4 cup flour
½ tsp. salt

2/3 cup brown sugar
1 egg, beaten slightly
1 tsp. vanilla extract
2tsps. baking powder
1 cup semi-sweet chocolate chips

Directions

1. Preheat the oven to 175°C. Grease and bake a 10x15-inch baking pan.
2. Beat the butter, white sugar, and brown sugar in a large bowl until light.
3. Beat the egg and vanilla.
4. Fold in the banana puree: mix baking powder, flour, and salt in another bowl.
5. Mix the flour mixture into the butter mixture. Stir in the chocolate chips. Spread in the pan.
6. Bake for 20 minutes.
7. Cool before cutting into squares.

Nutrition: Calories: 174 Fat: 8.2 g. Protein: 1.7 g.

Milky Peachy Dessert (Italian)

Prep Time: 15 minutes **Cooking Time:** 10 minutes
Servings: 2

Ingredients

1 fresh peach, peeled and sliced
1 tsp. brown sugar

1 tbsp. milk

Directions

1. Prepare a baking dish with a layer of peaches and toss in the milk.
2. Top the peaches with sugar, and bake at 350ºF for 5 minutes.

Nutrition: Calories: 366 Fat: 22.5 g. Protein: 1.9 g.

Citrus Sections (Greek)

Prep Time: 20 minutes **Cooking Time:** 5 minutes
Servings: 2

Ingredients

1 grapefruit, peeled and sectioned
1 small orange, sectioned into chunks
½ tsp. butter, low fat and unsalted, melted

½ cup pineapple, chunks
½ tbsp. brown sugar,

Directions

1. Preheat an oven tray at 350ºF.
2. Set the fruits on the tray, top with the brown sugar mixed with the butter, and bake for 5 minutes.
3. Transfer to a platter.

Nutrition: Calories: 279 Fat: 5.9 g. Protein: 2.2 g.

Mediterranean Watermelon Salad (Greek)

Prep Time: 4 minutes **Cooking Time:** 0 minutes
Servings: 4

Ingredients

1 cup watermelon, peeled and cubed
2bananas, cut into chunks

1tbsp. coconut cream
2 apples, cored and cubed

Directions

1. Incorporate watermelon with the apples and the other , toss and serve.

Nutrition: Calories: 131 Fat: 1.3 g. Protein: 1.3 g.

CHAPTER 11
Dinner Recipes

Salad Skewers (Greek)

Prep Time: 10 minutes **Cooking Time:** 0 minutes
Servings: 1

Ingredients

1wooden skewers, soaked in water for 30 minutes before use.
1 yellow pepper, cut into eight squares.
3.5-oz. (about 10cm) cucumber, cut into four slices and halved.
For the dressing:
Juice of ½ lemon.
A right amount of salt and freshly ground black pepper..

8 cherry tomatoes.
8 large black olives.
oz. feta, cut into 8 cubes
½ red onion, chopped in half and separated into eight pieces.
1 tsp. balsamic vinegar
Leaves oregano, chopped
1 tbsp. extra-virgin olive oil.
Few leaves basil, finely chopped (or ½ tsp dried mixed herbs to replace basil and oregano).
½ clove garlic, peeled and crushed.

Directions

1. Thread each skewer in the order with salad olive, tomato, yellow pepper, red onion, cucumber, feta, basil, olive, yellow pepper, red ointment, cucumber, feta.
2. Put all the ingredients of the dressing in a small bowl and blend well together. Pour over the spoils.

Nutrition: Calories: 315 g. Fat: 30 g. Protein: 56 g. Carbs: 45 g. Cholesterol: 230 mg. Sugar: 0 g.

Artichoke Petals Bites (Spanish)

Prep Time: 10 minutes **Cooking Time:** 10 minutes
Servings: 8

Ingredients

8 oz. artichoke petals, boiled, drained, without salt.
4 oz. Parmesan, grated.

½ cup almond flour.
2 tbsps. almond butter, melted.

Directions

1. In the mixing bowl, mix up together almond flour and grated Parmesan.
2. Preheat the oven to 355º F.
3. Dip the artichoke petals in the almond butter and then coat in the almond flour mixture.
4. Place them in the tray.
5. Transfer the tray to the preheated oven and cook the petals for 10 minutes.
6. Chill the cooked petal bites a little before serving.

Nutrition: Calories: 140 g. Fat: 6.4 g. Fiber: 7.6 g. Carbs: 14.6 g. Protein: 10 g.

Turkey With Cauliflower Couscous (Italian)

Prep Time: 20 minutes **Cooking Time:** 50 minutes
Servings: 1

Ingredients

3 oz. turkey.
1 pepper Bird's Eye.
1 tsp. fresh ginger.
1 clove of garlic.
oz. dried tomatoes.
0.3-oz. parsley.
¼ fresh lemon juice.

1-oz. cauliflower.
2 oz. red onion.
3 tbsps. extra virgin olive oil.
2 tsps. turmeric.
Dried sage to taste.
1 tbsp. capers.

Directions

1. Blend the raw cauliflower tops and cook them in a tsp. of extra virgin olive oil, garlic, red onion, chili pepper, ginger, and a tsp. of turmeric.
2. Leave to flavor on the fire for a minute, then add the chopped sun-dried tomatoes and 5 g of parsley. Season the turkey slice with a tsp. of extra virgin olive oil, the dried sage, and cook it in another tsp. of extra virgin olive oil. Once ready, season with a tbsp. of capers, ¼ of lemon juice, 5 g of parsley, a tbsp. of water and add the cauliflower.

Nutrition: Calories: 120 g. Fat: 10 g. Protein: 56 g. Carbs: 45 g. Cholesterol: 230 mg. Sugar: 0 g.

Italian Style Ground Beef (Italian)

Prep Time: 10 minutes **Cooking Time:** 20 minutes
Servings: 4

Ingredients

2 lbs. ground beef
Salt
3tbsp olive oil
1/2 tsp dried sage
2tsp thyme

2eggs, lightly beaten
1/4 tsp dried basil
11/2 tsp dried parsley
1 tsp oregano
1 tsp rosemary Pepper

Directions

1. Pour 1 1/2 cups of water into the instant pot then place the trivet in the pool.
2. Spray loaf pan with cooking spray.
3. Add all ingredients into the mixing bowl and mix until well combined.
4. Transfer meat mixture into the prepared loaf pan and place loaf pan on top of the trivet in the pot.
5. Seal pot with lid and cook on high for 35 minutes.
6. Once done, allow to release pressure naturally for 10 minutes then release remaining using quick release. Remove lid.
7. Serve and enjoy.

Nutrition: Calories 365 Fat 18 g Carbohydrates 0.7 g Sugar 0.1 g Protein 47.8 g Cholesterol 190 mg

Chicken Merlot with Mushrooms (Spanish)

Prep Time: 10 minutes **Cooking Time:** 40 minutes
Servings: 2

Ingredients

6 boneless, skinless chicken breasts, cubed.
¾ cup chicken broth.
¼ cup Merlot.
2 tbsps. basil, chopped finely.
1 (10 oz.) package buckwheat ramen noodles, cooked.

1 large red onion, chopped.
2 cloves garlic, minced.
1 (6 oz.) can tomato paste.
3 tbsps. chia seeds.
Salt and pepper to taste.
3 cups mushrooms, sliced.
2 tbsps. Parmesan, shaved.
2 tsps. sugar.

Directions

1. Rinse chicken; set aside.
2. Add mushrooms, onion, and garlic to the crockpot and mix.
3. Place chicken cubes on top of the vegetables and do not mix.
4. In a large bowl, combine broth, tomato paste, wine, chia seeds, basil, sugar, salt, and pepper. Pour over the chicken.
5. Cover and cook on low for 7–8 hours or on high for 3 ½–4 hours.
6. To serve, spoon chicken, mushroom mixture, and sauce over hot cooked buckwheat ramen noodles. Top with shaved Parmesan.

Nutrition: Calories: 213 g. Fat: 10 g. Protein: 56 g. Carbs: 45 g. Cholesterol: 230 mg. Sugar: 0 g.

Stuffed Beef Loin in Sticky Sauce (Italian)

Prep Time: 15 minutes **Cooking Time:** 6 minutes
Servings: 4

Ingredients

1 tbsp. Erythritol.
½ tsp. tomato sauce.
½ cup of water.
3 oz. celery root, grated.
3 oz. bacon, sliced.
¾ tsps. garlic, diced.

1 tbsp. lemon juice.
¼ tsp. dried rosemary.
9 oz. beef loin.
1 tbsp. walnuts, chopped.
2 tsps. butter.
1 tbsp. olive oil.
1 tsp. salt.

Directions

1. Cut the beef loin into the layer and spread it with the dried rosemary, butter, and salt.
2. Then place over the beef loin: grated celery root, sliced bacon, walnuts, and diced garlic.
3. Roll the beef loin and brush it with olive oil.
4. Secure the meat with the help of the toothpicks.
5. Place it in the tray and add a ½ cup of water.
6. Cook the meat in the preheated to 365º F oven for 40 minutes.
7. Meanwhile, make the sticky sauce: mix up together Erythritol, lemon juice, 4 tbsps. of water, and butter.
8. Preheat the mixture until it starts to boil.
9. Then add tomato sauce and whisk it well.
10. Bring the sauce to boil and remove from the heat.
11. When the beef loin is cooked, remove it from the oven and brush it with the cooked sticky sauce very generously.
12. Slice the beef roll and sprinkle with the remaining sauce.

Nutrition: Calories: 248 g. Fat: 17.5 g. Fiber: 0.5 g. Carbs: 2.2 g. Protein:20.7 g.

Olive Feta Beef (Greek)

Prep Time: 10 minutes **Cooking Time:** 6 hours
Servings: 8

Ingredients

1lbs. beef stew meat, cut into half-inch pieces.
½ tsp. salt.
½ cup feta cheese, crumbled.

30 oz. can tomato, diced.
1 cup olives, pitted, and cut in half.
¼ tsp. pepper.

Directions

1. Add all ingredients into the crockpot and stir well.
2. Cover and cook on high for 6 hours.
3. Season with pepper and salt.
4. Stir well and serve.

Nutrition: Calories: 370 g. Fat: 12 g. Fiber: 1 g. Carbs: 10 g. Protein: 50 g.

Excellent Beef Meal (Spanish)

Prep Time: 15 minutes **Cooking Time:** 7 hours 4 minutes
Servings: 6

Ingredients

1 tbsp. vegetable oil
2 lb. beef stew meat
1 can artichoke hearts
1 container beef broth
1 can tomato sauce
1 tsp. dried basil
1 onion
1/2 tsp. ground cumin

4 garlic cloves
1 can diced tomatoes with juice 1/2 C.
Kalamata olives, pitted
1 tsp. dried oregano
1 tsp. dried parsley
1 bay leaf, crumbled

Directions

1. In a skillet, heat the oil over medium-high heat and cook the beef for about 2 minutes per side.
2. Transfer the beef into a slow cooker and top with artichoke hearts, followed by the onion and garlic.
3. Place the remaining ingredients on top.
4. Set the slow cooker on "Low" and cook, covered for about 7 hours.

Nutrition: Calories: 410; Carbohydrates: 0.9g; Protein: 53.1g; Fat: 14.2g; Sugar: 6.7g; Sodium: 1116mg; Fiber: 6.4g

Chicken and Tzatziki Pitas (Greek)

Prep Time: 10 minutes **Cooking Time:** 0 minutes
Servings: 8

Ingredients

2pita breads
8 teaspoons tzatziki sauce

10 oz chicken fillet, grilled
1 cup lettuce, chopped

Directions

1. Cut every pita bread on the halves to get 8 pita pockets.
2. Then fill every pita pocket with chopped lettuce and sprinkle greens with tzatziki sauce.
3. Chop chicken fillet and add it in the pita pockets too.

Nutrition: calories 106, fat 3.8, fiber 0.2, carbs 6.1, protein 11

Sunday Dinner Brisket (Spanish)

Prep Time: 10 minutes **Cooking Time:** 8 hours 10 minutes
Servings: 6

Ingredients

2 1/2 lb. beef brisket, trimmed	Salt and freshly ground black pepper, to taste
2 medium onions, chopped	1 (15-oz.) can diced tomatoes, drained
2 large garlic cloves, sliced	2 tsp. Dijon mustard
1 tbsp. Herbs de Provence	2 tsp. olive oil
1 C. dry red wine	

Directions

1. Season the brisket with salt and black pepper evenly.
2. In a non-stick skillet, heat the oil over medium heat and cook the brisket for about 4-5 minutes per side.
3. Transfer the brisket into a slow cooker.
4. Add the remaining ingredients and stir to combine.
5. Set the slow cooker on "Low" and cook, covered for about 8 hours.
6. Uncover the slow cooker and with a slotted spoon, transfer the brisket onto a platter.
7. Cut the brisket into desired sized slices and serve with the topping of pan sauce.

Nutrition: Calories: 427; Carbohydrates: 7.7g; Protein: 58.5g; Fat: 193.6g; Sugar: 3.7g; Sodium: 178mg; Fiber: 1.7g

Leg of Lamb with Rosemary and Garlic (Greek)

Prep Time: 15 minutes **Cooking Time:** 8 hours
Servings: 4–6

Ingredients

3–4-lb. leg of lamb	4 garlic cloves, sliced thin
5–8 sprigs of fresh rosemary, more if desired	1 lemon, halved
2 tbsps. olive oil	
¼ cup flour	

Directions

1. Put a skillet over high heat and pour the olive oil.
2. When the olive oil is hot, add the leg of lamb and sear on both sides until brown.
3. Spray the slow cooker with olive oil and then transfer the lamb to the slow cooker.
4. Squeeze the lemon over the meat and then place it in the pot next to the lamb.
5. Take a sharp knife, make small incisions in the meat, and then stuff the holes you created with rosemary and garlic.
6. Place any remaining rosemary and garlic on top of the roast.
7. Cook on low for 8 hours.

Nutrition: Calories: 557 Fat: 39 g. Protein: 46 g.

Lemon Honey Lamb Shoulder (Spanish)

Prep Time: 10 minutes **Cooking Time:** 8 hours
Servings: 4

Ingredients

3 garlic cloves, thinly sliced	1 tbsp. fresh rosemary, chopped
1 tsp. lemon zest, grated	4–5-lb. boneless lamb shoulder roast
½ tsp. each salt and pepper	
3 tbsps. lemon juice	6 shallots, quartered
1 tbsp. honey	2 tsps. Olive oil
2 tsps. cornstarch	

Directions

1. Stir the garlic, rosemary, lemon zest, salt, and pepper.
2. Rub the spice mixture into the lamb shoulder. Make sure to coat the whole roast.
3. Spray the slow cooker with olive oil and add the lamb.
4. Mix the honey and lemon juice and then pour over the meat.
5. Arrange the shallots beside the meat in the slow cooker.
6. Cook on low for 8 hours.
7. Serve. You can make a gravy by transferring the juice from the slow cooker to a medium saucepan. Thoroughly mix the cornstarch into a bit of water until smooth. Then mix into the juice and bring to a simmer. Simmer until mixture thickens.

Nutrition: Calories: 240 Fat: 11 g. Protein: 31 g.

Lemony Trout with Caramelized Shallots (Greek)

Prep Time: 10 minutes **Cooking Time:** 20 minutes
Servings: 2

Ingredients

For the shallots:	1tsp. almond butter
2shallots, thinly sliced Dash	For the trout:
1tbsp. almond butter	2(4 oz./113 g.) trout fillets
3tbsps. capers	¼ cup freshly squeezed lemon juice
salt	Dash freshly grounds black pepper
¼ tsp. salt	1 lemon, thinly sliced

Directions

1. For the shallots:
1. Place a skillet over medium heat, cook the butter, shallots, and salt for 20 minutes, stirring every 5 minutes.
2. For the trout:
3. Meanwhile, in another large skillet over medium heat, heat 1 tsp. almond butter.
4. Add the trout fillets and cook each side for 3 minutes, or until flaky. Transfer to a plate and set aside.
5. In the skillet used for the trout, stir in the capers, lemon juice, salt, and pepper, then bring to a simmer. Whisk in the remaining 1 tbsp. almond butter. Spoon the sauce over the fish.
6. Garnish the fish with lemon slices and caramelized shallots before serving.

Nutrition: Calories: 344 Fat: 18 g. Protein: 21 g.

Skillet Braised Cod with Asparagus and Potatoes(Spanish)

Prep Time: 20 minutes **Cooking Time:** 20 minutes
Servings: 4

Ingredients

4 skinless cod fillets	12 oz. halved small purple
1 lb. asparagus	potatoes
½ lemon zest, finely grated	½ lemon juice
½ cup white wine	¼ cup torn fresh basil
1 ½ tbsp. olive oil	leaves
1 tbsp. capers	3 garlic cloves, sliced
½ tsp. salt	¼ tsp. pepper

Directions

1. Take a large and tall pan on the sides and heat the oil over medium- high.
2. Season the cod abundantly with salt and pepper and put in the pan, with the hot oil, for 1 minute. Carefully flip for 1 more minute and after transferring the cod to a plate. Set aside. Add the lemon zest, capers, and garlic to the pan and mix to coat with the remaining oil in the pan, and cook for 1 minute. Add the wine and deglaze the pan. Add the lemon juice, potatoes, ½ tsp. salt, ¼ tsp. pepper and 2 cups of water and bring to a boil, reduce the heat, and simmer until potatoes are tender, for 10–12 minutes.
3. Mix the asparagus and cook for 2 minutes. Bring back the cod filets and any juices accumulated in the pan. Cook until the asparagus are tender, for 3 minutes.
4. Divide the cod fillets into shallow bowls and add the potatoes and asparagus. Mix the basil in the broth left in the pan and pour over the cod.

Nutrition: Calories: 461 Protein: 40 g. Fat: 16 g.

Savory Vegetable Pancakes (Greek)

Prep Time: 10 minutes **Cooking Time:** 40 minutes
Servings: 7

Ingredients

8 peeled carrots	2 garlic cloves
1 zucchini	1 bunch green onions
½ bunch parsley	1 recipe pancake batter
Salt to taste	3 tbsps. of olive oil

Directions

1. Grate chop the zucchini and carrots using the grater. Finely chop the onions, mince the garlic and roughly chop the parsley. Prepare the pancakes with your favorite recipe or buy them in the store, but use ¼ cup of liquid less than required, zucchini will add a large amount of liquid to the mix. Fold the vegetables in the prepared pancake batter.
2. Heat a pan over medium-high heat and brush it gently with the olive oil. Use a 1/3 measuring cup to scoop the batter on the heated pan. Cook for 3–4 minutes, until the outer edge has set, then turn over. Cook for another 2 minutes and remove from the heat.
3. Season the pancakes with plenty of salt. Serve with butter, sour cream, or even a salted jam.

Nutrition: Calories: 291 Protein: 24 g. Fat: 10 g.

Niçoise-inspired Salad with Sardines (Spanish)

Prep Time: 9 minutes **Cooking Time:** 16 minutes
Servings: 4

Ingredients

4 eggs	12 ounces baby red
6 ounces green beans, halved	potatoes (about 12 potatoes)
4 cups baby spinach leaves or mixed greens	1 bunch radishes, quartered (about 1 1/3 cups)
20 Kalamata or Niçoise olives (about 1/3 cup)	3 (3.75-ounce) cans skinless, boneless sardines packed in olive oil, drained
1 cup cherry tomatoes	
8 tablespoons Dijon Red Wine Vinaigrette	

Directions

1. Situate the eggs in a saucepan and cover with water. Bring the water to a boil. Once the water starts to boil, close then turn the heat off. Set a timer for minutes.
2. Once the timer goes off, strain the hot water and run cold water over the eggs to cool. Peel the eggs when cool and cut in half.
3. Poke each potato a few times using fork. Place them on a microwave- safe plate and microwave on high for 4 to 5 minutes, until the potatoes are tender. Let cool and cut in half. Place green beans on a microwave-safe plate and microwave on high for 1½ to 2 minutes, until the beans are crisp-tender. Cool.
4. Place 1 egg, ½ cup of green beans, 6 potato halves, 1 cup of spinach, 1/3 cup of radishes, ¼ cup of tomatoes, olives, and 3 sardines in each of 4 containers. Pour 2 tablespoons of vinaigrette into each of 4 sauce containers.

Nutrition: Calories: 450 Fat: 32g Protein: 21g

Tuscan Beef Stew (Spanish)

Prep Time: 10 minutes **Cooking Time:** 4 hours
Servings: 8

Ingredients

1lbs. beef stew meat	2 (14 ½ oz.) cans tomatoes
1 medium onion	1 package McCormick®
1 tsp. rosemary leaves	Slow Cookers Hearty Beef
8 slices Italian bread	Stew Seasoning
½ cup water	½ cup dry red wine
4 carrots	

Directions

1. Place the cubed beef in the slow cooker along with the carrots, diced tomatoes, and onion wedges.
2. Mix the seasoning package in ½ cup of water and stir well, making sure no lumps are remaining.
3. Add the red wine to the water and stir slightly. Add the rosemary leaves to the water-and-wine mixture and then pour over the meat, stirring to ensure the meat is completely covered.
4. Turn the slow cooker to LOW and cook for 8 hours, or cook for 4 hours on HIGH.
5. Serve with toasted Italian bread.

Nutrition: Calories: 329 Fat: 15 g. Protein: 25.6 g.

Chicken Kapama (Spanish)

Prep Time: 10 minutes **Cooking Time:** 90 minutes
Servings: 4

Ingredients

1 (32 oz.) can tomatoes, chopped	¼ cup dry white wine
3 tbsps. extra-virgin olive oil	2 tbsps. tomato paste
½ tsp. dried oregano	¼ tsp. red pepper flakes
2 whole cloves	1 cinnamon stick
½ tsp. sea salt	1 tsp. ground allspice
4 boneless, skinless chicken breast halves	1/8 tsp. black pepper

Directions

1. In a pot over medium-high heat, mix the tomatoes, wine, tomato paste, olive oil, red pepper flakes, allspice, oregano, cloves, cinnamon stick, sea salt, and pepper. Bring to a simmer, stirring occasionally. Adjust the heat to medium-low and simmer for 30 minutes, stirring occasionally. Remove and discard the whole cloves and cinnamon stick from the sauce and let the sauce cool.
2. Preheat the oven to 350°F.
3. Place the chicken in a 9-by-13-inch baking dish. Drizzle sauce over the chicken and cover the pan with aluminum foil. Bake for 45 minutes.

Nutrition: Calories: 220 Protein: 8 g. Fat: 14 g.

Spinach and Feta-Stuffed Chicken Breasts (Greek)

Prep Time: 10 minutes **Cooking Time:** 45 minutes
Servings: 4

Ingredients

2tbsps. extra-virgin olive oil	3garlic cloves, minced
1 lb. fresh baby spinach	1 lemon zest
½ tsp. sea salt	1/8 tsp. freshly ground black pepper
4 chicken breast halves	
½ cup Feta cheese, crumbled	

Directions

1. Preheat the oven to 350°F.
2. Preheat the oil and skillet over medium-high heat.
3. Cook the spinach for 3–4 minutes.
4. Cook the garlic, lemon zest, sea salt, and pepper.
5. Cool slightly and mix in the cheese.
6. Spread the spinach and cheese mixture in an even layer over the chicken pieces and roll the breast around the filling.
7. Hold closed with toothpicks or butcher's twine.
8. Place the breasts in a 9-by-13-inch baking dish and bake for 30–40 minutes.
9. Take away from the oven and let rest for 5 minutes before slicing and serving.

Nutrition: Calories: 263 Protein: 17 g. Fat: 20 g.

Steamed Trout with Lemon Herb Crust (Spanish)

Prep Time: 10 minutes **Cooking Time:** 15 minutes
Servings: 2

Ingredients

3 tbsps. olive oil	3 garlic cloves, chopped
1 tbsp. fresh mint, chopped	1 tbsp. fresh parsley, chopped
2 tbsps. fresh lemon juice	1lb. (454 g.) fresh trout (2 pieces)
¼ tsp. dried ground thyme	2 cups fish stock
1 tsp. sea salt	

Directions

1. Blend the olive oil, garlic, lemon juice, mint, parsley, thyme, and salt. Brush the marinade onto the fish.
2. Insert a trivet in the electric pressure cooker. Fill in the fish stock and place the fish on the trivet.
3. Secure the lid. Select the STEAM mode and set the cooking time for 15 minutes at high pressure.
4. Once cooking is complete, do a quick pressure release. Carefully open the lid. Serve warm.

Nutrition: Calories: 477 Fat: 30 g. Protein: 52 g.

Roasted Trout Stuffed with Veggies (Greek)

Prep Time: 10 minutes **Cooking Time:** 25 minutes
Servings: 2

Ingredients

1(8 oz.) whole trout fillets	¼ tsp. salt
1 tbsp. extra-virgin olive oil	1 poblano pepper
1/8 tsp. black pepper	1small onion, thinly sliced
½ red bell pepper	2–3 shiitake mushrooms, sliced
Cooking spray	1 lemon, sliced

Directions

1. Set the oven to 425°F (220°C). Coat the baking sheet with nonstick cooking spray.
2. Rub both trout fillets, inside and out, with olive oil. Season with salt and pepper.
3. Mix the onion, bell pepper, poblano pepper, and mushrooms in a large bowl. Stuff half of this mix into the cavity of each fillet. Top the mixture with 2–3 lemon slices inside each fillet.
4. Place the fish on the prepared baking sheet side by side. Roast in the preheated oven for 25 minutes.
5. Pull out from the oven and serve on a plate.

Nutrition: Calories: 453 Fat: 22 g. Protein: 49 g.

Fragrant Asian Hotpot (Spanish)

Prep Time: 15 minutes **Cooking Time:** 45 minutes
Servings: 2

Ingredients

1 tsp. tomato purée.
Small handful parsley, stalks finely chopped.
Small handful coriander, stalks finely chopped.
Broccoli, cut into small florets.
1 tbsp. good-quality miso paste. oz. raw tiger prawns.
oz. firm tofu, chopped.
500 ml chicken stock, fresh or made with one cube.

1-star anise, crushed (or ¼ tsp. ground anise).
Juice of ½ lime.
½ carrot, peeled and cut.
Beansprouts.
oz. rice noodles that are cooked according to packet instructions. Cooked water chestnuts, drained.
Little Sushi ginger, chopped.

Directions

1. In a large saucepan, put the tomato purée, star anise, parsley stalks, coriander stalks, lime juice, and chicken stock and bring to boil for 10 minutes.
2. Stir in the carrot, broccoli, prawns, tofu, noodles, and water chestnuts, and cook gently until the prawns are cooked. Take it from heat and stir in the ginger sushi and the paste miso.
3. Serve sprinkled with peregrine leaves and coriander.

Nutrition: Calories: 185 g. Fat: 30 g. Protein: 56 g. Carbs: 45 g. Cholesterol: 230 mg. Sugar: 0 g.

Turkey Burgers with Mango Salsa (Greek)

Prep Time: 15 minutes **Cooking Time:** 10 minutes
Servings: 6

Ingredients

1½ lb. ground turkey breast
1 tsp. sea salt, divided
2 mangos, peeled, pitted, and cubed
1 garlic clove, minced
2 tbsps. extra-virgin olive oil
1 lime juice

¼ tsp. freshly ground black pepper
½ red onion, finely chopped
½ jalapeño pepper, seeded and finely minced
2 tbsps. fresh cilantro leaves, chopped

Directions

1. Form the turkey breast into 4 patties and season with ½ tsp. sea salt and pepper.
2. In a nonstick skillet over medium-high heat, heat the olive oil until it shimmers.
3. Add the turkey patties and cook for 5 minutes per side until browned.
4. While the patties cook, mix the mango, red onion, lime juice, garlic, jalapeño, cilantro, and remaining ½ tsp. sea salt in a small bowl. Spoon the salsa over the turkey patties and serve.

Nutrition: Calories: 384 Protein: 3 g. Fat: 16 g.

Asian King Prawn Stir Fry with Buck wheat Noodles (Italian)

Prep Time: 10 minutes **Cooking Time:** 20 minutes
Servings: 1

Ingredients

oz. shelled raw king prawns, deveined.
2 tsps. tamaris.
1 garlic clove, finely chopped.
oz. celery, trimmed and sliced.
Red onions, sliced. Green beans, chopped.

oz. soba (buckwheat noodles).
2 tsps. extra virgin olive oil.
1 bird's eye chili, finely chopped.
1 tsp. finely chopped fresh ginger.
oz. kale, roughly chopped.
Little lovage or celery leaves. Chicken stock.

Directions

1. Heat a frying pan over a high flame, then cook the prawns for 2–3 minutes in 1 tsp. tamari and 1 tsp. oil. Place the prawns onto a tray. Wipe the pan out with paper from the kitchen, as you will be using it again.
2. Cook the noodles for 5–8 minutes in boiling water, or as directed on the packet. Drain and put away.
3. Meanwhile, over medium-high heat, fry the garlic, chili, and ginger, red onion, celery, beans, and kale in the remaining oil for 2–3 minutes. Add the stock and boil, then cook for 2–3 minutes until the vegetables are cooked but crunchy.
4. Add the prawns, noodles, and leaves of lovage/celery to the pan, bring back to the boil, then remove and eat.

Nutrition: Calories: 185 g. Fat: 30 g. Protein: 56 g. Carbs: 20 g. Cholesterol: 230 mg. Sugar: 0 g.

Herb-Roasted Turkey Breast (Greek)

Prep Time: 15 minutes **Cooking Time:** 90 minutes
Servings: 6

Ingredients

1 tbsps. extra-virgin olive oil
1 tbsp. fresh thyme leaves
2 tbsps. fresh Italian parsley leaves
¼ tsp. black pepper
1 cup dry white wine

1 lemon zest
1 tbsp. fresh rosemary leaves
1 tsp. sea salt
4 garlic cloves, minced
1 (6 lbs.) bone-in, skin-on turkey breast
1 tsp. ground mustard

Directions

1. Preheat the oven to 325°F.
2. Scourge the olive oil, garlic, lemon zest, thyme, rosemary, parsley, mustard, sea salt, and pepper. Layout the herb mixture evenly over the surface of the turkey breast, and loosen the skin, and rub underneath as well. Place the turkey breast in a roasting pan on a rack, skin-side up.
3. Pour the wine into the pan. Roast for 1–1 ½ hour. Take out from the oven and rest for 20 minutes, tented with aluminum foil to keep it warm, before carving.

Nutrition: Calories: 392 Protein: 84 g. Fat: 6 g.

CHAPTER 12
Snack Recipes & Appetizer Recipes

Garlic Parmesan Artichokes (Greek)

Prep Time: 9 minutes **Cooking Time:** 10 minutes
Servings: 4

Ingredients

4 artichokes, wash, trim, and cut top
¼ cup Parmesan cheese, grated
½ cup vegetable broth
1 tbsp. olive oil
2 tsps. garlic, minced Salt

Directions

1. Pour the broth into the electric pressure cooker, then place the steamer rack in the pot.
2. Place the artichoke steam side down on the steamer rack into the pot.
3. Sprinkle the garlic and grated cheese on top of artichokes and season with salt. Drizzle the oil over artichokes.
4. Seal pot with the lid and cook on high for 10 minutes.
5. Once done, release pressure using quick release. Remove the lid.
6. Serve and enjoy.

Nutrition: Calories: 132 Fat: 5.2 g. Protein: 7.9 g.

Manchego Crackers (Spanish)

Prep Time: 55 minutes **Cooking Time:** 15 minutes
Servings: 4

Ingredients

4 tbsps. butter, at room temperature
1 cup Manchego cheese
1 large egg
1 cup almond flour
1 tsp. salt, divided
¼ tsp. black pepper

Directions

1. Scourge butter and shredded cheese using an electric mixer.
2. Mix the almond flour with ½ tsp. salt and pepper. Mix the almond flour mixture to the cheese, constantly mixing to form a ball.
3. Put it onto plastic wrap and roll into a cylinder log about 1 ½-inch thick. Wrap tightly and refrigerate for at least 1 hour.
4. Preheat the oven to 350°F. Prepare 2 baking sheets with parchment paper.
5. For egg wash, blend egg and remaining ½ tsp. salt.
6. Slice the refrigerated dough into small rounds, about ¼-inch thick, and place on the lined baking sheets.
7. Top the crackers with egg wash and bake for 15 minutes. Pull out from the oven and situate in a wire rack.
8. Serve.

Nutrition: Calories: 243 Fat: 23 g. Protein: 8 g.

Greek Deviled Eggs (Greek)

Prep Time: 45 minutes **Cooking Time:** 15 minutes
Servings: 4

Ingredients

4 large hardboiled eggs
½ cup Feta cheese
2 tbsps. sun-dried tomatoes, chopped
¼ tsp. black pepper
2 tbsps. roasted garlic aioli
8 pitted Kalamata olives
½ tsp. dried dill
1 tbsp. red onion, minced

Directions

1. Slice the hardboiled eggs in half lengthwise, remove the yolks, and place the yolks in a medium bowl.
2. Reserve the egg white halves and set them aside.
3. Smash the yolks well with a fork.
4. Add the aioli, Feta cheese, olives, sun-dried tomatoes, onion, dill, and pepper and stir to combine until smooth and creamy.
5. Spoon the filling into each egg white half and chill for 30 minutes, or up to 24 hours, covered.

Nutrition: Calories: 147 Fat: 11 g. Protein: 9 g.

Burrata Caprese Stack (Greek)

Prep Time: 5 minutes **Cooking Time:** 0 minutes
Servings: 4

Ingredients

1 large organic tomato
¼ tsp. black pepper
8 fresh basil leaves
2 tbsps. extra-virgin olive oil
1 tbsp. red wine
½ tsp. salt
1 (4 oz.) ball of Burrata cheese

Directions

1. Slice the tomato into 4 thick slices, removing any tough center core, and sprinkle with salt and pepper. Place the tomatoes, seasoned-side up, on a plate.
2. On a separate rimmed plate, slice the Burrata cheese into 4 thick slices and place 1 slice on top of each tomato slice. Top each with 2 basil leaves and pour any reserved Burrata cream from the rimmed plate over the top.
3. Drizzle with olive oil and vinegar and serve with a fork and knife.

Nutrition: Calories: 153 Fat: 13 g. Protein: 7 g.

White Bean Hummus (Greek)

Prep Time: 11 minutes **Cooking Time:** 40 minutes
Servings: 12

Ingredients

2/3 cup dried white beans	2 garlic cloves, peeled and
½ tsp. salt	crushed
¼ cup olive oil	1 tbsp. lemon juice

Directions

1. Place the beans and garlic in the electric pressure cooker and stir well. Add enough cold water to cover the ingredients. Cover, set steam release to SEALING, select the MANUAL button, and time to 30 minutes.
2. Once the timer stops, release the pressure for 20 minutes. Select CANCEL and open the lid. Use a fork to check that beans are tender. Drain off the excess water and transfer the beans to a food processor.
3. Add the oil, lemon juice, and salt to the processor and pulse until the mixture is smooth with some small chunks. Pour into a container and refrigerate for at least 4 hours. Serve cold or at room temperature.

Nutrition: Calories: 57 Fat: 5 g. Protein: 1 g.

Kidney Bean Dip with Cilantro, Cumin, and Lime (Spanish)

Prep Time: 13 minutes **Cooking Time:** 51 minutes
Servings: 16

Ingredients

1 cup dried kidney beans	3 garlic cloves
¼ cup cilantro	¼ cup extra-virgin olive oil
4 cups water	1 tbsp. lime juice
2 tsps. lime zest, grated	½ tsp. salt
1 tsp. ground cumin	

Directions

1. Place the beans, water, garlic, and 2 tbsps. of cilantro in the electric pressure cooker. Close the lid, select steam release to SEALING, click on the BEAN button, and cook for 30 minutes.
2. When the timer alarms, let the pressure release naturally for 20 minutes. Press the CANCEL button, open the lid, and check that the beans are tender. Drain off the extra water and transfer the beans to a medium bowl. Gently mash the beans with a potato masher. Add the oil, lime juice, lime zest, cumin, salt, and the remaining 2 tbsps. of cilantro and stir to combine. Serve warm or at room temperature.

Nutrition: Calories: 65 Fat: 3 g. Protein: 2 g.

Crispy Green Bean Fries with Lemon-Yogurt Sauce (Greek)

Prep Time: 5 minutes **Cooking Time:** 5 minutes
Servings: 4

Ingredients

For the green beans	2 tablespoons water
1 tablespoon whole wheat flour	¼ teaspoon paprika
½ teaspoon garlic powder	1 egg
¼ cup whole wheat bread crumbs	½ teaspoon salt
½ cup nonfat plain Greek yogurt	½ pound whole green beans
1/8 teaspoon cayenne pepper	For the lemon-yogurt sauce
	¼ teaspoon salt
	1 tablespoon lemon juice

Directions

1. To make the green beans
2. Preheat the air fryer to 380°F.
3. In a medium shallow bowl, combine together the egg and water until frothy. In a separate medium shallow bowl, whisk together the flour, paprika, garlic powder, and salt, then mix in the bread crumbs.
4. Spread the bottom of the air fryer with cooking spray. Dip each green bean into the egg mixture, then into the bread crumb mixture, coating the outside with the crumbs. Situate the green beans in a single layer in the bottom of the air fryer basket.
5. Fry in the air fryer for 5 minutes, or until the breading is golden brown.
6. To make the lemon-yogurt sauce
7. Incorporate the yogurt, lemon juice, salt, and cayenne. Serve the green bean fries alongside the lemon-yogurt sauce as a snack or appetizer.

Nutrition 88 Calories 2g Fat 10g Carbohydrates 7g Protein

Homemade Sea Salt Pita Chips (Spanish)

Prep Time: 2 minutes **Cooking Time:** 8 minutes
Servings: 2

Ingredients

1 whole wheat pitas	½ teaspoon kosher salt
1 tablespoon olive oil	

Directions

1. Preheat the air fryer to 360°F. Cut each pita into 8 wedges. In a medium bowl, mix the pita wedges, olive oil, and salt until the wedges are coated and the olive oil and salt are evenly distributed.
2. Place the pita wedges into the air fryer basket in an even layer and fry for 6 to 8 minutes.
3. Season with additional salt, if desired. Serve alone or with a favorite dip.

Nutrition 230 Calories 8g Fat 11g Carbohydrates 6g Protein

Rosemary-Roasted Red Potatoes (Greek)

Prep Time: 5 minutes **Cooking Time:** 20 minutes
Servings: 6

Ingredients

1-pound red potatoes, quartered	¼ cup olive oil
½ teaspoon kosher salt	1 garlic clove, minced
4 rosemary sprigs	¼ teaspoon black pepper

Directions

1. Preheat the air fryer to 360°F.
2. In a large bowl, toss in the potatoes with the olive oil, salt, pepper, and garlic until well coated. Fill the air fryer basket with potatoes and top with the sprigs of rosemary.
3. Roast for 10 minutes, then stir or toss the potatoes and roast for 10 minutes more. Remove the rosemary sprigs and serve the potatoes. Season well.

Nutrition 133 Calories 9g Fat 5g Carbohydrates 1g Protein

Summer Tomato Salad (Greek)

Prep Time: 20 minutes **Cooking Time:** 0 minutes
Servings: 4

Ingredients

1 cucumber, sliced	¼ cup sun dried tomatoes
½ cup black olives	1 tablespoon balsamic vinegar
1 red onion, sliced	
¼ cup parsley, fresh & chopped	1 lb. Tomatoes, cubed
	2 tablespoons olive oil

Directions

1. Mix all of your vegetables together. For dressing, mix all your seasoning, olive oil and vinegar. Toss with your salad and serve fresh.

Nutrition: 126 Calories 2.1g Protein 9.2g Fat

Cheese Beet Salad (Italian)

Prep Time: 15 minutes **Cooking Time:** 0 minutes
Servings: 4

6 red beets	3 ounces feta cheese
2 tablespoons olive oil	2 tablespoons balsamic vinegar

Directions

1. Combine everything together, and then serve.

Nutrition: 230 Calories 7.3g Protein 12g Fat

Cauliflower and Cherry Tomato Salad (Greek)

Prep Time: 15 minutes **Cooking Time:** 0 minutes
Servings: 4

Ingredients

1 head cauliflower	2 tablespoons parsley
2 cups cherry tomatoes, halved	2 tablespoons lemon juice, fresh
	2 tablespoons pine nuts

Directions

1. Blend lemon juice, cherry tomatoes, cauliflower and parsley then season. Garnish with pine nuts, and mix well before serving.

Nutrition: 64 Calories 2.8g Protein 3.3g Fat

Veggie Shish Kebabs (Spanish)

Prep Time: 10 minutes **Cooking Time:** 0 minute
Servings: 3

Ingredients

Cherry tomatoes (9)	Olive oil (1 tsp.) Zucchini
Mozzarella balls (9 low-fat)	(3, sliced) Dash of pepper
For Servings:	Whole Wheat Bread (6
Basil leaves (9)	slices)

Directions

1. Stab 1 cherry tomato, low-fat mozzarella ball, zucchini, and basil leaf onto each skewer.
2. Place skewers on a plate and drizzle with olive oil. Finish with a sprinkle of pepper.
3. Set your bread to toast. Serve 2 bread slices with 3 kebobs.

Nutrition: 349 Calories 5.7g Fat 15g Protein

Spiced Salmon Crudités (Spanish)

Prep Time: 10 minutes **Cooking Time:** 15 minutes
Servings: 4

Ingredients

6 ounces smoked wild salmon	2 tablespoons Roasted Garlic Aioli
1 tablespoon chopped scallions, green parts only	½ teaspoon dried dill
4 endive spears or hearts of romaine	1 tablespoon Dijon mustard
2 teaspoons chopped capers	½ English cucumber, cut into ¼-inch-thick rounds

Directions

1. Roughly cut the smoked salmon and transfer in a small bowl. Add the aioli, Dijon, scallions, capers, and dill and mix well. Top endive spears and cucumber rounds with a spoonful of smoked salmon mixture and enjoy chilled.

Nutrition 92 Calories 5g Fat 1g Carbohydrates 9g Protein

Vegetable Fritters (Italian)

Prep Time: 15 minutes **Cooking Time:** 6 minutes
Servings: 5

Ingredients

Egg (3, beaten)	Whole wheat flour (8 oz)
Milk (8 Fl oz)	Baking powder (1 tbsp)
Maple syrup (1/2 oz)	Carrot (12 oz,)
Vegetables:	Salt (½ tsp)
Baby lima beans (12 oz)	Celery (12 oz)
Turnip (12 oz)	Eggplant (12 oz)
Cauliflower (12 oz)	Zucchini (12 oz)
Parsnips (12 oz)	Asparagus (12 oz)

Directions

1. Combine the eggs and milk.
2. Mix the flour, baking powder, salt, and maple syrup. Stir in to the milk and eggs and mix until smooth.
3. Set aside the batter for several hours in a refrigerator.
4. Stir the cold, cooked vegetable into the batter.
5. Drop with a No. 24 scoop into deep fat at 350 F. Toss the content from the scoop carefully in the hot oil. Fry until golden brown.
6. Drain well and serve.

Nutrition: 140 Calories 6g Fat 4g Protein

Avocado and Turkey Mix Panini (Italian)

Prep Time: 5 minutes **Cooking Time:** 8 minutes
Servings: 2

Ingredients

2 red peppers, roasted and sliced into strips	¼ lb. thinly sliced mesquite smoked turkey breast
2 slices provolone cheese	¼ cup mayonnaise
1 tbsp olive oil, divided	1 cup whole fresh spinach leaves, divided
2 ciabatta rolls	
½ ripe avocado	

Directions

1. In a bowl, mash thoroughly together mayonnaise and avocado. Then preheat Panini press.
2. Chop the bread rolls in half and spread olive oil on the insides of the bread. Then fill it with filling, layering them as you go: provolone, turkey breast, roasted red pepper, spinach leaves and spread avocado mixture and cover with the other bread slice.
3. Place sandwich in the Panini press and grill for 5 to 8 minutes until cheese has melted and bread is crisped and ridged.

Nutrition 546 Calories 34.8g Fat 31.9g Carbohydrates 27.8g Protein

Cucumber, Chicken and Mango Wrap (Greek)

Prep Time: 5 minutes **Cooking Time:** 20 minutes
Servings: 1

Ingredients

½ of a medium cucumber cut lengthwise	½ of ripe mango
1tbsp salad dressing of choice	1 whole wheat tortilla wrap
2 tbsp oil for frying	1-inch-thick slice of chicken breast around 6-inch in length
2tbsp whole wheat flour	Salt and pepper to taste
2 to 4 lettuce leaves	

Directions

1. Slice a chicken breast into 1-inch strips and just cook a total of 6-inch strips. That would be like two strips of chicken. Store remaining chicken for future use.
2. Season chicken with pepper and salt. Dredge in whole wheat flour. On medium fire, place a small and nonstick fry pan and heat oil. Once oil is hot, add chicken strips and fry until golden brown around 5 minutes per side.
3. While chicken is cooking, place tortilla wraps in oven and cook for 3 to 5 minutes. Then set aside and transfer in a plate.
4. Slice cucumber lengthwise, use only ½ of it and store remaining cucumber. Peel cucumber cut into quarter and remove pith. Place the two slices of cucumber on the tortilla wrap, 1-inch away from the edge.
5. Slice mango and store the other half with seed. Peel the mango without seed, slice into strips and place on top of the cucumber on the tortilla wrap. Once chicken is cooked, place chicken beside the cucumber in a line.
6. Add cucumber leaf, drizzle with salad dressing of choice.
7. Roll the tortilla wrap, serve and enjoy.

Nutrition 434 Calories 10g Fat 65g Carbohydrates 21g Protein

Raisin Rice Pilaf (Italian)

Prep Time: 13 minutes **Cooking Time:** 8 minutes
Servings: 5

Ingredients

1 tbsp. olive oil 1 tsp. cumin	1cup onion, chopped
½ cup carrot, shredded	½ tsp. cinnamon
2cups instant brown rice 1	1 cup golden raisins
¾ cup orange juice	
¼ cup water	½ cup pistachios, shelled
Fresh chives, chopped for garnish	

Directions

1. Place a medium saucepan over medium-high heat before adding in the oil. Add in the onion, and stir often, so it doesn't burn. Cook for 5 minutes, and then add in the cumin, cinnamon, and carrot. Cook for another minute.
2. Add in the orange juice, water, and rice. Boil before covering the saucepan. Turn the heat down to medium-low and then allow it to simmer for 6–7 minutes.
3. Stir in the pistachios, chives, and raisins. Serve warm.

Nutrition: Calories: 320 Protein: 6 g. Fat: 7 g.

Tuna Tartare (Spanish)

Prep Time: 15 minutes **Cooking Time:** 0 minute
Servings: 8

Ingredients

Sashimi quality tuna (26.5 g, well-trimmed)	Parsley (2 tbsp, chopped)
Fresh tarragon (2 tbsp, chopped)	Shallots (1 oz, minced)
Lime juice (2 tbsp)	Dijon-style mustard (1 Fl oz)
	Olive oil (2 Fl oz)

Directions

1. Use a knife to mince the tuna.
2. Mixed the rest of the ingredients with the chopped tuna.
3. Use a ring mold to make a beautifully presented tuna tartare.
4. Season to taste with pepper and salt.

Nutrition 200 Calories 12g Fat 21g Protein

Goat Cheese–Mackerel Pâté (Italian)

Prep Time: 10 minutes **Cooking Time:** 0 minute
Servings: 4

Ingredients

4 oz. olive oil-packed wild-caught mackerel	1 lemon zest and juice
2 tbsps. fresh parsley, chopped	2 oz. goat cheese
1 tbsp. extra-virgin olive oil	2 tsps. capers, chopped
2 tsps. fresh horseradish (optional)	2 tbsps. fresh arugula, chopped

Directions

1. In a food processor, blender, or large bowl with an immersion blender, combine the mackerel, goat cheese, lemon zest and juice, parsley, arugula, olive oil, capers, and horseradish (if using). Process or blend until smooth and creamy. Serve with crackers, cucumber rounds, endive spears, or celery.

Nutrition: Calories: 118 Fat: 8 g. Protein: 9 g.

Taste of the Mediterranean Fat Bombs (Greek)

Prep Time: 15 minutes 4 hours **Cooking Time:** 0 minute
Servings: 6

Ingredients

1 cup goat cheese, crumbled	12 pitted Kalamata olives
4 tbsps. jarred pesto	1 tbsp. fresh rosemary, chopped
½ cup walnuts, finely chopped	

Directions

1. Mix the goat cheese, pesto, and olives. Cool for 4 hours to harden.
2. Make 6 balls from the mixture, about ¾-inch diameter. The mixture will be sticky.
3. Place the walnuts and rosemary in a small bowl and roll the goat cheese balls in the nut mixture to coat.

Nutrition: Calories: 166 Fat: 15 g. Protein: 5 g.

Cream of Cauliflower Gazpacho (Spanish)

Prep Time: 15 minutes **Cooking Time:** 25 minutes
Servings: 6

Ingredients

1 cup raw almonds	½ tsp. salt
½ cup, plus 1 tbsp. extra-virgin olive oil	1 small head cauliflower
2 cups chicken stock	2 garlic cloves
¼ tsp. freshly ground black pepper	1 tbsp. red wine vinegar
	1 small white onion

Directions

1. Boil the almonds in the water for 1 minute. Drain in a colander and run under cold water. Pat dry. Discard the skins. In a food processor or blender, blend the almonds and salt. With the processor running, drizzle in ½ cup extra-virgin olive oil, scraping down the sides as needed. Set the almond paste aside.
2. In a stockpot, cook the remaining 1 tbsp. olive oil over medium-high heat. Sauté onion for 4 minutes. Add the cauliflower florets and sauté for another 3–4 minutes. Cook the garlic for 1 minute more.
3. Add 2 cups of stock and bring to a boil. Cover, reduce the heat to medium-low and simmer the vegetables until tender, 8–10 minutes. Pull out from the heat and allow to cool slightly.
4. Blend the vinegar and pepper with an immersion blender. With the blender running, add the almond paste and blend until smooth, adding extra stock if the soup is too thick. Serve warm, or chill in the refrigerator for at least 4–6 hours to serve a cold gazpacho.

Nutrition: Calories: 505 Fat: 45 g. Protein: 10 g.

Red Pepper Hummus (Greek)

Prep Time: 7 minutes **Cooking Time:** 34 minutes
Servings: 4

Ingredients

1 cup dried chickpeas	1 tbsp., plus ¼ cup extra-virgin olive oil, divided
4 cups water	
½ cup roasted red pepper, chopped, divided	1 tsp. ground cumin
½ tsp. ground black pepper	¾ tsp. salt
1/3 cup tahini	¼ tsp. smoked paprika
½ tsp. garlic, minced	1/3 cup lemon juice

Directions

1. Put chickpeas, water, and 1 tbsp. oil in the electric pressure cooker. Seal put steam release to sealing, select the manual button, and time to 30 minutes.
2. When the timer rings, quick-release the pressure. Click the cancel button and open it. Drain and next set aside the cooking liquid.
3. Process the chickpeas, 1/3 cup roasted red pepper, the remaining ¼ cup of oil, tahini, cumin, salt, black pepper, paprika, lemon juice, and garlic using a food processor. Serve, garnished with reserved roasted red pepper on top.

Nutrition: Calories: 96 Fat: 8 g. Protein: 2 g.

Crunchy Kale Chips (Italian)

Prep Time: 11 minutes **Cooking Time:** 2 hours
Servings: 8

Ingredients

2 tbsps. filtered water	½ tsp. sea salt
1tbsp. raw honey	2tbsps. nutritional yeast
1cup sweet potato	2bunches of green curly kale
1 cup fresh cashews	1 lemon, juiced

Directions

1. Prepare a baking sheet by covering it with unbleached parchment paper. Preheat the oven to 350 F.
2. In a large mixing bowl, place the kale.
3. In a food processor, process the remaining ingredients until smooth. Pour over the kale.
4. With your hands, coat the kale with marinade.
5. Evenly spread the kale onto parchment paper and pop in the oven. Dehydrate for 2 hours and turn leaves after the first hour of baking.
6. Remove from the oven; let it cool completely before serving.

Nutrition: Calories: 209 Protein: 7 g. Fat: 15.9 g.

Zucchini Lasagna (Greek)

Prep Time: 13 minutes **Cooking Time:** 45 minutes
Servings: 4

Ingredients

2 zucchinis, trimmed	1 cup Mozzarella, shredded
½ cup tomato sauce 1 onion, chopped	1 tbsp. olive oil
½ cup potato, boiled, mashed 1 tsp. Italian seasonings	¼ cup tomato sauce 1 tsp. butter softened

Directions

1. Heat the olive oil in a skillet.
2. Add the onion and roast it until light brown.
3. Meanwhile, slice the zucchini lengthwise.
4. Grease the casserole mold with butter from inside.
5. Put ½ part of sliced zucchini in the casserole mold to get the layer.
6. Then add the layer of cooked onion and a ½ cup of Mozzarella cheese.
7. After this, make the layer from the remaining zucchini.
8. Top the vegetables with a layer of mashed potatoes and Mozzarella.
9. Pour the tomato sauce over the cheese and cover the surface of the mold with foil. Secure the edges.
10. Bake the lasagna for 30 minutes at 365°F.
11. Then discard the foil and cook lasagna for 10 minutes more.

Nutrition: Calories: 103 Fat: 6.3 g. Protein: 4.1 g.

Quinoa with Banana and Cinnamon (Greek)

Prep Time: 10 minutes **Cooking Time:** 12 minutes
Servings: 4

Ingredients

1cup quinoa	2cup milk
1teaspoon vanilla extract	2bananas, sliced
¼ teaspoon ground cinnamon	1 teaspoon honey

Directions

1. Pour milk in the saucepan and add quinoa. Close the lid and cook it over the medium heat for 12 minutes or until quinoa will absorb all liquid. Then chill the quinoa for 10-15 minutes and place in the serving mason jars.
2. Add honey, vanilla extract, and ground cinnamon. Stir well. Top quinoa with banana and stirs it before serving.

Nutrition 279 Calories 5.3g Fat 4.6g Carbohydrates 10.7g Protein

Balsamic Eggplant Mix (Greek)

Prep Time: 10 minutes **Cooking Time:** 20 minutes
Servings: 6

Ingredients

1/3 cup chicken stock	2 tbsps. balsamic vinegar
2 large eggplants	1tbsp. rosemary
¼ cup cilantro	2tbsps. olive oil
1 tbsp. lime juice	

Directions

1. In a roasting pan, combine the eggplants with the stock, vinegar, and the rest of the ingredients. Put the pan in the oven and bake at 390°F for 20 minutes.
2. Divide the mix between plates and serve.

Nutrition: Calories: 201 Fat: 4.5 g. Protein: 3 g.

Wrapped Plums (Spanish)

Prep Time: 10 minutes **Cooking Time:** 0 minutes
Servings: 8

Ingredients

4 plums, quartered	2 ounces prosciutto, cut into 16 pieces
1 tablespoon chives, chopped	
A pinch red pepper flakes, crushed	

Directions

1. Wrap each plum quarter in a prosciutto slice, arrange them all on a platter, sprinkle the chives and pepper flakes all over, and serve.

Nutrition: Calories: 30 Fat:1 g Fiber:0 g Carbohydrates: 4 g Protein: 2 g

Easy and Healthy Baked Vegetables (Italian)

Prep Time: 9 minutes **Cooking Time:** 75 minutes
Servings: 6

Ingredients

2 lbs. Brussels sprouts, trimmed	1 lb. pork breakfast sausage
3 lbs. butternut squash	1 tbsp. fat from fried sausage

Directions

1. Grease a 9-inch baking pan and preheat the oven to 350ºF.
2. With medium-high heat, put a nonstick saucepan and cook sausage. Break up the sausages and cook until browned.
3. In a greased pan, mix browned sausage, squash, sprouts, sea salt, and fat. Toss to mix well. Pop into the oven and cook for 1 hour.
4. Remove from oven and serve warm.

Nutrition: Calories: 364 Protein: 19 g. Fat: 17 g.

Morning Tostadas (Spanish)

Prep Time: 15 minutes **Cooking Time:** 6 minutes
Servings: 6

Ingredients

½ white onion, diced	1 cucumber, chopped
1 tablespoon fresh cilantro, chopped	½ jalapeno pepper, chopped
1 tomato, chopped	1 tablespoon lime juice
6 corn tortillas	1tablespoon canola oil
2oz Cheddar cheese, shredded	½ cup white beans, canned, drained
½ teaspoon butter	½ teaspoon Sea salt
6 eggs	

Directions

1. Make Pico de Galo: in the salad bowl combine together diced white onion, tomato, cucumber, fresh cilantro, and jalapeno pepper. Then add lime juice and a ½ tablespoon of canola oil. Mix up the mixture well. Pico de Galo is cooked.
2. After this, preheat the oven to 390F. Line the tray with baking paper. Arrange the corn tortillas on the baking paper and brush with remaining canola oil from both sides. Bake the tortillas until they start to be crunchy. Chill the cooked crunchy tortillas well. Meanwhile, toss the butter in the skillet.
3. Crack the eggs in the melted butter and sprinkle them with sea salt. Fry the eggs until the egg whites become white (cooked). Approximately for 3-5 minutes over the medium heat. After this, mash the beans until you get puree texture. Spread the bean puree on the corn tortillas.
4. Add fried eggs. Then top the eggs with Pico de Galo and shredded Cheddar cheese.

Nutrition 246 Calories 11g Fat 4.7g Carbohydrates 13.7g Protein

Cheese Omelet (Italian)

Prep Time: 5 minutes **Cooking Time:** 10 minutes
Servings: 2

Ingredients

1 tablespoon cream cheese	¼ teaspoon paprika
½ teaspoon dried oregano	¼ teaspoon dried dill
2 eggs, beaten	1 oz Parmesan, grated
	1 teaspoon coconut oil

Directions

1. Mix up together cream cheese with eggs, dried oregano, and dill. Pour coconut oil in the skillet and heat it up until it will coat all the skillet.
2. Then fill the skillet with the egg mixture and flatten it. Add grated Parmesan and close the lid. Cook omelet for 10 minutes over the low heat. Then transfer the cooked omelet in the serving plate and sprinkle with paprika.

Nutrition 148 Calories 11.5g Fat 0.3g Carbohydrates10.6g Protein

Fruity Pizza (Italian)

Prep Time: 10 minutes **Cooking Time:** 0 minute
Servings: 2

Ingredients

1 tbsp fresh cilantro chopped	9 oz watermelon slice
1 tbsp Pomegranate sauce	2 oz Feta cheese, crumbled

Directions

1. Place the watermelon slice in the plate and sprinkle with crumbled Feta cheese. Add fresh cilantro. After this, sprinkle the pizza with Pomegranate juice generously. Cut the pizza into the Servings.

Nutrition 143 Calories 6.2g Fat 0.6g Carbohydrates 5.1g Protein

Herb and Ham Muffins (Greek)

Prep Time: 10 minutes **Cooking Time:** 15 minutes
Servings: 4

Ingredients

3 oz ham, chopped	2 tablespoons coconut flour
½ teaspoon dried oregano	¼ teaspoon dried cilantro
4 eggs, beaten	Cooking spray

Directions

1. Spray the muffin's molds with cooking spray from inside. In the bowl mix up together beaten eggs, coconut flour, dried oregano, cilantro, and ham. When the liquid is homogenous, pour it in the prepared muffin molds.
2. Bake the muffins for 15 minutes at 360F. Chill the cooked meal well and only after this remove from the molds.

Nutrition 128 Calories 7.2g Fat 2.9g Carbohydrates10.1g Protein

Appendix 1   Measurement Conversion Chart

VOLUME EQUIVALENTS(DRY)

US STANDARD	METRIC (APPROXIMATE)
1/8 teaspoon	0.5 mL
1/4 teaspoon	1 mL
1/2 teaspoon	2 mL
3/4 teaspoon	4 mL
1 teaspoon	5 mL
1 tablespoon	15 mL
1/4 cup	59 mL
1/2 cup	118 mL
3/4 cup	177 mL
1 cup	235 mL
2 cups	475 mL
3 cups	700 mL
4 cups	1 L

VOLUME EQUIVALENTS(LIQUID)

US STANDARD	US STANDARD (OUNCES)	METRIC (APPROXIMATE)
2 tablespoons	1 fl.oz.	30 mL
1/4 cup	2 fl.oz.	60 mL
1/2 cup	4 fl.oz.	120 mL
1 cup	8 fl.oz.	240 mL
1 1/2 cup	12 fl.oz.	355 mL
2 cups or 1 pint	16 fl.oz.	475 mL
4 cups or 1 quart	32 fl.oz.	1 L
1 gallon	128 fl.oz.	4 L

TEMPERATURES EQUIVALENTS

FAHRENHEIT(F)	CELSIUS(C) (APPROXIMATE)
225 °F	107 °C
250 °F	120 °C
275 °F	135 °C
300 °F	150 °C
325 °F	160 °C
350 °F	180 °C
375 °F	190 °C
400 °F	205 °C
425 °F	220 °C
450 °F	235 °C
475 °F	245 °C
500 °F	260 °C

WEIGHT EQUIVALENTS

US STANDARD	METRIC (APPROXIMATE)
1 ounce	28 g
2 ounces	57 g
5 ounces	142 g
10 ounces	284 g
15 ounces	425 g
16 ounces (1 pound)	455 g
1.5 pounds	680 g
2 pounds	907 g

Appendix 2   Dirty Dozen and Clean Fifteen

The Environmental Working Group (EWG) is a nonprofit, nonpartisan organization dedicated to protecting human health and the environment Its mission is to empower people to live healthier lives in a healthier environment. This organization publishes an annual list of the twelve kinds of produce, in sequence, that have the highest amount of pesticide residue-the Dirty Dozen-as well as a list of the fifteen kinds ofproduce that have the least amount of pesticide residue-the Clean Fifteen.

THE DIRTY DOZEN

- The 2016 Dirty Dozen includes the following produce. These are considered among the year's most important produce to buy organic:

Strawberries	Spinach
Apples	Tomatoes
Nectarines	Bell peppers
Peaches	Cherry tomatoes
Celery	Cucumbers
Grapes	Kale/collard greens
Cherries	Hot peppers

- *The Dirty Dozen list contains two additional itemskale/collard greens and hot peppers-because they tend to contain trace levels of highly hazardous pesticides.*

THE CLEAN FIFTEEN

- The least critical to buy organically are the Clean Fifteen list. The following are on the 2016 list:

Avocados	Papayas
Corn	Kiw
Pineapples	Eggplant
Cabbage	Honeydew
Sweet peas	Grapefruit
Onions	Cantaloupe
Asparagus	Cauliflower
Mangos	

- *Some of the sweet corn sold in the United States are made from genetically engineered (GE) seedstock. Buy organic varieties of these crops to avoid GE produce.*

Appendix 3   Index

Leave a Review

As an independent author with a small marketing budget, reviews are my livelihood on this platform. If you enjoyed this book, I'd appreciate it if you could leave your honest feedback. I read EVERY single review because I love the feedback from MY readers!

Thank you for staying with me.

.

Made in the USA
Monee, IL
09 January 2023

24889500R00063